Towards a Cognitive Mode in Global Finance

Torsten Strulik is Heisenberg-Fellow of the German Research Foundation (DFG) and assistant professor of sociology at the University of Bielefeld in Germany.
Helmut Willke is professor of sociology at the University of Bielefeld in Germany.

Torsten Strulik, Helmut Willke (eds.)

Towards a Cognitive Mode in Global Finance

The Governance of a Knowledge-Based Financial System

Campus Verlag
Frankfurt/New York

Distribution throughout the world except Germany, Austria and Switzerland by

The University of Chicago Press
1427 East 60th Street
Chicago, IL 60637

Gefördert durch die VolkswagenStiftung.

Bibliographic Information published by the Deutsche Nationalbibliothek.
Die Deutsche Nationalbibliothek lists this publication in the Deutsche Nationalbibliografie; detailed bibliographic data are available in the Internet at http://dnd.d-nb.de.
ISBN 978-3-593-38156-5

Printed on acid free paper.
Printed in Germany

For further information:
www.campus.de
www.press.uchicago.edu

Contents

Preface and Acknowledgements

The essays in this volume were first presented at an international conference organized by the Institute for World Society Studies at the University of Bielefeld in October 2005. The underlying idea is that while the implications of the knowledge intensity of contemporary life have received increasing attention in recent years, there has not been a systematic effort to understand the distinctive characteristics and ambivalent consequences of the knowledge production of the global financial system. This book attempts to identify important indications of a shift from a predominantly normative to a predominantly cognitive (learning-oriented) mode of managing financial and political risks. It will be analyzed to what extent the expansion of global finance is accompanied by a cognitive turn of the financial system from normatively regulated national capital markets to a knowledge-based global superstructure.

We are indepted to many people who supported the production of this volume. The VolkswagenStiftung generously funded the conference and this publication. Sven Kette, Matthias Kussin and Ben Penlington very efficiently helped to organize the conference. Pascal Spreen lent great support in the editorial production of the book. We are very grateful to all of them.

Torsten Strulik and Helmut Willke

Introduction

Torsten Strulik

1. The Governance of Global Finance

The end of the Bretton Woods System in 1973 is widely seen as the starting point of the global financial business. Although the first global financial market had already been established in the form of the Euromarket in 1958, the transition to flexible exchange rates set financial economic dynamics in motion which reflected both a globalization of transactions and high-speed innovation. For the governance of the financial system, the developments of the last three decades have meant a massive expansion of the range of opportunities for market actors. With the support of new information technologies and communication media, domestic and offshore financial markets have been opened and integrated into a single global market, including all industrial as well as a growing number of developing countries. At the same time, social expectations regarding the ability of public actors to intervene have grown disproportionately to their ability to keep up with the new opportunities and competencies of the market actors. There is a discernable institutional gap between the global nature of finance and the domestic charter of central banks and supervisory agencies. On the basis of this diagnosis numerous observers have attributed current problems in regulating global finance to a transition from a government-led international monetary system to a market-led international monetary system (Padoa-Schioppa/Saccomanni 1994). The corresponding research question is: Which new forms of governance respond to an increasing exterritorialization and autonomy of financial transactions? Instructive analyses can be found not only of institutional and regulatory adaptations on the national, international and supranational levels (e.g. Dale 1984; Kapstein 1996; Eichengreen 1999; Scholte 2002; Wood 2005) but also of the increasing relevance of private actors (e.g. Sinclair 1994; Tsingou 2003) and mixed public-private arrangements (e.g. Strulik 2000).

This book aims at opening up a complementary perspective. On the one hand, diagnoses of exterritorialization and the autonomy of finance are addressed. On the other hand, a shift of research towards the relevance of knowledge for governance might produce new insights in light of the continuing development of the regulatory field as well as the intensification of the debate on the characteristics and effects of the knowledge society (e.g. Adhikari/Sales 2001; Willke 2002). This introduction will argue that, for an adequate understanding of the current governance problems of global finance, it is important to consider the characteristics and consequences of the knowledge production of the global financial system as well as the relevance of knowledge for politics. The starting point of this analysis is the assumption that the globalization of the financial business is not only accompanied by a spatial incongruity of financial economic and political opportunities for action. Considering Niklas Luhmann's (1991) thoughts on the emergence of a world society, it appears instructive to examine the present problems of the governance of global finance in respect to different expectation structures towards which the functionally specialized societal subsystems of politics, law and the economy orient themselves.

Referring to the structure of modern functionally differentiated societies, it can be seen that because of their social function, politics and law are designed to normatively react to disappointed expectations while the expectation structures which direct the operations of the economy, and the global financial system in particular, are characterized by the predominance of cognitive, adaptive and learning-oriented expectations. The economy and the financial system are therefore taking on leading roles both in defining the problems of governance and in formulating ways of dealing with them. In contrast, politics and law are not only incapable of counteracting the exterritorialization of markets by developing and implementing globally binding norms but are also lacking the »cognitive competence« (Nonet/Selznick 1978: 112) to keep up with the innovation dynamic of the economy. Empirical studies on the »regulatory dialectic« (e.g. Kane 1981; Finnerty 1985) have shown that political and legal measures actually contribute to the acceleration of innovation processes and the intensification of regulatory problems. Consider the impact of the 1988 Basel Accord, which is commonly recognized as the greatest achievement in the history of global banking regulation. In the meantime, it has become apparent that these regulations have contributed not only to an expansion of the especially risky derivatives business (Strulik 2000: 175) but also to higher fluctuation within, and instability of, credit markets by favoring short-term over long-term credits, an effect which may have promoted the outbreak of the Asian Crisis in 1997 (Griffith-Jones 2000: 7).

An outstanding example of the cognitive orientation of the financial system is the rapid expansion of the risk-management industry in the 1970s. After the final collapse of Bretton Woods, a normatively-oriented international monetary system, the financial business was confronted with new uncertainties. It was not only the exchange rate volatility that increased dramatically but, as the liberalization of capital movements progressed, investors also started to look at opportunities offered by financial markets abroad. Accordingly, a demand for effective hedging and arbitrage instruments developed which can be used for protection *from,* as well as speculation *with,* risks. What these instruments have in common is that they are based on the anticipation of future developments and, to some extent, make the expectations of expectations tradable. This example of risk management demonstrates that the expectation structures of the global financial system are attuned to adaptation. Disappointments are reacted to by the development of new expectation structures. The learning-orientation is so pronounced that potential disappointments are anticipated and used as scenarios for the development of alternative strategies. This is clearly seen in the various simulation techniques that are employed by the risk management departments of banks.

Interestingly, the accelerated cognitive orientation of the global financial system which accompanied the separation of the financial business from the normatively-regulated national capital markets has been largely neglected in the writings of political scientists. Perhaps the traditional emphasis on the role of nation states and the perceived importance of hierarchy as a control medium have impeded a shift in attention to the cognitive aspects of governance. With the exception of some isolated studies addressing the impact of societal »knowledge structures« (Strange 1988; Porter 1999) and »epistemic authorities« (Cutler/Haufler/Porter 1999), the cognitive aspects of governance have only been explicitly dealt with in regime studies. Ernst B. and Peter M. Haas have elaborated cognitive conditions for international problem solving. While Ernst B. Haas (1990) has emphasized the importance of »consensual knowledge«, i.e. generally accepted knowledge that guides regulatory politics, Peter M. Haas (1992) stresses the importance of epistemic communities. He defines these as a »network of professionals with recognized expertise and competence in a particular domain and an authoritative claim to policy-relevant knowledge within that domain or issue area« (ibid.: 3). Such experts could potentially come from many different scientific disciplines or backgrounds but should be able to refer, to a »shared set of normative and principled beliefs«, »shared causal beliefs«, »notions of validity« and »a common policy enterprise« (ibid.).

While these considerations indicate the relevance of knowledge for governance, the heuristic range of an exclusive recourse to consensual knowledge and its connection to causal assumptions is severely limited. Firstly, from the perspective of the theory of self-referential social systems the non-consensual aspects of knowledge become visible. Luhmann (1998) stresses the observer-dependency of knowledge, which means that knowledge has no ontological quality and that it is actively constructed by social systems which are guided by specific criteria of observation. Observing systems bring a two-sided difference into existence, highlighting one of these sides while neglecting the other. For example, while observations of the economic system are oriented towards the difference between payment and non-payment, those of the political system focus on the difference between power and non-power, and those of the legal system on the difference between legal and illegal. The importance of this is that the dissimilarity of observations has made it impossible for perceptions and definitions to be in agreement with one another. Although economic, political and legal actors are able to agree on abstract definitions of problems (e.g. hedge funds must be better controlled), their perception of the details as well as their operative implementation of respective solutions are tied to their system-specific observation criteria. Thus, they are incapable of reaching more than a complementary combination of heterogeneous observations.

Secondly, it is obvious that causality assumptions are increasingly losing their problem-solving function. The growing relevance of ambiguous uncertainties (Bonß 1995) marks a transition from linear to complex risk constructions. In the case of derivatives, for example, there is no linearity between return of capital, fluctuation and deviation rates on the one hand and the performance of the position on the other. Because derivatives are based on other financial instruments (e.g. stocks, credits and other derivatives) and which often combine various additional risks, the potential for loss cannot be fully measured. Another example of the increasing relevance of ambiguous uncertainties in finance are risks that are grouped under the heading of operational risk, i.e. the risk of loss resulting from inadequate or failed internal processes, people and systems or from external events (BCBS 2002: 2). Because it is impossible to relate all the relevant elements of risk to one another, the assessment of operational risks is extremely difficult. Furthermore, considerations of the system risk of the global financial system illustrate that the innovation dynamics in global finance result »in a concatenated risk chain, enhancing the overall risk by unknown leverages and combinatorial effects« (see Willke in this volume). All in all it is apparent that the governance of global finance is being confronted with demands which can no longer be satisfied by the notion of consensual knowledge or with the help of causal constructions.

In contrast, newer approaches are more promising which address the particularities of knowledge production in the financial business as well as the potential of knowledge policy. From a sociological perspective, Karin Knorr Cetina and Alex Preda (2001) draw attention to the epistemic embeddedness of economic activities. Their concept of an epistemization of economic transactions refers to situations where these transactions rely and are interstitched with multiple analysis processes and systems in a variety of ways. The epistemic work which is addressed here is not the work of academic economists developing fundamental insights at a distance from market events. Rather, it is work inscribed in and constitutive of economic objects as relevant to the practical activities of economic agents, such as analysts, strategists, specialists and other knowledge workers in banks, rating agencies, investment, accounting and consulting firms. Besides this, sociological and political science studies are of importance which illustrate the ongoing fragmentation of societal knowledge production (e.g. Willke 2002; Rammert 2002). It is becoming clear that the production of new knowledge under the conditions of functional differentiation is divided between various institutional actors in science, the economy, politics and law. As mentioned above, it is not consensual knowledge that is being produced, but rather knowledge which is emerging from the more or less coordinated interplay of system specific forms of knowledge production.

In consequence, there is an interest in institutional arrangements which transcend not only the boundaries of nation states but also the self-referential operations of functionally specialized societal subsystems. The limitations of the governance of knowledge can be seen as rooted mainly in two paradoxical processes:

»Firstly, the heterogeneity of the enrolled actors – scientists and managers, politicians and administrators [...] – and the diversity of their perspectives cause problems of a successful concertation that does not level out the creative differences between disciplines or institutional rationality standards, and that does not destroy the complementary competencies of functionally specialized actors. Secondly, the specificity of knowledge to be an intangible asset and incompletely explicable set of competencies sets limits to the complete control [...] of knowledge« (Rammert 2002: 3).

Thus, political strategies which aim at enabling intelligent forms of governance

»should encourage the diversity of actors and perspectives. It should cultivate the differences in and between communities of practice. It should enable the criss-crossing between different disciplines of knowledge. And it should keep on spaces and places where collective learning between heterogeneous actors can take place. A policy of quantitative knowledge growth should be complemented by a qualitative policy of knowledge diversity« (ibid.: 14).

In order to put such ›boundary-spanning‹ arrangements in more concrete terms, it is instructive to refer to the concept of »collective intelligence« (Willke 2002: 174). This concept marks an emerging characteristic of social systems, which is not founded on the mere aggregation of individual intelligence, but on systemic intelligence as an emergent property of social systems that combine distributed intelligence. Collective intelligence focuses on the structures, processes and systems of rules that encourage (or hinder) collective learning processes. From the perspective of the theory of self-referential systems (e.g. Willke 1986, 1990; Luhmann 1995) it becomes clear that governments can initiate and promote collective intelligence by using a political strategy which is based on contextual interventions instead of direct, decree-type regulations. Contextual interventions consist of two complementary parts: a reflexive, decentralized framing of contexts which may serve as common source of orientation for the problem-relevant social systems (interactions, organizations, functionally specialized societal subsystems); and the self-guidance of these systems within the limits of their autonomy. A »decentral framing of contexts« (Willke 1990) means that a minimum of common ›world view‹ among social systems seems indispensable for managing collective problems. This aspect of self-guidance is important because only the systems themselves can implement changes in their basic operating procedures. If they are implanted from outside by directive measures, they provoke resistance, circumvention or even the collapse of the system's autonomy. Contextual intervention by the state can, however, operate according to a legal approach which respects the autonomy of social systems and makes use of their specific problem-solving abilities. Instead of directing administrative action through purposive programs and goal-directed forms of intervention, the state develops »relational programs« (Willke 1986) that serve to involve relevant social systems in the process of formulating programs, reaching a decision, and implementation. Such relational programs are intelligent because they focus on the aspect of self-guidance, use the differences between various expert cultures beyond system boundaries and make way for reciprocal learning processes in managing mutually created societal problems.

Considering the potential of the conceptual deliberations addressed here, it would appear promising to advance an integrative understanding of how forms of knowledge processes, structures, organizations and practices act as part of an ongoing shift towards a cognitive mode in global finance. Particularly, in light of the increasing risk-appetite of the global financial system the ambivalence of knowledge as a resource for societal guidance and productivity should be given special attention. In the context of global finance it is particularly apparent that intelligent organizations, work, and products are creating ›intelligent problems‹. Such problems, firstly, result from the intensive application of knowledge and, secondly, utilize attempts for problem solving (e.g. regulations) as an impulse and material for complex self-modification. Consider for example the increasingly sophisticated investment strategies, such as those practiced by hedge funds, and the difficulties economic and political actors have to adequately control and monitor this intransparent field of business.

2. Normative and Cognitive Expectations

New terminology such as »knowledge-based economy« (e.g. Amin/Cohendet 2004), »capitalisme cognitif« (e.g. Moulier-Boutang 2001) and »Wissensökonomie« (e.g. Strulik 2004) signalize a close relationship between the economy and knowledge. Obviously, a form of economic management is emerging which is oriented towards cognitive (learning-oriented) expectation structures to a previously unheard of extent. It can be assumed that this has something to do with the nature of modernity. A time characterized by change and acceleration is oriented towards the future. In contrast to the traditional model of relating to the experiences of the past, this new form of economic management focuses on the exploration and utilization of the potentials of an unknown future. Like a »faustischer Drang« (Bloch 1971) a change of emphasis is taking place in society from the application of existing knowledge to the creation of new knowledge. Besides the effects that these changes have had on science, they appear to be having the greatest impact on the economy and to be contributing to the acceleration of societal knowledge production (with various consequences). In addition to the classic basic factors of economic production information, knowledge and expertise have become of paramount importance. Increasingly more products have embedded intelligence. In the field of finance, for example, highly sophisticated financial instruments like Asset-Backed Securities (ABS) divide and recombine risks to create products which react to the risk-appetite of specific investors. Or think of the services of the leading rating agencies. Using their »global expertise« (Willke 2003) they analyze the creditworthiness of countries, supranational organizations, banks, insurance companies, industrial companies as well as investment funds (see Sinclair and Strulik in this volume).

The increasing knowledge-intensity in the fields of organization and labor is equally striking. Financial service providers in particular can be seen as »knowledge intensive firms« (Starbuck 1992): their operations are usually based on the use of sophisticated information and communication technologies, the combination of heterogeneous business fields and processes, the employment of experts and the continual innovation of financial products. Even traditional financial services like retail banking are transforming themselves into knowledge-intensive services with an emphasis on consulting and elaborating tailor-made financial solutions. At the same time, the share of knowledge work is increasing. According to Helmut Willke's

(2001) definition of knowledge work, »relevant knowledge is seen as (1) continually revised, (2) permanently amendable, (3) in principle, as a resource rather than as truth and (4) inseparably coupled with ignorance, so that specific risks are inherent to it« (ibid.: 21). One needs only to look into the departments of investment banks to recognize the cognitive orientation of their respective practices. Hence, adaptability is becoming the central criterion for knowledge driven competition.

»Although the experts in the departments of the investment banks know that they are not free from errors in their prognoses, day in day out they continue to analyze their stock charts, seek instructive correlations, assess the strategies and the management of young technology companies, examine the development potential of entire industries and national economies with the hope of generating better and more useful knowledge than their colleagues at other banks. In spite of all this, they are always ready to exchange existing knowledge for new, better knowledge. [...] The experts' willingness to learn must know no limits« (Vopel 1999: 14, translation T.S.).

The result of this focus on the generation and application of new knowledge is that the competition for adequate knowledge, that is, knowledge that contributes to solving relevant problems, is becoming fiercer and more fast-paced.

For an understanding of the ongoing shift towards a cognitive mode of global finance it is instructive to follow Luhmann's ideas (1991) on the emergence of a world society. From a system-theoretical perspective, Luhmann explains that a world society first emerged in interactions in which cognitive expectations became stable in respect to the expectations and actions of others (ibid.: 55). In the case of the economy, normative arrangements of (inter-)national economic policy are being replaced by structures, processes and regulation systems that incorporate the risk of a purely cognitive orientation to price and market fluctuations. The emergence of a highly innovative risk management industry in the 1970s is a striking demonstration of these developments. Luhmann sees the same process happening also in other areas of society, such as science, technology, and the media: cognitive, adaptive, and learning-oriented expectations have clearly become prominent while normative and prescriptive expectations are fading out. The increasing importance of cognitive expectations can be observed even in politics and law, the social functions of which consist both of »maintaining the capacity for collectively binding decision-making« (Luhmann 2000) and »stabilizing normative expectations« (Luhmann 2004). Examples of this trend are the growing number of approaches to a regulation of economic self-regulation (Power 2002) and the initiatives for a proceduralization of law (Ladeur 1995).

In order to find reasons for the shift of emphasis in the societal expectation structures and identify the consequences of the governance of global finance, it is advisable to start with a clarification of the difference between normative and cognitive expectations. According to Luhmann (1991) the difference lies in what actions are taken in the case of disappointment:

»Normative expectations are resolutely held on to, even when disappointed, and are based on the respective resources such as inner-conviction, sanctions and consensus. Cognitive expectations, in contrast, are characteristically learning-oriented, can be corrected by disappointments and are based on the respective resources, particularly on the expectation that disappointments are sufficient to quickly and clearly redirect expectations. Cognitive expectations seek themselves, normative expectations seek their objects to be changed. Learning or not learning – that's the difference« (ibid.: 55, translation T.S.).

What is important is that a blending and complex interrelationship of both expectation modi are apparent in societal practice. Hence, one tends to adapt differently to different situations: to situations without clear and immediate learning opportunities one adapts normatively while situations which promise no help in dealing with disappointed expectations provoke a cognitive adaptation. On the one hand, regulations such as the Sarbanes-Oxley Act comes to mind in the context of the governance of global finance. The problem of avoiding future balance fraud is addressed by public regulation which primarily operates with definitions of permissible and prohibited activities and determinations of accountability and responsibility. This primarily serves to determine the normative demands on the function of auditing and the trustworthiness of businesses. On the other hand, the recent developments in the field of banking supervision (Basel II) provides an example of cognitive forms of regulation. Not only because of growing uncertainty about *whether* there will be undesirable effects, but also *what* they will be, the Basel Committee presently recommends, to emphasize the process of risk management in banking supervision and to refine regulation techniques in accordance with the size, the risk structure and the potential liability of the banking institute. In establishing a more flexible and learning-oriented institutional arrangement, both the growing economic and societal demands for stability as well as for innovation are expected to be met.

Seen analytically, normative and cognitive expectations are direct opposites in respect to the way disappointments are seen and dealt with. In societal practice, however, they constitute functionally equivalent strategies for the treatment of uncertainty. Nevertheless, the choice of one strategy over the other does not appear to be random but to correlate with other factors. Assuming that the structure and the environment of a social system have an effect on the dominance of one of these expectation modi, the question could also be asked which factors stimulate shifts from one modus to the other. Here Luhmann (1991: 56) assumes that in the course of societal evolution the normative style of expectation precedes the cognitive style. This can be seen for instance in religious standards for the truthfulness of scientific research or in the attempts to tie legislation to natural law. With the increasing differentiation of society into autonomous subsystems with specific functions, normative guidelines based on religion, politics and law are reaching their limits. On the one hand, for example, the legal authority of the state enabled the establishment of highly contingent, complex social relationships which were structurally stable and psychologically bearable. On the other hand, there are visible deficits in the regulation of risks which transcend national territories and in situations where one is confronted with the demand for risky as well as welfare-promoting innovations.

Current debates on the effects of economic globalization and technological innovations illustrate that in the past decades a shift has taken place towards the evolutionary and functional primacy of the subsystems of science and the economy. Both systems are particularly cognitively-oriented and define the problems to be dealt with by society today as well as the conditions for and the limits to their solutions (ibid.: 58). As new considerations and empirical studies on knowledge politics demonstrate, public actors appear increasingly occupied with their own learning ability and the facilitation of learning processes within other functional systems (e.g. Willke 2003; Strulik/Kussin 2005). Initiatives for the promotion of a learning administration and the implementation of strategic models for the management of public organizations, such as the European Foundation of Quality Management's (EFQM) model for »Business Excellence«, indicate that political actors are trying to improve their cognitive competence to deal with rapid changes in their environment. At the same time, the emergence of mixed public-private governance regimes is leading to closer interactions between politics and other social spheres. Accordingly, the role of the political system can less often be understood in terms of ›normative integration‹ but is seen more often as a way to enable ›cognitive cooperation‹, that is the creation of optimal conditions for a combination of heterogeneous functional logics, governance structures and knowledge resources. As such, knowledge politics must take a diversity of perspectives and instruments into consideration and put them in relation to one another in order to promote collective learning processes.

It should be noted that today's economy, and global finance especially, are based on distinctively cognitive styles of expectation. The associated orientation towards learning and innovation has, on the one hand, led to a massive expansion of opportunities for action. Above all, the example of a highly knowledge-based risk management has demonstrated that the financial system has managed to suppress normative (political) guidelines, to raise (its own) acceptance of uncertainty, creating ways to make more expectations expectable and giving improbabilities a structuring function. As a result, there has, on the one hand, been a substantial increase in productivity: at the end of the last decade the volume of the ›symbolic‹ financial economy had reached roughly the sixty-fold of the volume of the ›real‹ economy (Held et al. 1999: 209; Kurtzman 1993: 12). On the other hand, the increasingly cognitive orientation of global finance poses fundamental challenges to governance. Today, the financial business is so complex and knowledge-intensive that even those who are directly involved are hardly able to understand or assess the criteria for, and results of, their decisions. As Philip Cerny (1994: 331) points out: »The mathematical complexity of financial innovations and transactions has been running ahead not only of the ability of regulators to follow (much less to control a priori) but also of the ability of many firms and financial firms to understand.«

3. Governance as a Cognitive Problem

The analytical differentiation of expectation modes discussed above is instructive for an adequate understanding of the recent problems of the governance of global finance. While a normative expectation mode operates with the difference between conforming and deviating behavior, a cognitive expectation mode uses the difference between *knowledge* and *ignorance*. With regard to the cognitively oriented financial system, it is first of all important to see that it is not a matter of minimizing or dissolving the difference between knowledge and ignorance through the use of knowledge. Rather, the orientation to learning, which is characteristic of the global financial system, indicates a »progressive reproduction of ignorance« (Luhmann 1995a: 177) in this respect. According to Willke (2002: 18), contemporary society is being confronted with a crisis of knowledge because essentially »no one can rely on existing knowledge as long as the complementary ignorance is not similarly registered and made as manageable as knowledge itself. The knowledge crisis designates the inability to competently manage ignorance« (ibid., translation T.S.). Crucial to an understanding of the particular dynamics and complexity of global finance as well as concrete governance problems, appears to be a detailed study of the function of ignorance: what is the importance of ignorance for the acquisition and reproduction of knowledge, the emergence and change of institutions and, not least, for the creation of risks?

The above mentioned change of emphasis in the societal treatment of knowledge, in the sense of an increase in the importance of the production of new knowledge obviously goes hand in hand with a new perspective on ignorance. Ignorance is no longer simply perceived as a deficit in rational decision-making, but increasingly often as an opportunity for creative action. Michael Smithson (1989) stresses this view:

»Not long ago, the dominant methods of coping with ignorance were to try eliminating it or absorbing it. The emerging frameworks now seem to have jettisoned the assumption, that ignorance is ultimately reducible, and the new style is ›managerial‹ in the sense of attempting to understand, tolerate, and even utilize certain kinds of ignorance« (ibid.: viii).

The importance of a more active and utilitarian treatment of ignorance becomes clear in connection with Robert K. Merton's (1987) discussion of the culture of science and the relationship between knowledge and ignorance. Assuming that science develops by replacing ignorance with knowledge, Merton refers to the dynamic cognitive role played by a form of ignorance that he calls specified ignorance. Scientific processes of knowledge-production

»repeatedly adopt the cognitively consequential practice of specifying this or that piece of ignorance derived from having acquired the added degree of knowledge that made it possible to identify definite portions of the still unknown. In workaday science, it is not enough to confess one's ignorance; the point is to specify it. That of course, amounts to instituting, or finding, a new, worthy, and soluble scientific problem« (ibid.: 8).

What is important is that economic realms are also increasingly defined by a utilitarian treatment of ignorance. Analysts and salespeople in investment banks, for example, exploit uncertainty regarding the development of markets, companies and products by transforming it into specific problems (e.g. market risk, credit risk). They then use these problems to develop tailor-made financial instruments to offer to their customers. Within such working contexts, ignorance appears not as a hindrance to decision-making, but as a source of innovation and productivity.

For the governance of global finance it is important to note that the active treatment of ignorance is accompanied by ever more complex problems of risk. A special type of ignorance has emerged which leads to decision-making situations that cannot be managed in traditional ways with the help of probability calculations. Ignorance presents itself here as an unsolvable information problem (delimitation of contingency). A very good example of such »unspecified ignorance« (Luhmann 1995a: 177), as well as the corresponding decision-making constellations, is how many financial institutions treat the above mentioned operational risks. These risks have become not only particularly prominent in connection with the massive losses in the financial sector (e.g. Barings Bank, Prudential, Metropolitan Life, Banca Nazionale del Lavoro), but also, and more importantly, in the balance frauds of large companies which have been uncovered since the beginning of 2002. As the Enron, WorldCom and Global Crossing cases illustrate, the potential for illegal practices has increased not least because of high performance information technologies and the complexity of corporate structures. Remarkably, the cases which have gained public attention are to some extent the result of inter-organizational fraud networks, which include not just the top management of the companies but also banks and accounting firms. The world-wide decline of stock markets in the wake of these scandals first of all reflects a massive loss of trust in an instrument which until then had stood for rationality, calculability and credibility: the balance sheet. Secondly, it demonstrates the growing interdependence and fragility of the economy. The massive consequences of the drastic decline in value of the companies have been felt, not only by many small investors, but also in other economic sectors.

The aspect of interrelated effects brings up a second type of ignorance relevant to the question at hand: »systemic ignorance« (Willke 2002: 29). This type corresponds to risk theoretical considerations referring to the social, factual and temporal delimitation of risk situations (e.g. Beck 1986;

Bonß 1995). What is important about systemic ignorance is that it no longer reflects the »normal risk« (Perrow 1989) typical of industrial societies, but designates a constellation within which too many events are connected to too many other events in a way that transcends the decision-making of individual actors. This phenomenon, as well as the explosiveness of systemic ignorance, can most clearly be seen in the context of global finance. The interaction of technological developments, the deregulation of financial markets, the regulation of financial institutions, and the ever more sophisticated financial innovations have led to a new level of systemic risk. This development is particularly visible in the highly knowledge-intensive derivatives business. This fact accounts for the assessment by the International Monetary Fund (1994):

»(D)erivative instruments tend to strengthen linkages between market segments and between individual financial institutions in ways that are difficult to identify or quantify. Consequently, disruptions or increased uncertainty in one market may now be more likely to spill over into other derivatives markets and into the cash markets« (ibid.: 51).

Considering the relationship between knowledge and ignorance it is evident that the cognitive orientation of the global financial system can be seen in its highly innovative dynamic and productivity. On the other hand, forms of risks are gaining significance which cannot be treated with traditional economic and political instruments. Governance is thus becoming a cognitive problem, or to put it differently: a matter of intelligent adaptation. In respect to the global financial business, five essential problem areas can be identified:

(1) *The exterritorialization of financial transactions*: Tailor-made financial innovations as well as information technologies enable complex investment and arbitration strategies, which bring about networks of markets that used to be fragmented. Central problems for large financial services firms are the elaboration, integration and assessment of globally dispersed data (e.g. business results, risk analysis) no less than the utilization of such data in decision-making. At the same time, the regulatory institutions are confronted with the fact that the consequences of the collapse of markets or organizations may transcend spatial and sectoral boundaries.

(2) *The asymmetry between private and public knowledge*: The acceleration of knowledge production in global finance has resulted in a forced asymmetry between private and public knowledge. Increasingly, regulatory institutions are less prepared to confront private actors with sufficient external knowledge. While this is related to a well-known problem of regulation, the spe-

cial innovation dynamics, the global dimension of business and the central position of finance within the economy make this fact more prominent. Public actors are thereby confronted with the task of generating suitably wide-ranging supervisory knowledge.

(3) *The emergence of unquantifiable risks*: The innovation dynamics of finance are accompanied by an increasing relevance of market and operational risks which are either very difficult to quantify or cannot be quantified at all. Any attempt at institutional risk management and supervision based on traditional quantitative approaches alone is no longer sufficient. Financial services firms are thus faced with the need to create complementary qualitative risk management mechanisms on the basis of which it will be possible to internally observe and deal with the problems of locating and forecasting the consequences of decisions. This results in the analogous need for regulatory arrangements that support and monitor organizations in implementing and applying such mechanisms.

(4) *The regulatory dialectic*: Political strategies of regulation are always confronted with the problem of being countered by the ›regulated‹ (Kane 1981). Corresponding dynamics are accelerated by an increasing knowledge intensity of the regulatory field. For global finance, it is apparent that political measures aimed at a higher degree of safety simultaneously stimulate financial services firms to develop economically motivated divergence while creating new insecurities. For example, globally operating banks have answered the regulatory demands for improvements in equity (in keeping with the Basel Accord of 1988) with an increase in non-balance sheet business (in particular innovations in derivatives) which does not have an effect on the supervisor's equity demands. Consequently, a more intensive dialogue between financial services firms and regulatory institutions is required.

(5) *The relevance of systemic risk*: Globalization and knowledge intensity both increase the systemic risk of the financial system, i.e. the probability that the difficulties of an individual institution will affect the functional ability of the entire system. The global economy experienced a foretaste of such a ›linkage‹ shock in 1974 with the failure of the German Bankhaus Herstatt, which was active in the expanding foreign exchange market. Other anxious moments for market participants were the 1995 failure of Barings Bank or the 1998 turbulences of Long-Term Capital-Management (LTCM). There is a lot of theoretical and empirical evidence that the problem of systemic risk increases not only with the global reach and interdependency of financial transactions but, as the Barings and LTCM

cases indicate, also with the knowledge intensity of financial firms and products.

4. Towards a Cognitive Mode of Global Finance?

The contributions to this volume all deal with cognitive aspects of global finance. Using different approaches from sociology and political science questions regarding the relevance of a cognitive mode of global finance are addressed. The first section presents complementary theoretical perspectives on the interrelationship of finance and knowledge. Particular emphasis is placed on the characteristics of the contemporary financial system and the relevance of normative and cognitive expectation structures for the (re-)production of its operations (Willke, Pahl, Sinclair). The second section deals with different modes of managing the insecurities of financial business, such as the accounting profession, the risk-management of international banks, and the functions and consequences of (self-)regulatory arrangements (Vollmer, Kalthoff, Hessling). The third section investigates the role of private actors and their expertise for the governance of global finance. Special attention will be drawn to the Group of Thirty (G30), a non-state organization, and the leading US-American credit rating agencies, which have become an essential part of the world's financial infrastructure (Tsingou, Strulik). The fourth section finally concentrates on an outstanding knowledge-intensive field of the governance of global finance, namely the regulation of globally operating banks. Referring to the new framework published by the Basel Committee on Banking Supervision in 2004 (Basel II), the role of standards and the meaning of politics are analyzed (Holzer, Kussin/Kette).

In the first section, where theoretical approaches to finance are linked to considerations of the relevance of normative and cognitive expectation structures, Helmut Willke describes the specific operative logic of global finance. Using concepts of sociological systems theory, three basic ideas are at the center of his argument: the idea of money as a generalized medium of communication, the idea of communication as an element of social systems, and the idea of emergence as a generative principle that creates a new system level. From this perspective Willke not only illustrates the preconditions and consequences of the financial system's autonomy but also the increasing significance of a cognitive mode in handling uncertainties. On the basis of his considerations a cognitive turn becomes evident: of the economy in general – from industrial economy to knowledge economy – and of the financial system in particular – from normatively regulated national capital markets to a knowledge-based global superstructure.

In elaborating the characteristics of global finance, Hanno Pahl focuses on the general relationship of finance and the economy. While some authors emphasize de- or uncoupling of the financial sphere from the real economy of goods and others claim an increasing causal interdependence of both realms, he aims at developing an integrative perspective able to deal with these contradictory findings in a theoretically sound way. Thus, Pahl raises the fundamental question of the unity *and* difference of finance and the economy. In search for an adequate answer he refers to the relationship of money and finance and analyses the theoretical legacies of Karl Marx's and Niklas Luhmann's work with special attention to core elements which contribute to a theory of money and a more sophisticated theory of finance. On this basis, the rise of the financial markets is interpreted as a further shift toward the autonomy of the economic system from society. External points of reference that normatively govern the shortage of money as the system's medium – whether political or extra-social – are increasingly offset by system-internal structures which are primarily oriented to adaptation.

Starting with the assessment that structure, in global finance, cannot be understood as invariant and unaffected by the meaning attributed to the situation by participants, Timothy J. Sinclair presents an institutional approach to the politics of global finance. His basic suggestion is that the analyses of finance must start with cognitive or social facts. A constructivist perspective is therefore developed that complements rationalist approaches, in which the heuristic is the struggle between rational actors with fixed preferences. Special attention is given to the processes through which the preferences and subsequent strategies of actors (such as corporations and states) are socially constructed. Using the concept of embedded knowledge networks, Sinclair shows that knowledge-based recommendations, rankings or ratings play a crucial role in constructing markets in a context of less-than-perfect information and considerable uncertainty about the future. The example of the leading US-American rating agencies Standard & Poor's and Moody's shows that their specific expertise in assessing the creditworthiness of financial actors and products adjusts the

›ground rules‹ inside international capital markets and thereby shapes the international organization and behavior of institutions seeking funds.

The second section starts with a contribution by Hendrik Vollmer. On the basis of the diagnosis that the amount and significance of financial numbers mobilized for purposes of governing public and private economies is immensely increasing, he analyses the driving forces behind an escalating commitment to acting, reacting, inspecting and regulating by numbers. From his sociological perspective he shows that financial numbers, rather than simply referring to monetary assets and liabilities, come to figure as symptoms of a broadening range of past, present and future aspects of economic reality. While this symptomatic quality of financial numbers on the one hand expresses the genuine and growing fixation of contemporary governmentality on getting, elaborating and improving information, it is on the other hand a mere shadow of contested social situations in which financial numbers are not of a narrowly cognitive, but of a more comprehensively existential significance deriving from basic behavioral problems of situated economic activity. How these problems are dealt with by participants of an activity, which is embedded in a circulation of numbers across social settings, is exemplified by an illustration of regulatory drama. From a conceptual point of view, Vollmer argues in detail that an exchange-based reconstruction of governing by numbers offers a promising approach towards analyzing contemporary forms of financial governance.

Focusing on the role and importance of calculation in modern societies, Herbert Kalthoff presents an outline of an empirical sociology of calculation. To illustrate the relevance of a corresponding empirical research program, three core dimensions are addressed: the use and function of operative modes of writing, the performativity of representation devices and the social practices of interpretation. On the basis of these conceptual considerations, he uses his empirical findings in the field of the risk management of international banks to suggest that in the bank's credit process numbers contribute to a necessary reduction of complexity and thereby make investment decisions possible. However, it emerges from the sociological perspective outlined that numbers should not be seen as hard facts but rather as ambivalent. As Kalthoff points out the function of risk management departments is not to avoid economic risk at all but to document it and to transform it into economic benefits for the bank.

Alexandra Hessling focuses in her essay on the ambiguities of accounting and the resulting regulatory problems. Using the critical accounting discourse and instructed by the sociological systems theory, she explores the paradoxical phenomenon that accounting involves the construction of selective visibilities which facilitates a distinctive mode of cooperation and coordination, but that these constructions are on the other hand highly ambiguous. Hessling argues that accounting produces regulatory problems that accountants, auditors and investors have to face. Special emphasis is given to the role of ignorance in the regulatory field of accounting. By using recent approaches to ignorance she shows that these regulatory problems are basically caused by the ignorance that accounting creates. On the basis of an elaboration of three concepts of ignorance – usable ignorance, exploitation of ignorance, latent ignorance – she illustrates not only the cognitive efforts of accounting professionals and other experts to specify this or that regulatory problem and the complex interactions between regulations and regulated but also the way regulatory bodies deal with these issues.

The third section investigates the role of private actors and their expertise for the governance of global finance and starts with a contribution by Eleni Tsingou. With reference to theoretical debates in International Political Economy (IPO) to explain the growing importance of non-state actors in policy processes, she analyses how financial governance is generated and offers a critical examination of the role of policy communities in global financial governance. With the Group of Thirty (G-30) she focuses on a non-state organization that has had an important impact on financial regulatory and supervisory practices both at the national and the global levels. Her critical analysis provides not just a comprehensive picture of a type of organization positioned halfway between an interest group and a think tank, but also gives a series of explanations for the rise and development of the G-30 and of how it has found its niche in the global financial governance framework by concentrating on the ›details‹ of the system that require private technical expertise. In sum, her examination of the Group of Thirty underlines that traditional debates on the relative merits of self-regulation and prescriptive regulation have been superseded by a shared understanding of what constitutes good financial governance and the appropriate role of private sector initiatives and standards within that structure.

My own contribution deals with the functions and consequences of the leading US-American credit rating agencies and refers to the role of ignorance in finance as well as the increasing relevance of system trust for enabling the reproduction of the global financial system. Using theoretical concepts from sociological systems theory, it is first demonstrated that the agencies' increasing relevance in global finance corresponds with the economies' shift towards a more active and utilitarian treatment of ignorance. With their global expertise, rating agencies actively grasp the indeterminateness of markets, interpret it and translate it into practicable expectations on the basis of which market actors can take risks and make profits accordingly. In a second step emphasis is given to the agencies' trust-producing function. It is shown that trust in the financial system's operations has become more relevant not just for the coordination of decisions, but also for enabling productive risk-taking. In light of this, I argue that a knowledge-based financial system requires organizations which are specialized in a knowledge-based production of system trust. With their expertise in credit assessments rating agencies not only observe the trustworthiness of states, firms and financial instruments, they also expand the risk-processing capacity of the global financial system.

In the last section of this book, Boris Holzer's contribution focuses on the role of politics and administration in the process of rule-making. By referring to the political-science diagnosis of a democratic deficit in financial regulation, he argues that the process of elaborating and negotiating a new approach in banking supervision is not so much characterized by a lack of democracy but a lack of politics. Based on a study of the Basel II-related media discourse in Germany he illustrates this thesis and discusses to what extent the lack of politics in the Basel II process is symptomatic of a shifting balance between administration and politics in the regulation of financial and other risks. It appears that both the unusual political fault lines involved in regulating financial risks and the emergence of a more cognitive style of regulation diminish the salience of politics in the decision-making process. On the other hand Holzer also shows that the inclusion of cognitive elements into administration itself may well be a functional equivalent of the (probably unrealistic) expectation that the increasing demand for the regulation of risks can be met by politics alone.

Matthias Kussin and Sven Kette analyze the operational logic of global standards as elements of soft law. Their focus is on the cognitive quality of such standards and the implications for the governance of the global financial system. Starting from the observation that norms as classical instruments of political and legal regulation cannot keep up with the global and future-oriented logic of the financial system they discuss to what extent the normative structure of expectations can be cognitively opened by standards. Kussin and Kette argue that standards are similar to norms in the way they operate, while legitimating principles and acquiring potentials constitute an apparently different mode of coordination. Empirically, they concentrate on Basel II and describe the recommendations by the Basel Committee on Banking Supervision as a standards-based framework that enables social coordination through the complementary use of normative expectations and elements of a cognitive mode of expectation. By enriching normative expectations with elements of cognitive indetermination, standards gain processing capacity for heterogeneous and knowledge-based circumstances. On the basis of their conceptual and empirical considerations the authors conclude that standards can contribute to more complex and adaptable forms of governance and therefore provide special capabilities to keep up with the innovation dynamics of global finance.

References

Adhikari, Kamini/Sales, Arnaud (2001), »New directions in the study of knowledge, economy and society«, in: *Current Sociology*, Vol. 49, 1–25.

Amin, Ash/Cohendet, Patrick (2004), *Architectures of Knowledge. Firms, Capabilities, and Communities.* Oxford.

Basel Committee on Banking Supervision (BCBS) (2002), *Sound Practices for the Management and Supervision of Operational Risk.* http://www.bis.org (07/19/06).

Beck, Ulrich (1986), *Risikogesellschaft. Auf dem Weg in eine andere Moderne.* Frankfurt a.M.

Bloch, Ernst (1971), »Über den Begriff der Weisheit«, in: Ernst Bloch, *Pädagogica.* Frankfurt a.M., 96–145.

Bonß, Wolfgang (1995), *Vom Risiko. Unsicherheit und Ungewißheit in der Moderne.* Hamburg.

Cerny, Philip G. (1994), »The dynamics of financial globalization. Technology, market structure and policy response«, in: *Policy Sciences*, Vol. 27, 319–342.

Cutler, Claire A./Haufler, Virginia/Porter, Tony (1999) (eds), *Private Authority and International Affairs.* New York.

Dale, Richard (1984), *The Regulation of International Banking.* Cambridge.

Eichengreen, Barry (1999), *Towards a New International Financial Architecture. A Practical Post-Asia Aagenda.* Washington (D.C.).

Eichengreen, Barry/Lindert, Peter H. (1989) (eds), *The International Debt Crisis in Historical Perspective.* Cambridge (Mass.).

Finnerty, John D. (1985), »Zero coupon bond arbitrage. An illustration of the regulatory dialectic at work«, in: *Financial Management*, Vol. 14, 13–17.

Griffith-Jones, Stephany (2000), »Developing countries and the new financial architecture«, http://www.ids.ac.uk/ids/global/finance/pdfs/finarc.pdf (03/01/02).

Haas, Ernst B. (1990), *When Knowledge is Power. Three Models of Change in International Organizations*. Berkeley.

Haas, Peter M. (1992), »Introduction: epistemic communities and international policy coordination«, in: *International Organization*, Vol. 46, 1–35.

Held, David/McGrew, Anthony/Goldblatt, David/Perraton, Jonathan (1999), *Global Transformation. Politics, Economics and Culture*. Cambridge.

International Monetary Fund (IMF) (1994), »Banks and derivatives markets: A challenge for financial policy«, in: *IMF Survey*, 02/21/94, 49–51.

Kane, Edward J. (1981), »Impact of regulation on economic behavior. Accelerating inflation, technological innovation, and the decreasing effectiveness of banking regulation«, in: *The Journal of Finance*, Vol. 36, 355–367.

Kapstein, Ethan B. (1996), *Governing the Global Economy. International Finance and the State*. Cambridge (Mass.).

Kurtzman, Joel (1993), *The death of Money. How the Electronic Economy has destabilized the World's Markets and created Financial Chaos*. New York.

Ladeur, Karl-Heinz (1995), *Das Umweltrecht der Wissensgesellschaft. Von der Gefahrenabwehr zum Risikomanagement*. Berlin.

Luhmann, Niklas (1991), »Die Weltgesellschaft«, in: *Soziologische Aufklärung*, Vol. 2. Aufsätze zur Theorie der Gesellschaft, 4th edition. Opladen, 51–71.

Luhmann, Niklas (1995), *Social systems*. Stanford.

— (1995a), *Gesellschaftsstruktur und Semantik. Studien zur Wissenssoziologie der modernen Gesellschaft*, Vol. 4. Frankfurt a.M.

— (1998), *Observations of Modernity*. Stanford.

— (2000), *Die Politik der Gesellschaft*. Frankfurt a.M.

— (2004), *Law as a Social System*. Oxford.

Merton, Robert K. (1987), »Three fragments from a sociologist's notebook: Establishing the phenomenon, specified ignorance, and strategic research materials«, in: *Annual Review of Sociology*, Vol. 13, 1–28.

Moulier-Boutang, Yann (2001), »Marx in Kalifornien: Der dritte Kapitalismus und die alte politische Ökonomie«, in: *Aus Politik und Zeitgeschichte*, B 52–53/2001, 29–37.

Nonet, Philippe/Selznick, Philip (1978), *Law and Society in Transition. Towards Responsive Law*. New York.

Padoa-Schioppa, Tommaso/Saccomanni, Fabrizio (1994), »Managing a market-led gobal financial system«, in: Peter Kenen (ed.), *Managing the world economy*. Washington (D.C.), 235–268.

Perrow, Charles (1989), *Normal Accidents: Living with High Risk Technologies*. Princeton.

Porter, Tony (1999), »The Late-Modern Knowledge Structure and World Politics«, in: Martin Hewson and Timothy J. Sinclair (eds), *Approaches to Global Governance Theory*. New York, 137–155.

Power, Michael (2002), »Standardization and the regulation of management practices«, in: *Soziale Systeme*, Vol. 8, 191–204.

Rammert, Werner (2002), »The governance of knowledge: The rising relevance of non-explicit knowledge under a new regime of distributed knowledge production«, in: *TUTS Working Papers* 8/2002. Berlin.

Scholte, Jan Aart (2002), »Governing global finance«, in: *CSGR Working Paper*, No. 88/02. Warwick.

Sinclair, Timothy S. (1994), »Passing judgement: credit rating processes as regulatory mechanisms of governance in the emerging world order«, in: *Review of International Political Economy*, Vol. 1, 133–159.

Smithson, Michael (1989), *Ignorance and Uncertainty. Emerging Paradigms*. New York.

Starbuck, William H. (1992), »Learning by Knowledge-Intensive firms«, in: *Journal of Management Studies*, Vol. 29, 713–740.

Strange, Susan (1988), *States and Markets*. New York.

Strulik, Torsten (2000), *Risikomanagement globaler Finanzmärkte. Herausforderungen und Initiativen im Kontext der Bankenregulierung*. Frankfurt a.M.

— (2004), *Nichtwissen und Vertrauen in der Wissensökonomie*. Frankfurt a.M.

Strulik, Torsten/Kussin, Matthias (2005), »Finanzmarktregulierung und Wissenspolitik. Basel II – Die aufsichtsrechtliche Konstitution kollektiver Intelligenz?«, in: *Zeitschrift für Rechtssoziologie*, Vol. 26, 101–129.

Tsingou, Eleni (2003), »Transnational policy communities and financial governance: the role of private actors in derivatives regulation«, in: *CSGR Working Paper*, No. 111/03. Warwick.

Vopel, Oliver (1999), *Wissensmanagement im Investment Banking. Organisierte Wissensarbeit bei komplexen Finanzdienstleistungen*. Wiesbaden.

Willke, Helmut (1986), »Three types of legal structure: The conditional, the purposive and the relational«, in: Gunther Teubner (ed.), *Dilemmas of Law in the Welfare state*. Berlin, 280–299.

— (1990), »Political intervention – Operational preconditions of generalized political exchange«, in: Bernd Marin (ed.), *Governance and Generalized Exchange*. Frankfurt a.M., 235–254.

— (2001), *Systemisches Wissensmanagement*. 2nd edition. Stuttgart.

— (2002), *Dystopia. Studien zur Krisis des Wissens in der modernen Gesellschaft*. Frankfurt a.M.

— (2003), *Heterotopia. Studien zur Krisis der Ordnung moderner Gesellschaften*. Frankfurt a.M.

Wood, Duncan (2005), *Governing Global Banking. The Basel Committee and the Politics of Financial Globalization*. Aldershot.

Part 1

Theoretical Perspectives on Knowledge and Finance

The Autonomy of the Financial System: Symbolic Coupling and the Language of Capital

Helmut Willke

1. Introduction

Modern economies are functionally differentiated subsystems of societies. These societies continue to be organized around a political and legal identity based on the concept of national sovereignty. In spite of these fundamentals, the national economies have transcended their traditional boundaries, building global exchange networks which today constitute a *world economy* with global reach, perspective and concerns.

The evolution of modern capitalism radicalizes the uses and utilizations of money (as generalized symbolics of economic communication) which began in biblical times with the invention of usury, followed by the invention of banks and formalized bookkeeping in Renaissance Italy. By mid 19th century, the separation of a first economy based on labor, and a secondary economy based on capital, creates the dividing lines that give Karl Marx reason to describe, in *Das Kapital*, the inner workings of the system of »industrial capital« and capital in general. His most pristine observation concerns a separation of logics and rationalities of the real (primary) economy on the one hand and finance as a secondary economy on the other.

In terms of modern sociological systems theory, in the primary economy money serves as a generalized symbolic medium of communication, facilitating the exchange of goods (commodities and services). In the secondary economy, the financial system, money itself becomes the commodity. The business of banks is to organize chains of payments and promises of future payments (Baecker 1991). In the primary economy money is used (in addition to serving as a store of value, as a medium of settlement and account and as a unit of account) as a common denominator to express prices in a market. A market extends as far as the relevant goods can be observed (evaluated) in terms of money. The function of money is to attach abstract prices to goods for the purpose of comparison in exchanges. In the secondary economy money is applied to itself in a reflexive way (Luhmann 1971): People and organizations buy and sell money (and its more sophisticated derivatives which for now are included in the term money) for a price expressed in money. A price is attached not to goods but to money itself. The financial system constitutes and is constituted by a market for money. In short: The primary economy is about the allocation of things, finance is concerned with the allocation of money (McGoun 2001: 2).

The financial system is by now a global »regime«, including structures (principles, norms, values), procedures and rule systems. It consists of a loosely coupled set of powerful states such as the G7 and international, transnational and global institutions such as the World Bank, the IMF, the BIS and the Basel Committee on Banking Superivsion, the IOSCO (International Organization of Securities Commissions) and the IAIS (International Association of Insurance Supervisors), the Central Banks of large economies and new institutions like the Financial Stability Forum. »The international financial regime includes but is not limited to norms and institutions governing exchange rate practices, regulation of all private cross-border financial flow, and management of the international financial institutions ...« (Armijo 2001: 380).

Financial capital (as opposed to e.g. cultural or intellectual capital) is a reflexive form of money and as such a commodity. It evolves like other commodities by means of successful innovations (for a review of literature on financial innovation see Frame and White 2002; for the role of crises see Knutsen 2004: 8). However, its evolution is guided by the specific rationality and rationale of money as a purely symbolic good. The goods of the primary economy derive their value (given supply) from their usefulness for the direct appetites of consumers, particularly their estimates of the relative weight of direct physical and psychological needs. The prices of the goods of the secondary economy (given supply) build on their usefulness for the deferred appetites of investors, particularly their risks/opportunities calculations of assets in specific future circumstances. The core roles of the primary economy are consumer and producer, those of the secondary economy are investor and saver. The saver »produces« money, and the investor »consumes« it as a commodity.

Elton McGoun has stated the normalized myths about the relations between the primary and the secondary economy succinctly:

»In both our scholarship and our society, we are wedded to the notion that the financial economy (of money) exist for, refers to, and is meaningless without the so-called real economy (of things). But is it? What if ›real‹ finance (finance which refers to the real economy), is in fact ›hyperreal‹ finance (finance which refers to nothing but itself)?« (McGoun 2001: 3)

In a sociological perspective, the most intriguing part of the evolution of the financial system pertains to observations articulated since Karl Marx which point to a separation or detachment or estrangement of the »real« economy from the financial system as a capital economy. If functional autonomy and operative closure (Varela 1981: 37pp) of various subsystems of society are defining traits of modern complex societies, then the case of an autonomous financial system is not singular at all. It should therefore be possible to describe the preconditions and some of the consequences of the detachment of the capital economy in sociological terms. The research question of this paper is not located in economics or finance but it is a sociological one: How can we describe the operative logic of a complex symbolic system of communication that is centered around the function of a self-referential mode of saving and investing money?

The gist of »financial capital« and of the ensuing logic of the financial system is the symbolism of reflexive money, of money applied to itself. The selective principle of the financial system which directs all communications in the sense of providing a »key difference« (Leitdifferenz) seems to be the difference of opportunities and risks. However, the key difference is directly related to the societal function of the financial system. The function, therefore, specifies and considerably narrows down the *types and kinds* of relevant opportunities and risks. The operative focus of the financial system is opportunities and risks *in strategies of saving and investing money.*

It is this detachment of the logic of the financial system from the »real« economy that sets it apart from the standard laws of (the sciences of) economics. Marx has obviously been a major force in thinking about this issue of a disconnection between the realm of ›real‹ things and commodities that are used by people to satisfy their ›real‹ (physical) needs on the one hand and the realm of abstract and generalized *value* on the other. However, Marx never ceased to affiliate value with the commodity of labor (more precisely with Ricardo's labor theory of value) or abstract value with the value of labor, and, therefore, he maintained a commodity of last resort, labor, as a cord coupling the economy with »industrial capital«, in spite of all his speculations about a detached sphere of capital.

Modern sociological systems theory provides a set of means to describe the global financial system as an autopoietic system in the sense of a self-referential, operationally closed system. This does *not* imply that it is an autarkic system. It is still coupled in specific, selective ways to its environments. However, it is the financial system itself that defines the avenues and gates through which it is willing to relate to the societal context. In systemic thinking this kind of relating autonomy and selective interrelations is called structural coupling. I prefer the term symbolic coupling since we are talking about symbolic systems that relate to each other by a complex transformation of symbols and symbolic logics.

All this is not a statement of truth but rather a description from a specific theoretical perspective. The proof lies not in its »truth« but in its explanatory and exloratory power. The guiding question is: What can be seen from this perspective that is hidden by other perspectives? The concepts elaborated by Hegel as »Entäußerung« and by Marx as »Verselbständigung der Wertsphäre« can be reconstructed by means of alternative theoretical instruments.

In a first step, I provide a general description of the financial system, focusing on three basic systemic concepts: the idea of money as a generalized medium of communication (chapter 2), the idea of communication as an element of social systems (chapter 3). In a second step, the financial system will be analyzed in terms of the building blocks of operational autonomy. This includes the concepts of capital as a medium in the sense of a super-language (chapter 4), the complex temporal construction of capital (chapter 5) and some of the reasons for the quality of resilience that capital shares with other symbol systems and allows the financial system to ›live a life of its own‹ – just as language lives a life of its own.

2. Money as Medium: Language, Communication, and Symbolic Media

Talcott Parsons pioneered the analysis of money and power (and other media like commitments or influence) as »media of exchange«, mediating between the differentiated parts of society. However, he still considered money as »essentially a specialized mode of communication mediating in the circulation of expectations and binding commitments« (Parsons 1961: 66), thus stressing the role of media of exchange as specialized languages which enhance and expand the communicative function of natural languages.

Luhmann builds on this legacy. He specifies Parsons' notion of media by relating the concept of generalized media and the basic sociological problem of contingency (contingency understood in the old philosophical meaning of possibility). Media like money or power render communication faster, more efficient and semi-automatic in important respects, thus creating specialized languages with special capabilities. In addition to this, Luhmann argues, generalized media of communication also improve the selectivity of language, transmitting choices and preferences within the process of communication: »Therefore, we cannot describe generalized media as a linguistic code or a specialized language alone. Like social systems, media are mechanisms for narrowing choices which linguistically remain open« (Luhmann 1976: 511). This built-in prevalence for one side of their dualistic codes makes communication that is based on generalized media smooth, continuous and semi-automatic for all »regular« cases and processes, while irregular cases, disagreements, conflicts etc. can still be processed by going back to contingent choices ›which linguistically remain open‹.

»Media, then, solve the problem of double contingency through transmission of reduced complexity. They employ their selection pattern as a motive to accept the reduction, so that people join with others in a narrow world of common understandings, complementary expectations, and determinable issues« (Luhmann 1976: 512).

Money, then, is a prime example of a generalized medium of communication. What exactly does that mean? Spoken languages are the basic and »natural« media of communication. Language permits people to convey meaning by formulating messages (information) in a code (language) that links alter and ego in such a way that an instance of communication has happened as soon as alter observes ego engaged in a process of using language in order to convey a message. From the very beginning, communication is constructed in a self-referential way. It is *not* a sender-receiver-model, nor does communication presuppose that it creates consensus among alter and ego. Instead, it is perceived as a circular process, relating alter and ego in a situation of mutual observation. The content of the information is irrelevant, any difference that makes a difference for the people involved, suffices. The effect of the exchange of observations on alter and ego is irrelevant as long as there are effects. In particular, dissent or misunderstanding as effects of conveying messages back and forth are as valid as consent and ›correct‹ understanding in constructing and completing an instance of communication (for details see Luhmann 1984: 191pp).

For this basic form of communication, language serves as a medium of conveying or transmitting signals or messages. Again, transmission does not mean, as in a sender-receiver-model, that definite and fixed contents of meaning are transported. Instead, alter and ego as persons or psychic systems reconstruct meaning from observed messages according to their own cognitive structures and within the operative closure of their respective mental systems. However, since communication simply seems to happen all the time, a somewhat contrived alienation is necessary in order to see the »hidden improbability of communication« (Luhmann 1981: 26; 1997: 360 and 363) in spite of its ubiquitousness. The principle of operative closure radicalizes autonomy and recursiveness and thus increases the systems' independencies, because with elementary circularity, self-referentiality, and self-reproduction the systems become inner-directed not only in the self-organizations of their own structure but also in the recreation of their specific elements and operational procedures. Working basically self-referentially, a system will be impressed by events in its environment only very selectively and according to its own selective criteria.

This basic condition of mutual »double contingency« gives language a unique role in overcoming the improbability of successful communication. On the one hand, the ability to speak (in Maturana's term: »languaging«) is a result of lifelong learning and socialization processes which serve the purpose of establishing accommodated meanings of terms, sentences and stories and a common linguistic background that increases, against all odds, the probability of successful communication.

On the other hand, the directive power of language in establishing shared expectations, rules, and world views goes much further. This second side of language as a medium involves language as a symbolic system or rather, as a system of symbolics, as *langue* in Ferdinand de Saussure's sense (Saussure 2003). Language in this sense is not a specific spoken language but the general system or systemic model behind all languages. The reconstruction of this general model is highly contested, the theories ranging from Noam Chomsky's innate generative grammar (Chomsky 2002) to Terrence Deacon's theory of a co-evolution of language and mind (Deacon 1997) on the basis of »learning deficiencies« in early socialization. However, there is a broad common view, best expressed in Saussure's work, that language as a symbolic system, regardless of its origin, is characterized by highly elaborated orders, structures, rules, logics and operational modes that constitute language as an autonomous system.

No single person or group of persons »creates« language as *langue*. No person changes or commands language. Nobody prescribes the course and fate of language, not even of »Newspeak« or Esperanto. Nobody switches *langue* on or off. Instead, it is language itself as a concatenated and self-referential system of symbols that creates its own rules and orders, its semiotics, semantics, syntax, grammar and pragmatics. The idea of *self-referentiality* radicalizes the concept of intrinsic dynamics of complex systems of any kind – including symbolic and social systems. Only when considerable efforts in various natural sciences proceeded to clarify the idea of »non-linear dynamic systems« on the edge of equilibrium, began the predominance of linear models of »stimulus-response« and of system-environment-adaptation to crumble. There is a variety of different notions: »ultrastability« (Ashby), »order through fluctuations« (Prigogine), »order through noise« (v. Foerster), »complex adaptive systems« (Buckley), »organized complexity« (LaPorte), »autocatalysis« (Kauffman), »hypercycle« (Eigen), »autopoiesis« (Maturana) etc. Their common denominator lies in assuming that the rules of the game of understanding complex systems change fundamentally when systemic processes act upon themselves in positive feedback loops and thus create self-reinforcing cycles, and eventually self-creating hypercycles, which are able to stabilize an *improbable order* of elements organized into a systemic configuration. This creation of order contradicts the law of entropy. It sets complex living, symbolic and social systems apart from physics and the second law of thermodynamics. One case in point is language.

Of course, any language »lives« only by being used by people but, interestingly enough, still people nevertheless do not create language by speaking. They activate and recreate an existing system.

»Symbols do not, then, get accumulated into unstructured collections that can be arbitrarily shuffled into different combinations. The system of representational relationships, which develops between symbols as symbol systems grow, comprises an ever more complex matrix. In abstract terms, this is a kind of tangled hierarchic network of nodes and connections that defines a vast and constantly changing semantic space.« (Deacon 1997: 100, emphasis added)

Therefore, I conceive of language as a semiotic sign system, that in a historical process develops its own elaborated structures, processes and rules, its patterns, relations and operational modes. As an organized symbolic system it acquires a life and a logic of its own, operating self-referentially and eventually arriving at operative closure. As a system and as a medium it becomes independent of physical reality, creating its own symbolic reality: »*Langue* is a system that permits only its own order.« (Saussure in Fehr 2003: 76, translation H. W.) This does not deny that as a sign system or as a system of symbols language needs to be activated by people willing to speak. However, as soon as language is activated by speakers, it operates within its own logic. It is not the speakers who have to adapt to and cope with that symbolic logic, instead it is language that offers the field of options which delimits and specifies what can be said. »What can be thought and said at all, needs to be offered by the grammar of a language as a dispositive.« (Abel 2004: 263, translation H. W.)

The elementary operation of language (as *langue*) is to process semantic combinations in a context of a grammar of relational meanings. »It is of absolute, even a priori evidence, that there never will be a single/unique fragment of language (fragment de langue) based on something else but, in the sense of a last principle, on its non-identity or its degree of non-identity with the rest of language.« (Saussure 2003: 324) Since any process of this type reproduces language as a symbolic order, language appears as a self-referential, operationally closed system of symbols. It is not a living system in itself, to be sure, but rather a predisposition or a dispositive. It becomes and develops as a living system, and accordingly undergoes continuous, gradual historic changes, as it is used (activated, put into operation) by speakers (and later: writers) in innumerable, continuous communications.

In order to understand language as a medium (for communication) it is important to realize its *operational autonomy* in relation to the mental systems of people. Language as a medium forces mental systems to express themselves in a logic that is different from the logic of mental operations (thoughts, feelings, implicit knowledge). As soon as mental operations are to be expressed in language, and not e.g. in non-verbal signs or behavior, the operational mode of language takes over and prescribes the ways in which things can be said. These »things« seem to become organized, clarified, systematic and explicit, as is the case in particular, when implicit knowledge is made explicit and, therefore, explicated and externalized in terms of a specific language (Willke 2004). At the same time, of course, these »things« being said, become estranged from what is »really« felt, separated from »real« internal emotions, intuitions etc. They acquire a quality and reality of their own even as verbal communications, and even more so as written texts: *libri sua fatem habent.*

A basic understanding of language as a medium of communication is obviously a prerequisite to proceeding from there to conceptualize more powerful and more generalized media of communication. In spite of its illustrious achievements as a medium, language soon reaches some limits of its operating power in the course of the evolution of societies. Talking and writing take too much time, effort, negotiation, and they invite misunderstanding and trigger dissent. Hence, more abstract and powerful media of communication evolve, conspicuously in the areas of magic/mythologycal/religious activity, economic activity, and »political« activity (domination, defense, collective endeavors). The focus here will be on money as a generalized medium of economic communication.

Money as an intrinsically worthless token symbolizes value, value meaning the exchange-value of real goods. Money as a common denominator for prices creates more transparent markets, actually allowing the market to become a »mirror«, as Harrison White puts it, in which the actors observe each other through the looking glass of prices: »Markets are tangible cliques of producers observing each other. Pressure from the buyer side creates a mirror in which producers see themselves, not consumers« (White 1981: 543–544). From a systemic view, of course the same self-referentiality pertains to consumers: they observe each other instead of observing the producers, thus creating self-serving trends, fads, and fashions independent of the intentions of the producers.

The market greatly facilitates the observation of price movements and thus allows the emergence of a complex market intelligence from the distributed intelligence of a great number of market participants (Hayek 1945). In these functions, money replaces an enormous amount of (spoken or written) language, putting economic communication almost on auto-pilot. However, these achievements come at a price. The costs of the use of money as a medium of economic communication lie in an even higher degree of symbolization, abstraction, generalization, and estrangement in comparison to natural language. Like language and on the basis of the logic of language, money as a symbol (symbolizing value) refers to itself. To fulfill its function it necessarily operates in a self-referential way. This takes money-based economic communication even further away from real life and natural experiences of real people. Instead, these real people transform to operators of economic roles, e.g. producer, consumer, buyer, seller etc. These roles are components of an artificial world, called the economic subsystem of a functionally differentiated society. And these roles follow the logic of the operational requirements of an economic system, defying the original desires and motives of »real« people.

Money as a generalized medium of communication forces people as economic actors to express themselves in a logic that is different from the logic of mental operations, even different from the logic of natural languages. It forces actors to calculate costs and benefits of goods of all kinds in a highly compressed and reduced code of an operation called ›payment‹. This code only knows two states: payment yes or payment no. The criterion for participating in economic communication (not: communication about economics) becomes the ability and willingness to transfer and/or defer payments.

An even more consequential side of the evolution of money as a symbolic medium of economic communication concerns its power to instigate an economic system that in modern societies has become a functionally autonomous, operationally closed system (Luhmann 1988: 43pp). Money drives an economy that exhibits surprising, unexpected or *emergent* traits which do not stem from the motives or desires of people but from the operational logic of a highly specialized, autonomous system: Competition and the creation of market-prizes (Adam Smith), the contradiction of labor and capital (Marx), formal rationality (Weber), innovativeness (Schumpeter), systemic intelligence (Hayek), the competitive advantages of firms (Coase 1937), the institutionalization of scarcity (Luhmann 1988: 177pp), and many more.

At very early stages of the evolution of money as a system of symbols, the medium already appears to operate not only self-referentially but also reflexively in the sense that it invites and enables actors to use money as a commodity. The use of money produces the idea of *credit* as soon as shortages (debitor) or excesses of money (creditor) occur and their mediation becomes manageable. This reflexive mechanism opens the gates for further steps in symbolizing symbols, thus adding layers of confirmed structures, routine processes and rules to the operational range of options that constitute and expand the grammar of money as a medium of communication.

3. The Financial System as an Autonomous System

The elementary operation of a modern, money-based economy is payment. The flow of payments is powered by money. Therefore, the logic of money implants and imposes itself on an economy that is still concerned, at least in the minds of people, with producing the goods for exchange transactions allowing a better living based on division of labor. Already at the level of an economy, there is a separation of an intrinsic economy logic, the formal rationality of an economic system driven by the flow of payments on the one hand, and a personal or organismic logic of subsistence production on the other.

Things become even more entangled at the level of financial capital. Money itself becomes the focus of business and economic activity. Now, this is strange. If economic activity serves to guarantee subsistence at the relevant level of human needs and individual motives, and if money serves nicely as a means to acquire goods but cannot be used itself as food or clothing or shelter, why then is there an economy of money, a market and business of money? An answer can be found by looking at the different logics of the economic and the financial system as specified and embodied by their different elementary operations. Whereas the elementary operation of the economy is payment, the elementary operation of the financial system is *deferred return on payment* and in this sense *investment.* Note should be taken of the fact that a return on payment is nothing but a payment itself. Hence, an investment is an intrinsically self-referential operation, positing payments in expectation of future payments. There are different kinds of capital goods and, therefore, different kinds of aspects of the financial system. This text focuses exclusively on pure financial markets, on investments in financial capital (securities, monetary and derivative assets).

Operations within the financial system are concerned with the economic use of money as a commodity, i.e. with saving/lending and investing, implying promises or expectations of payments or returns *at a later point in time.* This later point in time may be more or less exactly specified, yet it is always conditioned in the temporal dimension. Whereas payments for goods within the primary economy (insofar: »real« payments) are aligned primarily in the social dimension, connecting economic roles (producer/consumer, seller/buyer) via the medium of money to a social network of interacting people, the operations of the financial system are primarily aligned in the temporal dimension. They connect financial roles via the medium of capital to a temporal architecture of principally unlimited complexity, since the future is always open and can always be extended to more distant and more improbable and uncertain horizons, inculcating different types of investment risks.

Karl Marx bases his elaborate answer to the question of a distinct logic of capital on two *different* approaches. On the one hand he is concerned with the motives and interests of people, mainly capitalists and workers and their collective identities in terms of social classes, and on the other hand he explores the abstract logic of capital as a medium of economic circulation (»Zirkulationsmittel«), in an attempt to uncover the general form or formula of capital (»die allgemeine Formel des Kapitals«). This ambivalent approach has produced endless debates in spite of the failures and catastrophes of the practical and political sides of Marxisms and socialisms. Indeed, the theoretical discussion of the logic of capital, capitalism, the financial capital and the financial system is not finished at all. A global financial system, that Marx had to envision as a distant future possibility, only recently has come into being as an empirical reality, positing all the old questions with a new urgency.

Instead of following the trodden paths of Marxist, neo-Marxist, post-Marxist etc. discussions, a systems theoretical view might facilitate a turn towards a comparative perspective, understanding capital and the financial system as just one of many instances of a fundamental historical process that inexorably separates the logic or the operational modes of people as personal systems and the logic or the operational modes of symbolic systems as parts of complex modern societies. The financial system with its generalized medium of financial capital can then be compared with other subsystems of society, elaborating similarities and differences that make a much stronger case than pursuing a singular case. In particular, all the strange diabolizations (the Greek term *díabolon* means to take apart, *sýmbolon* means to put together) of a specific case of symbolization, the symbol system of capital, appear as unexplained and unwarranted over-extensions and overgeneralizations of a perspective that takes the economy for the entire system and grossly neglects the interplay and interdependencies of all the other functional subsystems of a modern society.

From a comparative view it becomes evident that operational closure, which in the cases of economy and financial capital Marx never ceases to castigate as deplorable estrangement, is the evolutionary fate of all complex systems, including mental systems, organizations and all subsystems of society. Jean Piaget is a good witness for the case of mental systems. In spite of this potential risk, operational closure seems to mark an indispensable ingredient of a system on its way to autonomy and an identity of its own. From the vantage point of persons as individual mental systems, assembling their own knowledge base, Piaget states succinctly:

»This extension (of the organism into its environment via behavior, H. W.) must, then be translated into a language which expresses its effective functioning; it is essentially a search for the means to close the system simply because it is too ›open‹. From the probabilistic point of view, which is the only valid one in this case, the risk adhering to the open system is the fact that its immediate environment or frontier does not supply the elements necessary for its survival.« (Piaget 1971: 351)

The case of organizations is even more obvious. If one cares to observe real organizations it is not particularly difficult to »see« self-reference and operational closure, if one knows what to look for. They account for those parts of organizational reality which lead organizations, particularly old and traditional ones, to disregard external signals stubbornly and eventually ruin themselves, although this does not lie in the interest of its members (which raises the question of how useful the concept of ›rational choice‹ can be at the level of individual decisions). Even when there are alarming external signals, even when other organizations in comparable situations are behaving differently, even when individuals and groups within the organization can read the signals and, in vain, try to change things, the organization as a system often clings to its internal procedures and priorities and eventually is punished by failure or extinction (for classic case studies see Allison 1971; Dörner 1989; Wohlstetter 1966). It is the operational logic of the organization as a system, frozen into its transpersonal rule systems and its collective mind which enforces self-referentiality in the very precise sense that the decisions and actions of the organization are directed with reference to its own criteria, values, and rules, disregarding external signals even if this incurs severe losses or even the disruption of the system. This shows that operational closure can be a mixed blessing. It may blindfold the organization and lead to various forms of »pathological learning« (Argyris and Schön 1996).

Finally, at the level of societal subsystems like polity, economy, the science system, education, health system etc., a recursive encapsulation of topical contexts of communication relies mainly on the »superlanguages« which evolve within these contexts. The generalized media of communication work as superlanguages insofar as they enhance and exceed the powers of language. The implications of this proposition are probably lost as long as language itself is considered a simple means for communicating, as a trivial system to convey meaning. When, on the contrary, language is seen as a highly organized symbolic system that superimposes its own logic on the minds of people, then the estrangement that Marx decries, is inevitable already at the level of natural languages – even if it is hard to see or realize this estrangement, since we live almost entirely within that estrangement and come to use and understand language as if it were a natural given, governed by the intentions of people.

If the range of feasible intentions, however, were constituted by language, because the mind can only think what language offers it to think, then the degrees of freedom and originality of any individual mind appears less impressive than imagined by the standard self-description of persons as individuals. Autonomy and individuality is still possible, mind you, because the mind can choose within a range of options. But it is a contextuated autonomy, symbolically coupled with the operational logic of (natural) language. The mind is shaped and conditioned by natural language. More elaborated projects of the mind, therefore, presuppose more elaborated means of a language. It is not out of the question, then, that the means provided by some superlanguage, for example by a generalized medium of communication like power or knowledge or money, exceeds the faculties of the mind.

In the line of this argument, the idea of generalized media of communication (beyond natural language) acquires a novel meaning. It points to an estrangement between mind and media and a separation of logics that expands further with every level of symbolization. The more symbolic systems are in a position, owing to their accumulated internal complexity, to reflexively operate on themselves, building reflexive mechanisms, self-referential loops, cyclical modes of »eigen-behavior« (Foerster 1993: 103pp) and other stable patterns of an organized complexity (LaPorte 1975), the more symbolic systems establish semiotics, semantics and grammars of their own.

By means of compressing contexts of meaning into more abstract and generalized symbols, using every level of symbolization as building blocks for more advanced symbolization, symbolic systems carry an expansion of symbolically patterned relations as compound figures or forms of communication onto very remote levels of synthetic meaning, far away from the innate logic of minds.

For example, money as a symbolic medium, simply symbolizing value, is easily grasped by the mind with little training and without any formal education. Once established as a symbolic medium, money lends itself to towering edifices of reflexive symbolization, from money to credit to obligations to shares to even more distant symbolizations of some measure of expected value change like derivatives, credit default swaps, CDOs, synthetic CDOs etc. Somehow the mind gets lost under way. It has some experience with reflexivity, being able to think about thinking and speak about speaking in terms of meta-communication. But that is about it. Any further level of reflexivity, thinking about thinking about thinking as well as communication about meta-communication appear to be excessively awkward for mind and language. Surprisingly, even some generalized media resist extended reflexivity. Like mind and language, this concerns media that are, in spite of being symbol systems, still quite close to the material/physical side of persons, i.e. to the body – in particular the media of the sport system (competitive exertion) and of the family system (love/intimacy).

On the other hand, besides power and knowledge, it is above all money that seems to know no limits of reflexive recursiveness. Under the banner of ›financial innovation‹ the modern financial system is constantly producing new symbolic forms leading to an exceedingly intransparent architecture of financial instruments, models and business processes. The financial system distances itself from ›regular‹ thinking and communication, provoking various kinds of desperate responses from people who are unable to cope with the fact that generalized media, and money in particular, cannot be controlled any more by thinking and communicating. Rather, elaborate organizational and institutional precautions and preconditions are necessary to provide even a semblance of ›control‹ over a financial system with global reach and global impact. At times this semblance of governability of the financial system gives the erroneous signal to financial and political actors that all is well and under control. However, those who command the most advanced expertise in financial operations and regulations are the very persons who are most worried about the real danger of ungovernabilty and possible systemic risks (Eatwell 2004).

One of the reasons why the mind is at a loss with the detached logic of the medium of financial capital lies in the surprising observation that it seems to be impossible to determine the real value of financial assets. In the primary economy this task is quite easy. People simply have to find out what value of use or what value of exchange they attach to a thing (›good‹). In the secondary economy, there is endless dissent on how to determine value. ›Intrinsic‹ value, ›economic‹ value, ›true investment‹ value etc. are circumscriptions in economic terms of something that probably needs a different language. Since capital is reflexive money, the value of capital expresses the value of a value and, therefore, some entity beyond real economics, i.e. an entity that is constructed symbolically at a societal level (see the discussion by McGoun 2001: 4pp).

Observations and descriptions of a serious severance or alienation between the operational modes of mental systems and those of advanced social systems based on generalized media of communication are not without precedent. In exemplary ways, Hegel and Marx have contributed refined arguments, even if from opposing vantage points, for an inevitable process of separation of worlds that once were united, possibly. These worlds become separated as soon as, within a context of concatenated events, self-reference becomes feasible and, therefore, the faculty of observing includes the observation of internal events or elements. For then the fundamental difference of internal/external creates separate worlds which appear to develop along their own trajectories. Hegel has extended this argument into the depths of a logic of difference and identity, following the »exteriorization« or expulsion of a symbolic entity (»Geist«) from the level of personal mind or consciousness: »Dieser Geist bildet sich daher nicht nur *eine* Welt, sondern eine gedoppelte, getrennte und entgegengesetzte aus.« (This symbolic entity creates for itself not just *one* world but a duplicated, severed and juxtaposed one.) (Hegel 1986: 361; for an elaboration see Willke 2005: chapter 3)

Marx builds on this idea of exteriorization but falls behind Hegel in two ways. He moralizes the inevitable separation of two worlds by depreciating exteriorization to estrangement, thus implying the possibility or even moral correctness of some form of reunification of the separations created by money as a medium. And secondly, Marx never accepts the full, unconditional detachment of a symbolic sphere from what he considers the real basis of it all, labor and its value. With the famous formula of W-G-W (Ware, Geld, Ware; goods, money, goods) and its reversal through capital to G-W-G (Geld, Ware, Geld; money, goods, money) he acknowledges the evolution of two distinct circulations, one of material goods and one of a symbolic medium (Marx 2005: 149pp). However, Marx insists on tying capital to the value of labor in spite of stating explicitly:

»Commodities are thus sold, not in order to buy commodities, but in order to replace their commodity-form by their money-form. Instead of being merely a way of mediating the metabolic process, this change of form becomes an end in itself« (Marx 1976: 227).

Financial capital evolves as a medium constituting a financial system of its own, when the operational logic of capital becomes based on references to capital itself (i.e. on real and expected movements, transfers, flow etc. of capital). By predominantly referring to its own operations, capital becomes self-referential and drifts away from references to the material world of real goods. An illustrative case in point is the creation and the effects of the famous Black-Scholes-Merton formula for determining adequate prices for options. Options are no »real« goods, there are no real markets and no real prices. »Indeed, options were often seen simply as gambling, as betting on stock price movements« (MacKenzie 2003a: 12). Accordingly, the first modern models for determining prices for options were based on the idea of random movements of stock prices, on the »random-walk model«.

The Black-Scholes-Merton equation changed all that in an instructive way. The equation *constructed* a model for the operational logic of capital movements which, in a first empirical test, produced only an approximate fit (MacKenzie 2003a: 52). However, within a few years, the discrepancies between patterns of option price movements (in Chicago and New York) and the prices predicted by the equation *diminished* and the traders actually used the equation to construct prices that were then considered fair market prices: »It was a delightful loop of performativity: the model being used to make one of its key assumptions a reality« (MacKenzie 2003a: 56).

Donald MacKenzie interprets this impressive case as an instance of performativity, which it certainly is. However, there seems to be more to the case if seen from the perspective of the workings of a symbolic system. Michel Callon maintains, and MacKenzie endorses this view, that economics as a science is not predominantly descriptive but performative in that it brings a world, that is modeled at first, into being by guiding and shaping economic practice (MacKenzie 2003b: 11). If this is a plausible assumption for the economy, it makes all the more sense for the financial system. Money as a medium of (economic) communication lends itself to indulgence in successive levels of meta-communication as long as the resulting operations still make sense *within* the logic of the symbolic system of capital. That logic hinges on the elementary operation of deferred return on payment. Since deferred payments may be tied to principally unlimited options and variations of conditions that structure future events, there seem to be no built-in limits to conjuring up innovative financial instruments and models.

Reframed in a systemic theoretical perspective, the autonomy of the financial system is based on its own specific structures, processes and rules for instituting an operational logic for handling the symbolics of money. Money is the *common* symbol system of the economic and the financial system – this is exactly what makes a symbolic coupling of the two distinct systems possible. However, the operational logics of the two systems are clearly different, following different codes and core differences (Leitdifferenzen). In Marx' terms the different codes are expressed by the formulas W-G-W vs. G-W-G. In systemic terms the different codes can be denoted by the formulas payment-goods-payment vs. investment-return-investment. The economy is based on a self-referential circle of payments, mediated through goods, whereas the financial system is based on a self-referential circle of investments, mediated through returns on investments (ROIs).

4. Capital as Medium: The Language of Investments

From the perspective of this text, investments of money in money (in the form of financial products) are the elementary operations of the financial system. Investments imply a recursive and reflexive use of money, decoupling the financial system from its linkage with the real economy. In addition, investments always refer to future events, including expectations about the future flow of capital, implying expectations about the risks involved in an investment. The financial system thus exhibits two constituting traits: (1) its recursive use of money and (2) its dependence on future events for completing connecting operations. These two preconditions for setting the works of the financial system in motion conditionalize and shape the logic of investments and thereby the language of the financial system.

In order to reconstruct what is going on here, it seems necessary to reiterate some insights into the operational modes of language as *langue*. Language does not speak itself. It needs people to activate the symbolic system of language by deciding to communicate. In spite of this, however, language as a symbolic system creates its own internal logic *independent* of specific people by assembling in the course of long waves of evolution specific internal structures, processes, and rules that form a specific set of semiotics, semantics, syntax and grammar. This internal logic prescribes the ways language can be used as a means and medium of communication. People cannot just pick some words and tie them together in haphazard ways as they think fit. The rules of the symbol system of language prevent this random or deliberate use. Rather, people wanting to communicate have to accept the internal logic of language and speak accordingly.

The relation between money on the one hand and the economy and financial system on the other can be described in a similar way. Money is the superlanguage, the medium of communication for both systems. It is set in motion by actors, organizations and people, as natural languages are set in motion by people, but it is not ruled by them. As a single natural language lends itself to building and perpetuating very different social systems, in modern societies for example politics, health, education, family, economy, religion etc., depending on the guiding core perspectives or core differences, so the general medium of money lends itself to building the economy as one social system and finance as another social system within the context of society (today: the global society).

Whether a communication via the medium of money relates to the economy or to the financial system, depends on the core perspective, or intentions or core differences of the actors involved: when a payment is related to acquiring or selling goods we are entering the territory of the economy; when a payment is related to investing in deferred payments or reaping the returns on investment the actors have entered the land of finance. It is even possible that one and the same payment is interpreted by different actors as pertaining to different systems. One communication can *uno actu* have effects in different social systems and fuel the operations of different systems (Teubner 2000).

In this sense, the immanent logic of the financial system is derived from its evolution as a symbol system governed by the recursive mode of capital as its medium and by an utterly improbable foundation of its operational *modus vivendi* on future constellations of events. These creative restrictions format and formalize a symbol system that expands, seemingly without restrictions, in the pertinent dimensions of time and risk. From a sociological view, these two dimensions describe the growth paths for internal complexity of the financial system on the one hand, and the very aspects where the operational modi of the financial systems strain and at times exceed the capacity of the mind to fathom the implications of the system's autonomy.

5. The Temporal Construction of Capital: Option Space and Future Liability

Financial capital occupies a very improbable and radical position on the horizon of time. Like religion it has nothing to offer but promises (and their complementary risks). It relies exclusively on future contingent events to drive its operations. Still, for some almost incomprehensible reasons these uncertain expectations about possible futures seem to provide enough motives for people to engage in present activities to bring about expected financial returns in the future. If there is a grammar of motives at work then the motives might as well be derived from mental systems. Their grammar, however, is provided by the options offered by a different kind of system – the symbol system of capital. With regard to actions, Luhmann succinctly states this hiatus between motives and events, where events are produced by a specific grammar or architecture of concatenation. »Actions are not produced by subjective motives or intentions. They are produced by the system of cross-references between these actions themselves. Actions are events« (Luhmann 1983: 993).

The conclusion is inescapable: the mind is corrupted by the siren songs of a system it has no way to direct or command. This type of corruption has nothing to do with morals. It is a completely amoral operational corruption (in the sense of Luhmann 1994) by association and structural coupling. As Lord Acton has observed, power tends to corrupt and absolute power corrupts absolutely. A century later one has to realize that this form of corruption has nothing to do with specific people or with the moral quality of people. Rather, ordinary people are mostly helpless when confronted with the gyrations of elaborated media of communication. The cases of power and money are quite obvious. In the special case of capital, knowledgeable observers even liken the quality of corruption that befalls actors in the financial system to the effects of drugs. Donald MacKenzie and Yuval Millo report an interviewee comparing (the financial instrument of) options to »marijuana and Thalidomide« (MacKenzie and Millo 2003: 13). In a study of The Center For The Study of Financial Innovation, one respondent refers to prime brokerage as »the crack cocaine of the financial system« (Plender 2005).

Natural language offers »thinkable« options to the mind, and the mind seems to be able to cope with these options because mind and language have co-evolved with mutual accommodations. Superlanguages or symbolic media of communication appear to offer an option space to the mind which the mind has serious difficulty grasping and coping with. It should not come as a surprise that the mind is at a loss when coupled with the »artificial« edifices, or rather labyrinths, of symbol systems that expand into the depth of multi-layered recursions. In particular, the financial system and its medium capital constitute an intricate temporal deep-structure of its operations that overwhelm the relatively simple means of the mind to cope with temporal complexities (for interesting experimental evidence involving recursive time loops see Dörner 1984; 1989).

The trouble starts with the uncertainty of the future. Since all transactions in the field of financial capital involve multiple references to future events (such as discount rates, fate of expectations, market movements, capital flow) and since these temporally conditioned categories interact in a non-trivial way, the task for the mind is literally mind-boggling. It has to make some sense of hypothetical future constellations it cannot comprehend in its own logic. In addition, the future does not stand still but it is a moving target. The movements of the target are influenced less by the motives of the individuals and more by the collective fantasies and expectations of a money »market« that behaves quite differently from a market for real things. Whereas the beauty of the market within the primary economy lies in its reliance on individuals to produce private and collective goods as well as collective welfare (within the range of the market), as Adam Smith has taught, the market of the secondary economy turns out to be a beast constructed by the transpersonal emergent properties of a collective symbol system. It is rather doubtful whether the beauty and the beast ever will get together again. Unfortunately, the modern financial system is not a fairytale and it remains to be seen whether it will turn out to be a heroic saga or as a tragedy.

An option space – in the sense of possibilities open to choice – is created by an architecture of relations between elements, when the established relations do not connect each element with all other elements (›fully connected‹) but when some elements are connected to some others selectively (›selectively connected‹) and when the selectivity of connections can be conditioned by a systemic value or criterion. Money creates an option space in that it selectively connects, within the relational architecture of a specific market, some elements (items of money) with some other elements (goods), directed by the criterion of price. The connections are not fixed but open to choice and strategy. Hence, an option space is created, giving market participants alternatives of choices and strategies. So far, it is economic common sense.

However, there is a second part to it. Money as a symbol system that is detached from the physical limitations of real goods and the urgency of physical needs of real people, offers options that cannot be found in goods or people themselves. It takes on, as Marx has said, a life of its own. As soon as money operates self-referentially, being applied to itself, it extends the option space into a virtual future beyond present needs for present goods. Its function of *symbolizing* value allows money to offer options that amount to manipulating or influencing or even steering future events. To be sure, this amazing quality of symbol systems starts with language. It is simply extended and powered by superlanguages, by symbolic media of communication. The famous Thomas-theorem (»If men define situations as real, they are real in their consequences«) becomes even more powerful, since it is not only men who define situations as real but symbols, too.

One corollary of extended options spaces is extended complexity. Indeed, Luhmann defines complexity

> »as a measure of the incapacity of a system to relate each element to every other one, be it in the system itself (system complexity) or in its environment (environmental complexity). Complexity means the necessity of selective relations and, since relations specify what elements are possible within the system, complexity also means contingent elements« (Luhmann 1983: 993).

In this sense the extended options space created by the medium of money and in particular by its reflexive forms like capital or derivatives means a vastly extended complexity of the financial system. The motives of people and the »actions« or operations following from an intricate interplay of symbolic events diverge drastically, or rather, they belong to different worlds created by different categories of symbols. Even the logic and rationality of established ›simple‹ supervisory systems seems to become overwhelmed by the complexities of the financial system:

»Indeed, the global operations of major financial institutions and markets have outgrown the national accounting, legal and supervisory systems on which the safety and soundness of individual institutions and the financial system rely« (Group Thirty 1997: V).

This argument can be illustrated with the financial instrument of ›options‹. Options provide the right to buy or sell a share (or any other property right) at a specific point of time in the future at a set price. Options were already widely traded in Amsterdam and London in the 17th century. (MacKenzie and Millo 2003: 10). As confirmed forms of economic communication through the symbolic medium of money they detach economic transactions from individual motives, opening up an option space of possibilities that become options because they are possible within the logic of the relevant system of symbols. It is not individual motives that make these types of transactions possible but the internal logic of a symbol system allowing combinations of symbols and thus symbolic constructions of realities (i.e. setting certain prices now for future events) which strain and probably exceed the capabilities of the mind to cope with future events. One way of expressing this detachment is the sound advice to players only to engage in the financial game if it is done, like gambling, with play money.

The questions of liability and risk arise, when ordinary people and firms are drawn into the complicated gyrations of this symbolic game because of motives that are indifferent or incompatible in relation to the logic of complex structured financial instruments. It happens to ordinary investors when their investments become part and parcel of long chains of packaging components of debts/credits, decomposing and recomposing different elements of risks and opportunities in complex financial instruments that are traded without leaving a trace of their initial motives. Famous cases in this respect are the bankruptcy of Orange County (US) or the breakdown of the Long-Term Capital Management Fund as documented in case studies (ERisk 2005), causing losses for investors because of events way beyond their reach and understanding.

These instances are also cases in point for a second, more problematic consequence of the autonomy of the financial system – the emergence of systemic risks. »A lack of focus on the changing *system* characteristics of the international financial system has become a characteristic of international regulatory developments in the past few years« (Eatwell 2004: 1). John Eatwell has given an exemplary account of two of the most acute factors of common concepts of regulation that actually create and enhance systemic risks: The factors he singles out are: (1) the focus on single firms instead of a focus on a conglomerated global system of finance, and (2) a misguided focus on homogeneity instead of a focus on heterogeneity as an optimal mix of risk factors.

(1) In principle, regulation and supervision of the financial system through central banks, regulatory and supervisory institutions aim at system-wide financial stability. In practice, however, critical standards and rules, i.e. the Sarbanes-Oxley Act or pillar one of Basel II, address single firms and their specific control architectures and risk models. To be sure, Basel II is an important step in establishing a learning mode of the new supervisory review process, aiming at a cognitive supervisory regime in banking. Still, the focus is on single firms and their risk behavior, neglecting structural issues and negative externalities of the risk strategies of single firms. New types of operational risks emanating from individual firms might coalesce to systemic operational risks and market risks that overwhelm the coping capacities of the individual actors of the financial system: »The internal risk management regime – for credit and market risk, operational risk, compliance risk – needs to meet a more exacting standard. The requirements for operational resilience for technology systems are necessarily more demanding« (Geithner 2004: 4).

The shifting grounds for regulatory supervision correspond with a marked change in risk perception within the last decade. In the 1990s, major risks derived from aberrant or criminal behavior of single firms and persons. By 2003, the sources of risks had shifted to complex financial instruments and adverse macroeconomic conditions for the business strategies of financial firms (Smutniak 2004: 16). At present, the systemic effects of individual risk taking are becoming more accentuated, because the traditional separation of different types of financial institutions, in particular the separation between banks, insurance companies, securities and funds, already loosened by the Gramm-Leach-Bliley Act of 1999 (for the USA) is undermined by an intransparent concatenation of risk propensities via diffusing effects of structured credit instruments (Plender 2005) (see the following table).

1996	2003	2005
Poor management Bad lending Derivatives Rogue traders Excessive competition	Complex financial instruments Credit risks Macroeconomic conditions Insurance Business continuity	Banks have diversified their credit exposure via derivatives such as structured credits, which can be used to *transfer risks to insurance companies,* pension funds, hedge funds and others outside the banking sector

Table 1: Shifts in Risk Perception. Sources: Plender 2005; Smutniak 2004.

As the option space within the financial system is extended into the depth of structured derivative instruments and into the labyrinths of prolonged chains of conditioned events, the chances and risks of aggregate or even systemic effects of mutual reinforcement, snowballing, leverage and positive feedback loops beyond single firms loom large. A complex array of options corresponds with chances of »low-probability, high-impact events« (Kohn 2004). A regulatory focus on single firms necessarily is blind for systemic turbulences. These turbulences certainly start with some actions and decisions of firms, like kids throwing snow balls, but theses actions then turn into avalanches by setting off chain reactions that follow the logic of the financial system and defy the motives and reasons of the people involved.

An important aspect of the logic of the financial system lies in the temporal deep-structure of capital. Since »financial markets are markets for stocks of current and future assets, the value of which today is dependent on the expectations of their future value« (Eatwell 2004: 2), present expectations of future asset-price movements and future value dynamics must be based on past experience as well as concurrent beliefs, assumptions, reasoning and extrapolations of distributed knowledge. No person nor institution commands the knowledge or covers the expertise to ›run the system‹. The system runs itself. Friedrich von Hayek has shown this convincingly for the ›simple‹ regular market, stressing that only the market itself is able to combine the complexities of distributed knowledge into a construction of operating market: »the knowledge of the circumstances of which we must make use never exists in concentrated or integrated form, but solely as the dispersed bits of incomplete and frequently contradictory knowledge which all the separate individuals possess« (Hayek 1945: 519). Even more so, then, the financial markets rely on a trans-individual aggregation of knowledge and non-knowledge (uncertainties, risks, and ignorance) that no single person nor institution is in a position to direct or escape.

(2) A second form of systemic risk exhibits the idiosyncratic logic of the financial system even more clearly. Whereas financial innovations and a more elaborate temporal deep-structure of financial transactions enhance the option space of the financial system, a complementary dynamic can reduce that option space to a dangerous level of uniformity. John Eatwell calls this result a state of homogeneity, as opposed to the crucial heterogeneity which allows markets to prosper: »Markets become illiquid when objectives become homogeneous. When everyone believes that everyone will sell, liquidity vanishes. Markets fall over the cliff when average opinion believes that average opinion has lost confidence in financial assets« (Eatwell 2004: 3). What aspects of capital as a symbolic medium drive financial markets towards homogeneity instead of preserving a more balanced heterogeneity of diverse objectives, methodologies, instruments, risk models, time horizons etc.?

Surprisingly, the culprits seem to be exactly those aspects of capital that are responsible for a global financial system coming into being in the first place: liberalization, disintermediation, internationalisation, global standards and methods of professionalization »and extensive conglomeration of financial institutions« (Eatwell 2004: 4). These factors combine to create a unified and uniform space of global finance, characterized by global infrastructures, global suprastructures (i.e. uniform methods, standards, and models of regulation and supervision), aligned core business processes and financial products, similar business visions, strategy maps, and core competencies, coordinated rule systems, risk management procedures, and control ideas.

At first glance, these factors seem innocent enough, since they contribute to establishing exactly what is at stake – a global financial system. The unintended consequences of their performance, however, appear detrimental to the stability and success of the very system they constitute. This basic ambivalence or built-in contradiction is of course reminiscent of Marx' characterization of the capitalist system as inherently self-destructive. Ironically, Marx' diagnosis was premature in presupposing circumstances of the deterritorialized deployment of capital that only the ultimate global breakthrough of the capitalist mode of financial operations have brought into existence – a constellation which Marx may have foreseen simply by following the logic of the medium of capital.

The astonishing self-defeating propensity of the financial system is closely related to its temporal deep-structure. In order to understand this it seems helpful to distinguish between three levels. The market economy as a functional subsystem of society fosters heterogeneity because the power of competition drives differentiation, specialization, a Schumpeterian propensity for innovations and a Porterian exploitation of differential competitive advantages of locations (Porter 1990). So, on a first level, in a ›simple‹ market economy there is little danger of forced homogeneity.

However, the trouble with »herd behavior« and the corresponding urge towards homogeneity begins on a second level, when the decisions to invest and the decisions to sell/buy are distant points in time and therefore lose their automated corrective response from the market. The famous »hog cycle« points to the problem of maintaining heterogeneity when extended time frames (i.e. investing in life stock, raising hogs, producing meat and selling the product) and committed resources prevent a fast and flexible reaction to market conditions. Hog cycles still exist today, causing serious problems of excess production capacity in many fields: automotive, memory chips, computers, mobile phones, ship building etc. The hog cycle builds on exaggerated expectations of investors in times of shortages and it results in overcapacities because »everybody does the same« (homogeneity) instead of everyone doing their own thing (heterogeneity).

On a third level, the level of the financial system, the long-term cyclicity of the real economy is replaced and enhanced by the short-term and ultra short-term cyclicity of electronic financial flow.

»Good risk management will result in firms holding a portfolio of assets that are not volatile and the prices of which are not highly correlated – not correlated in normal times that is. Suppose however that the volatility of a given asset rises sharply, the models will tell all the firms to sell. As all try to sell, liquidity dries up. As liquidity dries up, volatility spreads from one asset to another. Previously uncorrelated assets are now correlated in the general sell-off, enhanced by the model driven behavior of other institutions caught up in the contagion. Whilst in normal times such models may encompass a wide range of behavior, in extreme circumstances the models will encourage firms to act as a herd, charging toward the cliff edge together« (Eatwell 2004: 6).

In these cycles, the eigen-behavior and the autonomy of the financial system become evident, seemingly to the point of a self-defeating logic. This strange logic, however, is not a necessary feature of the operational laws of the financial system as such. Rather, it results from an interplay of a highly complex symbol system, finance, with the more or less sophisticated interventions of players (people, organizations and institutions) trying to influence the workings of the symbolic system. Like many other attempts at influencing operationally autonomous systems, i.e. interventions in therapy, education, foreign aid, political transformation etc., these interventions rarely succeed in the sense of producing the desired results. It takes considerable experience and expertise for people to direct their interventions in a way that avoids unintended or detrimental consequences. It is important to recognize »that we do not know a lot about the underlying dynamics of financial crises in the context of the evolving financial system« (Geithner 2004: 4).

Accordingly, quite a few elements of governing, controlling, and regulating the financial system lend themselves to producing unintended or detrimental results. During the Asian crisis, for example, »financial institutions followed the instructions of their risk models by reducing their exposure to emerging markets throughout the world. These cutbacks helped spread the crisis, as reduced lending and reduced confidence fed the financial downturn« (Eatwell 2004: 7). Similarly, strong incentives to create global standards for corporate governance, risk management, accounting and management control increase the system's propensity for homogeneity and pro-cyclical positive feedback loops (Power 2003).

A different kind of perverse effect resulting from the structural coupling of personal intentions and the logic of capital concerns the creation of future liabilities. Again, this pertains to the temporal construction of capital. Whereas capital as a medium of communication speaks the language of investments, when the capacity for present investments is derived from past savings and is directed towards future opportunities for returns on investment, the risk-side of investments deploys this complex temporal structure as a destructive futurization and diffusion of liabilities. As long as the opportunities and risks of investments were closely related, tied together by a specific economic actor, the liabilities could be considered a balanced matching of opportunities and risks. Increasingly, however, complex financial instruments structure and decompose risks into opaque entities as building blocks of designer risk outfits that at times appear to have the same purpose and appeal as designer drugs: to mitigate and distance the eventual call of the presence and its real liabilities by means of an obfuscated future.

This dynamic has not gone unnoticed by the financial and regulatory community. Basel II for example, a revised agreement on »international convergence of capital measurement and capital requirements« on the basis of the 1988 Basel Accord, came into effect as proposals in June 2004. The proposals have been accepted by the European Parliament in September 2005 and they will become operational at the beginning of 2007 and 2008 respectively. Basel II aims at creating a level playing field for the global competition of banks and other financial institutions, thus reducing the incentives for aggressive financial institutions to enhance risks and underestimate their future liabilities. It seeks to avoid over-extension of banks to credit risks by providing guidelines for adequate and necessary capital assets and for measuring the »value-at-risk« (VaR) of an existing credit portfolio.

The problems of measuring VaR are fundamental because financial innovation and the creation of complex structured financial instruments make it increasingly difficult to build reciprocal credit risk models that provide dynamic measurements of risk probabilities. Complex financial instruments like Asset-Backed Securites (ABS) or Collateralized Debt Obligations (CDOs) or Single-Tranche CDOs divide and recombine risks to create highly individualized risk-menus for specific investors. A complexly structured instrument usually has four common traits: (1) it involves non-standard customer specific transactions; (2) it is knowledge intense, costly and needs the collaboration of professionals from multiple backgrounds; (3) it is designed as part and parcel of a complex financial strategy, including economic, legal, tax, accounting and other objectives; and (4) it creates complex risks for both sides – the issuing financial institution *and* the specific customer (Schmidt Bies 2004: 2).

Valid (non-destructive) financial transactions depend on highly sophisticated cognitive fundamentals of various economic models. For example, the four major models for measuring credit portfolio risks each depend on underlying economic models that imply vast uncertainties. »CreditMetrics« depends on microeconomic calculations and ratings, »CreditRisk« depends on insurance mathematics, »Credit Portfolio View« depends on econometric calculations of macroeconomic risk factors, and »KMV Portfolio Manager« depends on simulations and (Moody's) credit ratings (for a detailed descriptions of the four models see (Schulte-Herbrüggen 2004).

Additional risks and uncertainties prevail. For example, demographic trends and ensuing changes in the composition of the work force, the impact of pension schemes and pension liabilities of firms or the financial impact of employee benefits such as share payments are very hard to specify even from a mid-term perspective. On the one hand, new global accounting standards – like IAS19 – force listed companies to disclose pension liabilities (Bruce 2005) and thus render their accounting more precise. On the other hand, pension liabilities are volatile and, therefore, imply additional risks. The emerging International Financial Reporting Standards (IFRS) that began affecting listed European firms in 2005 and will affect them more seriously in 2006, again change the basis for deducing the overall VaR by including measures that depend on market and price dynamics: »the biggest shake-up to the income statement will come from the inclusion of changes in the ›fair value‹ of assets and liabilities that have not been traded: derivatives, for instance« (Fuller 2005).

In practical terms this means that it is virtually impossible for regulators and supervisory institutions to arrive at »valid« measurements of the risks implied in a certain complex credit portfolio of a bank or other financial institutions. Since financial institutions give credit to firms on the basis of their balance sheet, their accounting and numerous additional indicators, all of which are highly sophisticated, knowledge based, and dependent on trend estimates and value judgements, the risk structure of firms is incorporated into the risk portfolios of banks. Financial innovations often include credit risk transfer operations between financial institutions and investors, e.g. credit default swaps or synthetic CDOs, which can enhance the mutual build up and intransparency of leveraged risks (Schmidt Bies 2004: 4).

This results in a concatenated risk chain, enhancing the overall risk by unknown leverages and combinatorial effects. Possible turbulences add »to the potential for nonlinear responses in the economy« (Kohn 2004: 3), indicating the point where possible *systemic risk* comes into play.

»The Federal Reserve reacted strongly to both the stock market crash of 1987 and the ›seizing up‹ of financial markets in the fall of 1998 after the Russian debt default and failure of Long Term Capital Management. In each of these situations, we were dealing with the aftermath of one low-probability, high-impact event – the market meltdown – in a manner also designed to limit another such event – snowballing disruptions to intermediation and spending« (Kohn 2004: 2).

The basic approach of Basel II, therefore, makes sense: It creates a »supervisory review process« that shifts from control to cooperation, from authoritative controlling to appreciative inquiry, from normative positioning to cognitive reasoning. This *cognitive turn* seems to be the most important paradigm shift in regulating the global financial system. In respect to Basel III, Schulte-Herbrüggen states: »Basel III should, therefore, be based on a new supervisory paradigm, that still needs to be developed« (Schulte-Herbrüggen 2004: 39, translation H. W.). A similar cognitive turn is discernible in the field of insurance and pension regulation around the framework of »Solvency II« and the Pension Act 2004. The minimum funding requirements (MFR) are being replaced by statutory funding objectives (SFO): »Where the MFR applies a highly prescriptive range of assumptions, the SFO is more flexible – hence the need for prudence« (Harrison 2005).

The cognitive turn in supervision follows a deeply seeded and ongoing cognitive turn of the economy in general – from industrial economy to knowledge economy – and of the financial system in particular – from normatively regulated national capital markets to a knowledge-based global superstructure that shows evidence of self-reference, operational closure and autonomy in the dynamics of its own specific symbolism.

References

Abel, Günter (2004), *Zeichen der Wirklichkeit.* Frankfurt a.M.

Allison, Graham (1971), *Essence of Decision. Explaining the Cuban Missile Crisis.* Boston.

Allport, Floyd (1954), »The structuring of events: Outline of a general theory with applications to psychology« , in *The Psychological Review*, Vol. 61, 281–303.

Argyris, Chris, Schön, Peter (1996), *Organizational Learning II. Theory, Method, and practice.* Reading, Mass.

Armijo, Leslie (2001), »The political geography of world financial reform: Who wants what and why?«, in *Global Governance*, Vol. 7, 379–396.

Baecker, Dirk (1991), *Womit handeln Banken?* Frankfurt a.M.

Chomsky, Noam (2002), *Syntactic Structures.* Berlin.

Coase, Ronald (1937), »The nature of the firm«, in: *Economica*, N.S. 4, 386–405.

Deacon, Terrence (1997), *The Symbolic Species. The Co-Evolution of Language and the Human Brain.* London.

Dörner, Dietrich (1984), »Modellbildung und Simulation«, in: Erwin Roth and Klaus Heidenreich (eds), *Sozialwissenschaftliche Methoden. Lehr- und Handbuch für Forschung und Praxis.* 4th edition, Oldenbourg, 327–340.

— (1989), *Die Logik des Mißlingens.* Reinbek.

Eatwell, John (2004), *International Regulation, Risk Management and the Creation of Instability.* Lecture at the IMF. 1st October 2004. http://www.cerf.cam.ac.uk.

Eigen, Manfred/Schuster, Peter (1979), *The Hypercycle: A Principle of Natural Self-Organization.* Berlin et al.

ERisk (2005), »Case study LTCM: Credit portfolio management workshop«. http://www.erisk.com.

Fehr, Johannes (2003), *Saussure: Zwischen Linguistik und Semiologie. Ein einleitender Kommentar. Erste Teil von: Ferdinand de Saussure. Linguistik und Semiologie.* Frankfurt a.M.

Foerster, Heinz von (1981), *Observing systems.* Seaside Cal.

— (1993), *Wissen und Gewissen. Versuch einer Brücke.* Frankfurt a.M.

Frame, Scott/White, Lawrence (2002), »Empirical studies of financial innovation: lots of talk, little action?«, in: *Federal Reserve Bank of Atlanta. Working Paper Series.* Working paper 2002–12, July 2002.

Fuller, Jane (2005), »Confusion, delays and a fex shocks. The accountantcy column«, in: *Financial Times.* January 13, 2005: 11.

Geithner, Timothy (2004), *Changes in the structure of the U.S. financial system and implications for systemic risk.* http://www.cerf.cam.ac.uk.

Harrison, Debbie (2005), »Dear prudence ...«, in: *Financial Times. Special Report.* FTfm Trustee summer school. July 18th, 2005. Part 4.

Hayek, Friedrich A. (1945), »The use of knowledge in society«, in: *The American Economic Review* XXXV, 519–530.

Hegel, Georg W. F. (1986), *Phänomenologie des Geistes. Werke Band 3. Auf der Grundlage der Werke von 1832–1845 neu edierte Ausgabe.* Redaktion Eva Moldenhauer und Karl Markus Michel. Frankfurt a.M.

Knutsen, Sverre (2004), *Financial Systems and Economic Growth – A Critical View on the ›Business Systems‹ Literature.* http://www.bindproject.nl/textfiles/kundsen.pdf.

Kohn, Donald L. (2004), »How should policymakers deal with low-probability, high-impact events? Remarks by Governor Donald L. Kohn«, in: *The Federal Reserve Board. Speeches.* http://www.federalreserve.gov/boarddocs/speeches/ 2004.

LaPorte, Todd (1975), *Organized Social Complexity. Challenge to Politics and Policy.* Princeton.

Luhmann, Niklas (1971), »Reflexive Mechanismen«, in: *Soziologische Aufklärung 2. 2nd edition,* Niklas Luhmann (ed.). Opladen, 92–112.

— (1976), »Generalized media and the problem of contingency«, in: Jan Loubser et al. (eds), *Explorations in General Theory in Social Science. Essays in Honor of Talcott Parsons.* Vol. 2, New York, 507–532.

— (1981), *Soziologische Aufklärung 3.* Opladen.

— (1983), »Insistence on systems theory: Perspectives from Germany – An essay«, in: *Social Forces,* Vol. 61, 987–998.

— (1984), *Soziale Systeme. Grundriß einer allgemeinen Theorie.* Frankfurt a.M.

— (1988), *Die Wirtschaft der Gesellschaft.* Frankfurt a.M.

— (1994), »Politicians, honesty and the higher amorality of politics«, in: *Theory Culture & Society,* Vol. 11, 25–36.

— (1997), *Die Gesellschaft der Gesellschaft, 2 Bände.* Frankfurt a.M.

MacKenzie, Donald (2003a), »An equation and its worlds: Bricolage, exemplars, disunity and performativity in financial economics«, in: *Social Studies of Science*, Vol. 33, 831–868.
— (2003b), »Opening the black boxes of global finance«, in: *Review of International Political Economy*.
MacKenzie, Donald/Millo, Yuval (2003), »Constructing a market, performing theory: The historical sociology of a financial derivatives exchange«, in: *American Journal of Sociology*, Vol. 109, 107–145.
Marc, Edmond/Picard, Dominique. n.d. *Bateson, Watzlawick und die Schule von Palo Alto*. n.p.
Marx, Karl (1976), *Capital*. London.
— (2005), *Das Kapital. Kritik der politischen Ökonomie. Der Produktionsprozess des Kapitals* (first published in 1867) Köln.
Maturana, Humberto (1981), »Autopoiesis«, in: Milan Zeleny (ed.), *Autopoiesis. A theory of living organization*. New York/Oxford, 21–33.
McGoun, Elton (2001), »Hyperreal finance« Unpublished Manuscript. Bucknell University, Deparment of Management. http://www.panopticon.scustan.edu/cpa96/pdf/mcgoun.pdf.
Minsky, Marvin (1988), *The society of mind*. New York.
Parsons, Talcott (1961), »An outline of the social system. General introduction II«, in: Parsons/Shils/Naegele/Pitts (eds), *Theories of society*. New York/London, 30–79.
Piaget, Jean (1971), *Biology and Knowledge*. Chicago.
Plender, John (2005), »Shock of the new: a changed financial landscape may be eroding resistance to systemic risk«, in: *Financial Times*, February 16, 11.
Porter, Michael (1990), *The Competitive Advantage of Nations*. New York.
Power, Michael (2003), »The invention of operational risk«, in: *LSE ESRC Center for analysis of risk and regulation. Discussion paper*, No. 16, June 2003. London, 1–20.
Saussure, Ferdinand de (2003), *Linguistik und Semiologie. Notizen aus dem Nachlaß. Texte, Briefe und Dokumente. Gesammelt, übersetzt und eingeleitet von Johannes Fehr*. Frankfurt a.M.
Schmidt Bies, Susan (2004), *Financial Innovation and Effective Risk Management. Remarks by Governor Susan Schmidt Bies to the Financial Service Institute 2004, Washington D.C.* http:// www. federalreserve.gov/boarddocs/speeches/2004/20040506, 1–6.
Schulte-Herbrüggen, Walter (2004), »Von Basel II zu Basel III: Die Herausforderungen«, in: *Deutsches Risk*. www.risk.net, 35–39.
Smutniak, John (2004), »Living dangeroulsy. A survey of risk«, in: *The Economist*, 3–22.
Teubner, Gunther (2000), »Global private regimes: Neo-spontaneous law and dual constitution of autonomous sectors in world society? http://www.uni-frankfurt.de/FB/fb01/spontaneous.pdf«, in: Karl-Heinz Ladeur (ed.), *Globalization and Public Governance*, Cambridge.
Thirty, Group of (1997), *Global Institutions, National Supervision and Systemic Risk. A Study Group Report*. Washington D.C.

Varela, Francisco (1981), »Autonomy and autopoiesis«, in: Gerhard Roth and Helmut Schwegler (eds), *Self-organizing systems*. Frankfurt a.M., 14–23.

White, Harrison (1981), »Where do markets come from?«, in: *American Journal of Sociology*, Vol. 87, 517–547.

Willke, Helmut (2004), *Einführung in das systemische Wissensmanagement*. Heidelberg.

— (2005), *Symbolische Systeme*. Weilerswist.

Wohlstetter, Roberta (1966), *Pearl Harbor. Signale und Entscheidungen*. Erlenbach-Zürich.

On the Unity and Difference of Finance and the Economy: Investigations for a New Sociology of Money

Hanno Pahl

1. Introduction

In the last years sociological research has contributed interesting insights into the dynamics of international financial markets. Empirical developments such as the so-called *take-off* of the financial markets during the new economy boom and bust have stimulated an interdisciplinary discourse on the financial sphere as some kind of emergent social reality sui generis (cf. MacKenzie 2003). Numerous contributions to the discourse on globalization address the financial markets as the main scenes of contemporary dynamics. For example, Castells (2001: 113) labels them as the *backbone* of globalization, Guttmann (n.d.) speaks of them as the *nervous system* of globalization and Luhmann (1997: 808) admits them to be the *centers of world society*. Giddens (1990: 21–22) speaks of a »disembedding of social systems« and Knorr-Cetina and Bruegger (2002) proclaim the emergence of *global microstructures* in the field of financial market trading. But on theoretical grounds the general relationship between finance and the economy remains for the most part unclear. While some authors emphasize the de- or uncoupling of the financial sphere from the real economy of goods and mark this as the *hyperreality of finance* (McGoun 1997; Schinckus 2005), others claim an increasing causal dependency between both realms and highlight phenomena of a *capture of business by finance* or *financialization* (Froud et al. 2000). The search for an integrative perspective that may be able to deal with these contradictory findings in a theoretically sound way leads us to the fundamental question of the unity and difference of finance and the economy. Although both economic sociology in general and the more specific sociological discourses on finance have questioned the neglect of money in neo-classical economics, there is still no genuine sociological theory of money and finance at hand. This article therefore scans the huge theoretical legacies of Karl Marx's and Niklas Luhmann's[1] work in search for core elements that can contribute to a theory of money and a more sophisticated theory of finance.

The first section of this essay discusses the neglect of money in orthodox neo-classical economics as well as in traditional economic sociology. It is argued that neither paradigm is able to grasp the dynamics of the modern monetary nexus. Moreover, both remain in a state of helplessness towards current empirical affairs. The second section develops the thesis that sociology needs to take into account the monetary nexus of modern economies in order to grasp their dynamics instead of primarily focussing on aspects of the social embeddedness of economic behavior. Using Karl Marx's critique of political economy, which will be read with an emphasis on form analysis,[2] and Niklas Luhmann's theory of the modern economy as an autopoietic system, core aspects of the modern economy's systemic features are sketched. This section also outlines further perspectives for a self-reliant sociology of money. The third and final section is dedicated to the question of the unity and difference of finance and the economy in

1 See also the contribution by Helmut Willke in this book. While my text focuses predominantly on Marx and refers to Luhmann mainly as a benchmark, Helmut Willke presents a more detailed and sophisticated systems-theoretical perspective on the question of the unity and difference between finance and the economy. While we mostly agree on systems theory, my appraisal of the ability of the Marxian theory to grasp the logic of the financial sphere is far less sceptical than Willke's.

2 Generally speaking, this means a sort of reading that concentrates primarily on qualitative and sociological aspects of the Marxian theory.

modern societies. The concluding remarks sum up the theoretical findings and apply them again to our main question. In contrast to the unsatisfactory alternative of describing finance either as a sphere of hyperreal referencelessness or as a causal coercion to the so-called real economy, I argue that both diagnoses do no more than merely highlight opposite sides of the same coin. Instead of voting for one of the alternatives my suggestion is to question the fruitfulness of the distinction itself.

I would like to make one final remark before I start my discussion, and this relates to the usual way of dealing with Marxian and systems theory: Of course, both traditions rival each other in their claim to be two of the *grand theories* of modern society. Therefore, it is not surprising that their relationship is still very unnatural/hostile today, marked by polemics or mutual neglect. But this state of affairs is not satisfactory at all concerning chances of fruitful mutual irritations. For this reason, my text should be regarded as some kind of *limbering-up exercise* to stimulate further encounters between the two schools.

2. On the Neglect of Money in Neoclassical Economics and Traditional Economic Sociology

In recent years, various authors from the field of heterodox economics have questioned the dominant view of money as a neutral veil as contended by the neoclassical orthodoxy (cf. Heinsohn, Steiger 2002; Riese 2000). But until now, only a small number of sociologists have adopted these criticisms and drawn consequences for a sociological approach to money (cf. Deutschmann 2001; Paul 2004; Ingham 2004; Dodd 1994). For the most part, we still face the traditional division of labour between the disciplines of economics and economic sociology that Ganßmann (1996) called *Oppenheimer's curse*. This expression refers to the unfortunate distinction drawn by the German sociologist and economist Franz Oppenheimer, who argued that economics deal with human/object-relations while sociology deals with human/human-relations. *The result of this division of labour is a neglect of money in both disciplines*: Neoclassical economics usually starts its analysis of the modern economy with a barter model. From this perspective, money gets into view only in a very limited sense as some kind of veil or as a neutral means of exchange. Neutrality here implies the assumption that when the economy is in an equilibrium, money simply mediates the production and exchange of goods, making no intrinsic difference to real economic variables (see Dodd 1994). Economics then, is about a mere aggregation of instrumental-rational actions. On theoretical grounds, this neglect of money results either in the emergence of dubious heuristic models, like Schumpeter's *social book-keeping* or Walras' *auctioneer* (cf. Spahn 2002) or the transintentional (unintended) qualities of the modern economies are illustrated with reference to the Smithian metaphor of the invisible hand of the market, which transforms a totality of selfish and strategic actions into the wealth of nations. *What remains unclear is how these transformations are achieved in reality.* Although economic sociologists have criticised the strong concept of rational behavior, they often tended to leave money as a topic to the economists. Focussing on the social embedding of economic agents, the core questions of social synthesis and coordination in the field of the modern societies' economies as well as its cataclysmic dynamics were largely ignored. Rather than posing a challenge, these attempts are complementary to existing economic theories of money. Even if we take a look at the famous *grand theories* of the discipline, we can find that money is the big blind spot of sociology, or, as Deutschmann (2001) has recently put it, *the mystery of sociology.*[3] A good example of this can be found in Parsons' huge theoretical legacy. Although Parsons developed a highly sophisticated theory of society, his approach to economic affairs more or less codified the usual division of labour. In his masterpiece *Economy and Society*, co-written with Neil Smelser (Parsons, Smelser 1956), a research frame is set up that offers many perspectives. Along the lines of a repetitive application of the AGIL-scheme, Parsons is able to analyse the boundaries between economic affairs and other realms of modern societies on different levels of abstraction. But what remains unclear for the most part are again the internal dynamics of the modern economy itself. Although Parsons introduced an interesting concept of money as a medium of interchange, it seems obvious to me that Parsons – focussing on societal integration – never fully exhausted the potential of his own concept of money (Hessling, Pahl 2006; Beckert 1997). Parsons, too, leaves the dynamic qualities of modern money to the economists.

Albeit even Habermas' findings on economy and money in general do not go beyond the traditional approach, they can nevertheless serve as a

3 Simmel's *Philosophy of Money* seems to be the exception that proves the rule.

starting point in our search for basic criteria for a sociological theory of modern money as an emergent and systemic sphere. In his *Theory of Communicative Action* Habermas (1981) starts with an action-theoretical framework, focussing on a hermeneutical approach in order to reconstruct the symbolic and material reproduction of societies. One striking attribute of modern societies, Habermas argues, is that political as well as economic affairs tend to detach from society and re-configure as autonomous social systems. While in Habermas' *lifeworld*, social coordination and integration is accomplished either by discourse (communicative action) or by unquestioned traditions, Habermas assumes that modern politics and the modern economy qua systems are marked by transintentional and, in this respect, emergent modes of reproduction and operation. To analyse the shift from pre-modern, socially integrated forms of economic and political states of affair to their detachment in modern societies, Habermas leaves hermeneutics and adopts the Parsonian theory of interchange media. While in the case of Parsons it remained unclear whether the media of interchange were regarded as purely heuristical instruments of analysis or as real structural properties of modern societies, Habermas clearly votes for the second alternative. He regards money and power as generalized media of communication that have emerged only in modern societies and that lead the differentiation of the political and economic systems from the lifeworld. To describe the logic of these systems Habermas (1986) uses the term *functionalist reason*. This term is meant to mark the emergent properties of modern politics and the modern economy that distinguish them as systemic units from a pure aggregation of instrumental-rational actions in the sense of Max Weber. On a phenomenological level I would agree with these findings, but on theoretical grounds Habermas himself offers no solution of how to conceive the decoupling effects of modern money. As Dodd (1994: 75) has stated correctly, in Habermas' approach, money suddenly

»expresses a capitalistic rationality which is altogether autonomous from the lifeworld. Habermas cannot explain how this process occurs. Money is dependent on a form of normative integration in order to work at all in society, while also being a focus of structural inequalities of wealth and power, a source and expression of major conflicts of interest. Habermas seems unable to reconcile these two facts« (for more detail see Reichelt 1998; Pahl 2004 and Meyer 2005).

If empirical findings suggest that the modern monetary economy is in fact mainly a transintentional occurrence – and it is not only the recent developments in the financial markets that undoubtedly suggest this – then one should look for a deeper understanding of money and its derivates than that offered by the positions discussed so far.

3. Modern Money as an Emergent Unity of Money's Three Basic Functions: On the Uncoupling of the Modern Economy

Both Marx[4] and Luhmann regard the modern economy as a sphere that has differentiated from society, following its own specific logic that is neither reducible to intentional agency nor explainable with recourse to a general theory of material reproduction. Although arguing from different theoretical positions, they agree in the core-assumption that this process of differentiation or detachment relates to specific qualities of modern money. Up to this point their position is also in accordance with Habermas and with many assumptions that can regularly be found in the field of heterodox economics. Where they differ, however, seems to be their understanding of money's new qualities. While Habermas drew the distinction between pre-modern money as a circulating medium and modern money as a catalyst of system-building without clarifying their differences, heterodox economists often argue that one of money's basic functions is the dominant one or that one function is more fundamental than the others and has led economic differentiation. The missing link has usually been seen in money as a store of value or in credit-contracts. Following Marx and Luhmann I would propose by contrast that the logical origin of the modern economy is a result of modern money as an *emergent unity of money's three basic functions*. From this perspective, the question which one of money's functions came first into being loses much of its importance for the explanation of its function in modern society. For example, while money as a medium of exchange might have emerged *at the intersections* of pre-modern communities, early forms of credit, requiring trust and assurance, presumably originated *within* pre-capitalist communities (Itoh, Lapavitsas 1999: 74). But what is remarkable about modern, capitalist money is that it links various functions of money, once independent, to a *systemic monetary*

4 Marx's approach in the *Grundrisse* follows a different path than his famous earlier writing *The German Ideology*. While in *The German Ideology* Marx argued more or less for an ontology of economic affairs, in the *Grundrisse* he draws a fundamental distinction between pre-modern economic affairs and the modern capitalist economy.

nexus. We will first take a look at the Marxian theory of money and afterwards turn – more briefly – to Niklas Luhmann's theory.

Within our line of argument, the Marxian *Grundrisse*, the rough draft of what later turned into the three volumes of *Capital*, becomes an important document. It is well known that Marx described the shift to modern capitalism with two different formulas: C-M-C (commodity-money-commodity) and M-C-M' (money-commodity-more money, see *Capital*, Volume I). As it is also commonly known that Marx used the distinction between both formulae to mark the crucial difference of the capitalist mode of production, I think it is more important to clarify the frame of reference Marx addressed with these formulas. The point is not that money has become an end in itself per se, which was of course the case in pre-modern times – just think of hoard-building or the behavior of merchants or money-lenders. Marx's question concerns the features that arise from the second formula when we take the whole economy into account. In *Capital*, Volume I, it remains somewhat unclear how Marx gets from the first formula to the second: Does he skip to the second formula by a simple inversion or does he understand the second formula empirically? In the *Grundrisse*, Marx pays much more attention to this shift, enquiring into the terms and circumstances that must be met for this movement to become true not only as single acts but as an ongoing, systemic process. To describe the C-M-C formula Marx, in the *Grundrisse*, uses the term *simple circulation* and speaks about capitalist circulation (M-C-M') as *mediated circulation*. At the same time, the distinction between both concepts of circulation is more sophisticated than the distinction between the two formulas because simple circulation contains both formulas (C-M-C *and* M-C-M'), without however bringing forth any systemic features. Although the concept of simple circulation has at least a double meaning and methodological function (see below), I want to concentrate mainly on one aspect: In contrast to his discussion in *Capital*, Volume I, Marx does not presume modern capitalism and a labour theory of value in the *Grundrisse*. Instead, he presents a *theory of the constitution of value* (Reichelt 1996) as an emergent and objective property that drives the process of economic differentiation. Marx himself characterized this method as follows: »To develop the concept of capital it is necessary to begin not with labour but with value, and, precisely, with exchange value in an already developed movement of circulation« (Marx 1973: 259). Here Marx states unmistakably his aim in *Grundrisse*, which is to derive capital – first of all – from circulation. We can understand the concept of simple circulation as an outcome of Marx' reconstruction of the emergence of monetary forms in pre-modern societies. For example, he argues that the first function of money – money as a measure (price-form) – emerged as soon as there were trading contacts between pre-modern communities. The same holds true for the second function of money. As soon as exchange becomes steady, money arises as a means of exchange (for more detail see Marx 1973: 146pp). And even in its third function – which, following Marx, presupposes »the first two [functions] and constitutes their unity« (Marx 1973: 216), money appears in pre-modern societies, for example in the form of hoard-building or credit-contracts.

While there is certainly also a connection between these different functions in which money appears historically as there is an inherent dynamic in those forms, Marx never contended the thesis – as claimed by the orthodox reading of his method as a unity of historical and logical analysis – that there is a tendency or even a necessity for modern capitalism to originate. The opposite is in fact the case: what he works out with the concept of simple circulation is the *improbability of modern capitalism to emerge*. Although we can find all three functions of money, including the derangement from money as a means to an end to money as an end in itself, in various pre-modern communities, as for instance in the ancient Greek cities or in European medieval societies, *none of these societies knew a differentiation of the economy such as modern society does*. As Marx puts it:

»But the mere presence of monetary wealth, and even the achievement of a kind of supremacy on its part, is in no way sufficient for this dissolution into capital to happen. Or else ancient Rome, Byzantium etc. would have ended their history with free labour and capital, or rather begun a new history« (Marx 1973: 506).

Marx regards the de-coupling of the modern economy as some kind of *chance encounter*. Modern industrial capitalism only emerged because two necessary prerequisites fell together historically: On the one side a developed sphere of circulation, on the other side a separation of work and property, including the constitution of a class of free wage-workers, being able and forced to sell their labour as a commodity. The second prerequisite only emerged in late European medieval societies, being a product of pre-modern merchant capitalism as well as of the political revolutions of that time. Insofar the origin of modern capitalism is for the most part *contingent*, although there surely was much reciprocation between both prerequisites. But it is Marx's argument that as soon as the reciprocity between circulation and production has reached a certain degree, capitalist economy takes off on its own, transforming contingency into *systemic dynamics* by unfolding economic laws and tendencies.

For our main point, the reconstruction of this shift as the constitution of a monetary nexus that links all forms and functions of money into a systemic unity, Marx offers many revealing comments on the difference between both forms of circulation: On the level of simple circulation Marx criticises the comparison of money with blood (Marx 1973: 162). He argues that simple circulation »does not carry within itself the principle of self-renewal. The moments of the latter are presupposed to it, not posited by it. Commodities constantly have to be thrown into it anew from the outside, like fuel into a fire. Otherwise it flickers out in indifference« (Marx 1973: 254–255). What is remarkable here is the use of the metaphor flicker out with reference to the circulation. Some pages below Marx notices about money's capacity to represent general wealth in simple circulation: »It collapses into its material, which is left over as the inorganic ashes of the process as a whole« (Marx 1973: 263). Here Marx addresses the fact that gold loses its economic determination to represent abstract value and regresses to a simple metal. Both metaphors refer to the non-systemic character of simple circulation. Although simple circulation includes the movement M-C-M', i.e. the shift from money as a means to an end to money as an end in itself, this derangement does not get stabilized with regard to the total economic process. Insofar, simple circulation »is merely a vanishing mediation« (Marx 1973: 269), but not the nexus of the economy's decoupling. Marx states that it is »in fact circulation only from the standpoint of the observer, [...], not posited as such« (Marx 1973: 261). In contrast to this, Marx characterizes capitalist circulation as a »perpetuum mobile« (Marx 1973: 516) or an »organic system« (Marx 1973: 278) and claims: »If anything needed to be compared with the circulation of the blood, it was not the formal circulation of money, but the content-filled of capital« (Marx 1973: 517). Marx's point is that those claims that are inherent to money as soon as it appears in the third function – that of the »material representative of wealth« (Marx 1973: 203), i.e. as an end in itself – need a counterpart in the structure of the process of production. In pre-modern societies, as mentioned above, circulation remained separated from production, which was embedded in traditional structures of power (feudalism). What establishes a systematic connection between circulation and production, however, is capitalism, which transforms both to subordinate moments of its boundless self-preservation. Or as Reichelt (1997: 16, translation H.P.) has put it:

»The false infinity[5] that arises within the process of derangement in exchange, reproduces itself on the level of production and reproduces those contradictions that arose with the third function of money: the contradiction between the quality of the form of wealth and its quantitative limitedness ceases to exist only in the mind of the hoard-builder or the trader, and determines the reality of work itself as a never-ending attempt to catch up to the absolute form of wealth by quantitative expansion. Work produces immediately commodities, i.e. value in unity with use-value«.

Here Reichelt gives reasons why it makes sense for Marx to tie up to the labour theory of value: In contrast to the Ricardian tradition, which is based naturalistically and anthropologically and does not distinguish between concrete labour and abstract labour (being a systemic category!), Marx first of all argues with social determinations of work that occur only in modern capitalism (see Backhaus 1996; Heinrich 2001). It is only in capitalism that a »supraindividual totality of work« (Backhaus 1992: 57) emerges, being itself the result of the subsumption of production under those claims originally constituted in circulation.

In contrast, money in simple circulation is – when regarded from a systemic perspective on the whole economy – unable to redeem its own claims. Marx sums up money's awkward nature in simple circulation as follows:

»Money in its final, completed character now appears in all directions as a contradiction, a contradiction which dissolves itself, drives towards its own dissolution. As the general form of wealth, the whole world of real riches stands opposite it. It is their pure abstraction – hence, fixated as such, a mere conceit. Where wealth as such seems to appear in an entirely material, tangible form, its existence is only in my head, it is a pure fantasy. Midas. On the other side, as material representative of general wealth, it is realized only by being thrown back into circulation, to disappear in exchange for the singular, particular modes of wealth. It remains in circulation, as medium of circulation; but for the accumulating individual, it is lost, and this disappearance is the only possible way to secure it as wealth. To dissolve the things accumulated in individual gratifications is to realize them. The money may then be again stored up by other individuals, but then the same process begins anew. I can really posit its being for myself only by giving it up as mere being for others. If I want to cling to it, it evaporates in my hand to become a mere phantom of real wealth. […] If the other riches do not [also] accumulate, then it loses its value in the measure in which it is accumulated. What appears as its increase is in fact its decrease. Its independence is a mere sem-

5 Hegel distinguishes between true and false infinity. False infinity, as cited above, refers to the impossibility of production ever to fully comply with the qualitative implications included in money.

blance; its independence of circulation exists only in view of circulation, exists as dependence on it« (Marx 1973: 233–234).

Of course, this text passage is hard to retrace. Helmut Reichelt (1996) has noticed that in these assertions Marx partly paraphrases the shift from the doctrine of being to the doctrine of essence in Hegel's *Science of Logic*. What Marx wants to accentuate by his paraphrase is on the one hand the same as mentioned above: Money is unable to fulfil its role as general form of wealth as long as circulation and production remain unlinked, as was the case in pre-modern economies. On the other hand, Marx criticizes the economists in the same way in which Hegel criticized the philosophers: They use economic categories but they have no consciousness of the inner connection between the categories they use. They simply grasp them empirically and start to build analytical models. Here, the second meaning of simple circulation comes into play because Marx criticizes the economists for neglecting the functional unity of production and circulation in modern capitalism, reducing capitalist circulation to simple circulation.

For our purposes we can leave this discussion aside and focus on the difference between the two forms of circulation with reference to systems-theory. Helmut Willke emphasizes in his contribution in this book that »systems-theories assume that complex systems change fundamentally when systemic processes act upon themselves in positive feedback loops and thus create self-reinforcing cycles or even hypercycles, which are able to stabilize an improbable order of elements into a systemic configuration«. Marx summarises the difference between simple circulation and capitalist circulation as follows:

»The circulation of money began at an infinite number of points and returned to an infinite number of points. The point of return was in no way posited as the point of departure. In the circulation of capital, the point of departure is posited as the terminal point and the terminal point as the point of departure« (Marx 1973: 516).

Because points of departure and terminal points coincide only in capitalist circulation, is it possible that processes of positive feedback arise. Only in this case is a specific order between the formerly independent elements (money and commodities) constituted that transforms them into *elements of a systemic whole*. It is also in this context that a phrase makes sense which Marx included in the first draft of Volume I of *Capital* but removed in later drafts for the sake of popularisation. There he determines the relationship between commodities and money in capitalism in the following dialectical manner: »It is as if alongside and external to lions, tigers, rabbits, and all other actual animals, which form when grouped together the various kinds [...] of the animal kingdom, there existed also in addition *the animal*, the individual incarnation of the entire animal kingdom« (Marx 1976: 27). We can find a similar phrase in *Grundrisse*: »Money – the common form into which all commodities as exchange values are transformed, i.e. the universal commodity – must itself exist as a *particular* commodity alongside the others« (Marx 1973: 165). In both quotations money is described as an existing form of unity of all commodities, linking them to a systemic nexus. These findings demonstrate another important point that plays a major role in the Marxian theory of credit-money as discussed in the next section: *The objectivity of value, in the sense of Marx, has nothing to do with materiality* (e.g. gold as money commodity). Instead, it only refers to social determinations. Marx only refers to gold as money because the natural attributes of gold answer the purposes given with money's form-determinations. Today, functional equivalents have arisen but these do not change the general setting in principle.[6]

To get a benchmark for our discussion of this Marxian approach to credit-money, let us first take a cursory look at Niklas Luhmann's conception of the modern economic system. Luhmanns' approach to the separation of the modern economy is placed within a broader concept of society. What Marx regards as a special feature of the capitalist economy, its differentiation from society and its self-referential dynamics, Luhmann generalises towards other social spheres (see Baecker 1998; Willke 2000). He assumes that modern society develops in parallel with a shift towards functional differentiation. This pattern of functional differentiation is neither seen from the perspective of the Durkheimian tradition as a sort of more or less harmonious division of labour nor is it a mere analytical tool in the sense of Parsons. Instead, Luhmann's conception of functional differen-

6 Duncan Foley (2005: 47–48), for instance, has this to say: »Since state credit, like land or other fictitious capital assets, is exchanged against produced commodities (though it is not a produced commodity) there is no formal inconsistency in viewing it as a general equivalent or socially accepted general equivalent in the framework of Marx' theory of forms of value. This line of thinking preserves the integrity of Marx' theory by extending it to embrace new historical institutions. It does leave a loose theoretical end in removing the production of price of the money-commodity as a determinant of the monetary expression of labour time, but even in the commodity-money theory this determinant operates only gradually over the long period. It also presents a picture of the world monetary system in which one national currency must take over the functions of world money, rather than a single produced commodity functioning as world money. [...] It is quite plausible that competition between major national (or regional) currencies for the functions of world money will be an increasingly salient feature of world political economy in coming decades«.

tiation is inspired by what Max Weber has called the *polytheism* of increasingly independent *value-spheres* in modern society: Max Weber

»portrayed the birth and composition of modern society as the emergence of a number of autonomous ›value-spheres‹. One after the other, science, law, art, politics, economics, sexuality, and others freed themselves from their former domination by religious ideas. These ›value-spheres‹ became societal domains of their own which cultivate their particular central value without concern for the value-orientations of other domains« (Schimank 2002).

While pre-modern societies are characterized by a hierarchical and to a certain degree total form of integration, with e.g. political or religious leaders claiming to represent and integrate all of society, modern society gets »decomposed in perspectives of function systems which cannot become organized as a whole« (Nassehi 2004: 5). Each function system is thought to constitute its own claims and to evolve its own imperatives of systems-continuation. To theorize these processes of real structural differentiation, Luhmann has worked out his own theory of generalized media of interchange, which is influenced by Parsons' earlier version, but has taken the argument much further. In the Parsonian framework, interchange mechanisms are seen as social phenomena that derive from processes of functional differentiation and solve problems of social integration at the same time. »The need for generalized media of interchange is a function of the differentiatedness of social structures: in this sense they are all partly integrative mechanisms« (Parsons 1968: 471). For this reason, »the differentiation of media follows the differentiation of systems and not vice versa« (Luhmann 1976: 507). However, one of the problems of this approach – as various critics have noticed – is that the epistemological and ontological status of the media remains somewhat unclear: Are they the results of real interchange in concrete interaction or are they only an outcome of the analytical theory of functional differentiation (e.g. Alexander 1984: 110pp; Habermas 1979: 69pp; Willke 1993: 233)? In contrast to Parsons' concept of interchange media which is developed deductively, Niklas Luhmann has turned the argument completely around: Generalized media (like power, money or truth) solve the problem of double contingency on the level of concrete interaction through the transmission of reduced complexity. They are regarded as meaningful constellations of combined selectivity that »employ their selection pattern as a motive to accept the reduction, so that people join with others in a narrow world of common understandings, complementary expectations, and determinable issues« (Luhmann 1976: 512). Following this conception, we can understand media of interchange as »catalytic principle(s) of subsystem-building within the internal environment of the society« (Luhmann 1977: 39).

Arguing on the level of empirical prices, Luhmann regards the distinction of payment/non-payment as the basic operation that accomplishes the differentiation and reproduction of the modern economic system. Against this it may be objected that this determination is not sufficient to explain the emergence of the modern economy because pre-modern societies knew payments as well. Even though Luhmann pays less attention to an analysis of money's functions than Marx had done, he draws a distinction between money as a *preadaptive advance* and modern money as a *catalyst of social differentiation* that we can broadly compare with Marx's description of the shift from the first (C-M-C) to the second formula (M-C-M'). While pre-modern money serves various functions but fails to establish a solid sphere of pure economic values, modern money is a totalizer of a function-specific perspective. This switch presumes what Luhmann (1995: 456) has called *over-determination of property by money* (»Zweitcodierung des Eigentums durch das Geld«). He introduces this term in order to describe the fact that property itself is more and more affected by, and incorporated into, economic purposes. While Marx made critical comments on the use of an organism-analogy to describe the autonomy and emergence of the capitalist economy, Luhmann incorporates the concept of *autopoiesis* from biology to understand the modern function systems' autonomy. Originally developed to describe living systems such as cells (cf. Maturana, Varela 1980), Luhmann has generalized this concept to put emphasis on the autonomy of social systems. On these theoretical grounds, the economic system is thought to have gradually emerged along with the constitution of recursive chains of monetary operations. Concerning system-to-system-relations, autopoiesis implies that no system can affect the internal structure of another system directly on the level of its operations. For example, political decisions such as introduction of taxes damage the economy, but inside the economic system these effects are only visible in the language of prices. ›Inputs‹ from the environment have to pass the filters of the system itself, or, more precisely, they are internal constructions of the prevailing system, only activated by external disturbances.

Although therefore Luhmann and Marx argue on different epistemological backgrounds, many assumptions on the dynamics of the modern economy are identical. The most important aspect here is perhaps an insight that we can find implicitly in Marx, but which is made more explicit in Luhmann: Closeness and openness should no longer be regarded as opposite conditions but should be regarded as conditions of mutual amplification. It is the modern economy's state of closeness and self-referential operation that has to be regarded as the cause of its opaque dynamics. Some characteristics that are basic to modern society and its economy, such as economic and financial hypergrowth as well as the economy's blindness to all kinds of external affairs, are the outcome of the economy's detachment from society. While pre-modern economies were socially embedded and integrated, the modern capitalist economy has autonomized its functioning, generating system-internal temporal structures as well as spatial demarcations and apperceptions in general. Luhmann's position thus stands in sharp contrast to central assertions of today's dominant economic schools. For example, both neoclassical orthodoxy and modern economic institutionalism refer to anthropological assumptions in order to grasp economic affairs. While neoclassical orthodoxy tends to regard the modern economy as a direct outcome of rational behavior, economic institutionalism regards the rise of capitalism and its triumph in the western world as an outcome of the successful correlation of economic institutions with fundamental human traits. Both Marx and Luhmann are far less affirmative concerning modern society's character (although they differed broadly in their opinions on chances to intervene). Or as Dirk Baecker (1998: 11, translation H.P.) has expressed it in an obituary on Luhmann:

»The world is not well ordered into systems, it resolves into systems that all have their own environment. In these systems, self-referential mechanisms are at work that only care about one thing: to enable the continuity of the system. This has nothing to do either with rationality or with progress. This form of observation applies the Marxian analysis of the economy to the whole of society. It therefore corrects the over-assessment of the economy (which with Marx has been an underestimation, too) and does not find a point of departure for the expectation of a revolution anymore«.

4. On the Unity and Difference between Finance and the Economy

Having introduced two concepts of the modern economy as a social system detached from society, we now can address the question of how to conceive modern finance on these theoretical grounds. First, I want to go back to Marx and sketch his thesis of modern credit as a necessary outcome of the circulation of industrial capital. On this basis, some remarks will be made about what Marx distinguishes as money-economy and credit-economy (or as monetary-system and credit-system), in other words, his approach to the question of the unity and difference between finance and the economy. Second, I will discuss the question whether it makes sense to describe modern finance from a systems-theoretical point of view as a process of internal differentiation and sub-system-building within the economic system itself. In my discussion, I will outline some basic assumptions by Luhmann on internal differentiation as well as newer contributions to a systems-theory of finance.

Returning to Marx, we should mention that his development of economic categories does not stop with what he called money *as money*, although we can understand the derangement of money from a means to an end to an end in itself as a kind of basic Marxian version of the modern economy's autopoietic character. As mentioned above, in *Grundrisse* Marx describes the »completed bourgeois system« as an »organic system« in which »every economic relation presupposes every other« (Marx 1973: 278). But in addition to this description of the systemic features of the modern economy, Marx highlights a second aspect: When he states that the economy's »development to its totality consists precisely in subordinating all elements of society to itself, or in creating out of it the organs which it still lacks« (Marx 1973: 278), he assumes that there is an inherent tendency in modern capitalism to breed new forms suitable for its reproduction, or to put it differently: Marx assumes morphogenesis to be a necessity of the modern economy as a system. This concept of morphogenesis helps us to understand Marx's approach to credit-money: In *Grundrisse*, we do not find a systematic elaboration of credit and interest, but only some programmatic remarks by Marx that show us the logical place of credit within his theory. He states for example that »it will be shown how capital, in credit, creates new products of circulation« (Marx 1973: 659). Elsewhere he defines credit as a »form of circulation« that is »directly posited by capital – which arises, hence, specifically from the nature of capital« (Marx 1973: 672). With such remarks, Marx suggests *that credit itself is a kind of internal differentiation of the modern capitalist economy*, or, as Martha Campbell (2002: 212) puts it: Marx »derives the credit system from capital, which he initially presents as industrial capital[7] by itself. That is, he appeals to the requirements and inherent tendencies of industrial capital to explain why the credit system evolves«. Of course, many forms of credit existed in the course of history before modern capitalism emerged. But this is not the point. The logical structure of the argument is the same as mentioned above in the context of money. Marx states:

»There was borrowing and lending in earlier situations as well, and usury is even the oldest of the antediluvian forms of capital. But borrowing and lending no more constitute credit than working constitutes industrial labour or free wage labour. And credit as an essential, developed relation of production appears historically only in circulation based on capital or on wage labour« (Marx 1973: 535).

Marx's argument is that modern credit differs qualitatively from any form of pre-modern credit, being a necessary outcome of modern capitalism itself.

A more concrete determination can be found in Volume II of *Capital*: There, Marx develops the same argument by criticizing the opinion that »natural economy, money-economy and credit-economy« can be »placed in opposition to one another as being the three characteristic forms of movement in social production« (Volume II: 119). Instead, he mentions that »the so-called credit-economy is merely a form of the money-economy«, arguing that »money-economy and credit-economy thus correspond only to different stages in the development of capitalist production, but [...] are by no means independent forms of exchange vis-à-vis natural economy« (ibid.). Here, as well as in the quotations from *Grundrisse* mentioned above, modern credit is addressed as a social form resulting from internal differentiations of the modern economic system. *These assumptions are central to our question concerning the unity and difference of finance and the economy.* Orthodox readings have always claimed that Marx suggested that

7 Please note that Marx's concept of industrial capital should not be conflated with the use regularly made of it in sociology, for example to distinguish industrial society from the knowledge society. While sociology uses the term *industrial* to refer to a prevailing mode of production (i.e. Taylorism), industrial capital in Marx's works is a value-theoretical category, relating to the actual forms of circulation, not to concrete modes of organising the production process. So far, no matter whether the commodities they produce are material or immaterial, today's knowledge firms have been types of industrial capital.

capitalism operates with commodity money because this is the way Marx introduces his theory of money in Volume I of *Capital*. If you accept this point of view, credit and finance always remain inferior superstructures, not affecting the system's basic dynamics. In the last section I have already briefly explained why Marx referred to gold. Again, I would agree with Martha Campbell (2002: 212–213) when she criticizes the orthodox views by stressing that commodity money »is simply the form of money capital does not create but inherits from previous society«. *What capital creates is credit money, and this form of money unfolds its own laws of motion that macro-determinate the whole system.* Marx himself addresses these emergent features of credit-money when he states: »In developed capitalist production, the money-economy appears only as the basis of the credit-economy« (Volume II: 119). But it is not until part four of Volume III of *Capital* that Marx has reconstructed the necessary economic forms to discuss this relationship between money-economy and credit-economy on an adequate conceptual basis. Of course, it is impossible to discuss the structure of volumes II and III in this article in any detail but what can be done is to outline some basic features concerning credit's dependency as well as relative autonomy according to Marx.

In the excursus on *Grundrisse* in the last section, we saw that the formula M-C-M' contains many more aspects than a simple inversion of C-M-C. In volume 2 of *Capital* Marx takes up and develops these considerations. The formula M-C-M' is no longer regarded as an *independent and single process*, but as an *ongoing process* that is mediated by a capitalist production process (Arthur 1998). While this is the *result* of the line of argument in the *Grundrisse* (and, on the basis of a popularised account, in volume I of *Capital*), now it is the *starting point* for an extended analysis of the *circulation of capital*. I will not discuss, but only mention that this extended analysis allows three different points of views, depending on where one fixes the starting and the end points: We get the *circuit of money capital* when we regard the formula as M-C…P…C'-M', we get the *circuit of productive capital* when we regard it as P…C'-M'-C…P, and we get the *circuit of commodity capital* when we regard it as C'-M'-C…P…C' (see Volume II: 25–102). Following Marx, the preceding schools of economic thinking altogether failed to analyse the circulation of capital properly. He characterized them as limited approaches, each displaying significant blind spots. For example, mercantilism only regarded the circulation of capital as a circuit of money capital, the classical political economic theory of Smith and Ricardo only saw it as a circuit of productive capital while the physiocrats only regarded it as a circuit of commodity capital (see Murray 1998). Marx himself claimed to be the first to dispose of an adequate method to fully describe the differentiation of the modern economy by taking into account the *unity-in-difference of all three circuits*. Money capital, productive capital and commodity capital in Volume II are neither empirical forms nor are they species of an abstract genus. Instead, Marx reconstructs them, as Chris Arthur (1998: 107) highlights, as »internal self-differentiations of a single whole« that »acquire their potency as shapes *of* capital only within this whole«. Following Arthur (ibid.), the Marxian treatment of the circulation of capital has to be regarded as »a special case of the phenomena of ›emergent properties‹ in which the emergent property does not merely passively reflect the epiphenomenal effects of the functioning of the ›original‹ or ›basic‹ elements, but itself has an active principle or law which turns its determinants into determined determinants and hence shapes the functioning of the base elements in accordance with the requirements of the emergent function«. In Volume II, one result of the analysis of the circulation of capital is that Marx derives the credit-categories of *hoards* and *commercial credit* that can be regarded as embryonal pre-forms of the credit-system that he discusses in Volume III. While hoards and commercial credit both emerge from the circulation of industrial capital but have only a limited capacity to overcome barriers to the expansion of capital on the level of the total social capital, the developed credit-system in Volume III possesses these qualities to a higher degree. By leaving aside the details of this conception in Volume II, we can briefly turn to some general aspects of Volume III before turning to the question of the unity of, and difference between, money-economy and credit-economy.

One main topic that Marx discusses in Volume III before he addresses credit is the *conversion of profit into average profit* (this includes the so-called transformation-problem from values to production prices[8], see Volume

8 The common criticism – first made by Boehm-Bawerk and since then repeated many times – misses the point: It is not a contradiction that Marx in Volumes I and II argues with values while in Volume III he argues with production-prices. Marx wrote the manuscript of Volume III before he wrote that of Volume I. Value and production-prices are arguments on different levels of abstraction. It is the emergent feature of the price form to enable the detachment of value and price. The important point is that Marx' version of a *quantitative* solution to the transformation problem is false (cf. Heinrich (2001) for a critique of Marx's quantitative solution). But one has to take into account that this failure does not affect a strictly qualitative reading of his development of economic categories.

III: 142–143). *Here, for the first time, an empirically valid systemic perspective on the total process of the capitalist economy is achieved.* What traditional economic theories describe by using metaphors or heuristic constructions, Marx is able to handle on a conceptual level by deriving the process of individual rates of profit to constitute an average rate of profit that impinges on different branches and markets. Marx regards the mechanisms that equalize the rate of profit on different capitals as the central »law on which the whole of capitalist production depends« (Campbell 2002: 216; see also Heinrich 2004: 16–17). Here we have a further, more concrete determination of the general assumption that has been expressed by saying that it is value that unifies and synthesizes the anarchic system of capitalism (Reichelt 1970). It is the credit-system that allows a distribution of capital over the economy as a whole and, by this, »unifies all individual capitals into one total social capital« (Campbell 2002: 216). Again, the *Grundrisse* include a phrase that may help to clarify the logical structure of the argument. Marx explains:

»Capital in general, as distinct from the particular capitals, does indeed appear (1) only as an abstraction; not an arbitrary abstraction, but an abstraction which grasps the specific characteristics which distinguish capital from all other forms of wealth – or modes in which (social) production develops. […] (2) however, capital in general, as distinct from the particular capitals, is itself a real existence. […] While the general is therefore on the one hand only a mental [gedachte] mark of distinction [differentia specifica], it is at the same time a particular real form alongside the form of the particular and individual« (Marx 1973: 449–450).

What might look at first glance like a reopening of the medieval debate about universals turns out to be again some kind of Marxian version of the phenomenon of emergent properties that deals with the problem of the whole and its parts in a special manner. The topic is economic synthesis, not metaphysics or epistemology. Marx claims that beneath, and external to, all concrete and empirical capitalist enterprises (»particular capitals«), their unity is itself a concrete form. While traditional epistemologies would accept generality only as a category of thinking, Marx is – via Hegel – forced to enrich formal logic with what is today called tangled hierarchies (cf. Reusswig 1993) to describe capitalism's inner law of motion. In a letter written while working on the *Grundrisse* (known as *Short Outline of the First Part*), Marx elucidates a central aspect of this real form of capital in general and identifies it as credit:

»Capital falls into 4 sections. a) Capital en général (This is the substance of the first instalment) b) Competition or the interaction of many capitals. c) Credit where capital, as against individual capitals, is shown to be a universal element. d) Share capital as the most perfected form (turning into communism) together with all its contradictions.« (MECW40: 296).

While we can regard the last assumption on share capital as a holdover from Marx' earlier thesis of a so-called dialectics of productive forces and the existing relations of production, the crucial point is that Marx addresses *credit* as that element »where capital, as against individual capitals, is shown to be a universal element«. This statement makes it clear once more that Marx does not regard all the empirical forms he deals with in Volume III commercial capital, money-dealing capital, interest-bearing capital, fictitious capital – as mere superstructures that do not affect the economic system. The statement leads, rather, to the assumption that Marx regards credit as some kind of non-intentional unit of economic synthesis (cf. Heinrich 2004: 167–168).

When Marx finally comes to discuss the credit system, he emphasizes the limited scope of his analysis, which results from the general level of abstraction: »An exhaustive analysis of the credit system and of the instruments which it creates for its own use (credit-money, etc.) lies beyond our plan. We merely wish to dwell here upon a few particular points, which are required to characterise the capitalist mode of production in general« (Volume III: 400). But this limitation does not have to be a disadvantage. On the contrary: Because the Marxian analysis remains on such a general level, we still can catch up with today's empirical affairs *in general* by using categories developed by Marx. In Volume III he approaches the treatment of core-aspects of finance from several angles, but for our purposes – the question of the unity and difference between finance and the economy – it seems preferable only to concentrate on his basic distinction between the monetary-system and the credit-system here,[9] all the more because there has recently been a debate on this point between Heiner Ganßmann (1996) and Martha Campbell (2002), which we would like to take up here. Throughout Volumes I and II of *Capital*, although Marx sketches the necessity of credit-money to arise, circulation is regarded along the lines of his commodity theory of money. What distinguishes the credit-system he deals with in Volume III from the early forms of credit developed in Vol-

9 As we can only deal with the basic relationship between money-economy and credit-economy, we leave aside here the question of fictitious capital (cf. Kraetke 2000) although it has of course to be taken into account when one wants to discuss the decoupling of finance in greater detail.

ume II is that it acts upon a banking system that concentrates society's total money-capital reserves:

»Generally speaking, this aspect of the banking business consists of concentrating large amounts of the loanable money-capital in the banker's hand, so that, in place of the individual money-lender, the bankers confront the industrial capitalists and commercial capitalists as representatives of all money-lenders. They become the general managers of money-capital« (Volume III: 402).

What Marx accomplishes here is that the »social character of capital is first promoted and wholly realised through the full development of the credit and banking system« (Volume III: 607). He also goes on to argue that the »banking system, so far as its formal organization and centralisation is concerned, is the most artificial and most developed product turned out by the capitalist mode of production« (Volume III: 606). Marx mentions two general features of this credit-system (cf. Campbell 2002: 216–217): On the one hand, it overcomes barriers to the expansion of capital to a higher degree than was possible by pure commercial credit. Marx here assumes that the »credit system accelerates the material development of the productive forces and the establishment of the world-market« (Volume III: 441). On the other hand, this socialisation of money-capital increases the interconnections among individual capitals and reduces the total reserve. These latter aspects increase both the complexity and the fragility of the systems. As Marx states: »it is the developed credit and banking system which creates this over-sensitiveness of the whole organism« (Volume III: 572). It has however to be taken into account that the functioning of the credit-system is not a mere outcome of institutional innovations (such as banks). Rather, it runs parallel to Marx's form-theoretical account of *interest-bearing capital* (cf. Volume III: 338–399). To quote Campbell's (2002: 217) recapitulation of Marx's assumptions, the circuit of interest-bearing capital »is completely external to the reproduction of real capital (meaning industrial and commercial capital)«. The circuit of interest-bearing capital can be displayed as M-M-C-M'-M' (cf. Volume III: 340).[10] Here, it becomes clear that Marx uses a *logic of emergence* (cf. Ganßmann 1996: 215–216) in his derivation of the credit-system. Ganßmann (ibid.) comments that this procedure is an attempt to derive new complex attributes and qualities (here: the credit-system and the

10 Marx already mentioned in the *Grundrisse* that as »interest, capital itself appears again in the character of a *commodity*, but a commodity *specifically* distinct from all other commodities; *capital as such* – not as a mere sum of exchange values – enters into circulation and becomes a *commodity*« (Marx 1973: 318).

circuit of interest-bearing capital) from simpler ones (here: the monetary-system and the circuit of industrial capital), without however predicting that the new features developed can be reduced to the initial conditions.

The point at issue in the recent debate has been the question of how to conceive the relationship between the monetary system and the credit system. Marx assumes on the one hand that the credit system unfolds emergent properties, but on the other hand he states over and over again that the credit-system is never fully emancipated from its basis in the monetary-system. Thus he claims that the »change-over from the credit system to the monetary system is necessary« (Volume III: 572) because »money – in the form of precious metal – remains the foundation from which the credit system, by its very nature, can *never* detach itself« (Volume III: 606). While Ganßmann (1996: 218) assumes that Marx regards the turnover from credit to money as a validation of his theoretical starting point (featuring gold as money-commodity), Campbell (2002: 223) argues that although Marx regards the turnover from the credit-system to the banking-system as caused by monetary constraints, this »has nothing to do with the metallic form of money«. As I already remarked in the last section, one has to distinguish between the metallic form of money and Marx's commodity theory of money. In as far as the metallic form of money can be replaced by functional equivalents, the distinction between the monetary system and the credit system is not identical with the assumption that in the case of financial crises the modern economy regresses to gold-money. Instead, I agree with Campbell (2002: 223) when she argues that the »credit system is eliminated in the sense that credit reverts to commercial credit by itself, outside the credit system (i.e., with no access to the pool of funds the credit system creates)«.

Turning now again to Niklas Luhmann's theory of social systems, we can develop another version of how to conceive the question of the unity and difference of finance and the economy. Against Marx, Luhmann rejects any concept of surplus value, referring instead only to empirical prices. This is why the borderlines that are drawn between economy and society as well as those between finance and the economy follow different paths from those of Marx. Before turning to the question of a systems-theoretical approach to finance, let us take a short look at these differences. A conspicuous instance concerns the way both theories handle the category of capital. While we have seen that for Marx, capital is the overwhelming principle of the economic system, Luhmann classifies capital on the secondary level of what he calls programs, that is specific determinations of how to handle the code payment/non-payment (Luhmann 1988: 250). For example, while households usually use payments only for consumption, enterprises accomplish payments for the sake of regaining the ability to pay, including profits (cf. Luhmann 1986: 109). Elaborating this position, Dirk Baecker (2001) regards capital as a mechanism of *structural coupling* between the economic system and its internal environments (markets, organizations). As a result of this divergence, Luhmann and Marx draw different system/environment-distinctions and ascribe to capital a different role concerning the whole system.

Let us now turn to the question of how to describe the uncoupling of the financial sphere from a systems-theoretical point of view. Although the design of Luhmann's theory suggests that we should think about this relationship in terms of processes of further differentiation, Luhmann himself never addressed the question of whether we should regard finance as an autopoietic system in its own right. Luhmann's main interest was to work out the autpoiesis-perspective for all primary function-systems, not least to demonstrate the validity of his assumption that functional differentiation is the primary form of social differentiation in modernity. Empirically, as I have stated above, this mainly refers to the shift from European medieval societies to modern society. From this perspective, processes of further system-internal differentiation seem less important. In the case of finance, Luhmann has only dealt with the financial sphere in the narrow sense of *financial markets*. Although notices that these markets represent the unity of the whole economic system because they are closely linked to all other markets, firms and households (Luhmann 1988: 118), he never raises the question of finance's systemic qualities. This might be thought consistent because autopoietic systems-theory regards markets not as systems but as internal environments of systems. On the other hand, the question of how to conceive structural shifts within the differentiated function-systems of modern society seems too important to be left aside, just think of the changes in the economy's financial architecture that we have witnessed over the last four decades. Proponents of systems-theory have, particularly during the last decade, taken up Luhmann's basic assumptions on finance and have begun to set up a more detailed theoretical framework for various aspects of this subject (e.g. Baecker 1988; Schmidt 1998; Strulik 2000; Willke 2001; Piel 2003). As far as I can see however, the question of the unity and difference between finance and the economy has not yet been fully clarified. Helmut Willke for example argues strongly for a position that regards finance as an autopoietic world-system detached from the world economy (Willke 1998 and his contribution in this book), while Dirk Baecker (2001) is more sceptical of treating finance as an autopoietic system in its own right and has instead focussed on the *unity in difference* of finance and the economy. One core argument offered by Willke (2003: 205) to underpin the uncoupling of the two stresses the fact that transactions in money-capital have their clues and benchmarks in expectations and conjectures that are generated within the financial sphere, leaving fundamental data aside. In contrast to this, Baecker (2001: 314) rejects the assumption of a detachment of finance and the economy, arguing that the self-referential nexus of the financial sphere is still – however mediated – bound to forms of external reference. It seems obvious that both claims are a bit exaggerated. What we need to do is to decide how to weight them and how to relate them to each other, for instance with regard to the different systems both statements refer to.

Some general remarks might help to fathom the ongoing debate. In contrast to Parsons' analytical version of functional differentiation, processes of further internal differentiations of social systems cannot in Luhmann's view be derived from a presupposed scheme. Instead, one would have to look inductively for specific communicative operations (decisions, operations) that share unique features and act as points of reference for other communications of the same kind. A second line of argument in systems theory supposes that social systems differentiate from society because they specialise on certain functions to be fulfilled on the level of society as a whole (cf. Luhmann 1988: 132). For example, Luhmann (1988: 65) treats the economic system's function as actually constituting and regulating lacks in order to satisfy future needs. Until now, most scholars have concentrated on asking whether other social spheres that Luhmann has not treated should not also be regarded as primary function systems (for example sport, sexuality etc.). The answer to this is obvious because Luhmann always emphasised that neither the number nor the type of primary function systems are predictable. But in our case, the problem is slightly different. I would refuse to regard finance as another primary function system because it operates within the same medium as the economy (money). What differs are the types of form-building (chains of payments) and expectations within this medium. While the economy is marked by the distinction payment/non-payment without any further determinations,

Baecker (1988: 281) regards *payments that anticipate the reproduction of payments through payments* as a typical element of finance. Willke (in his contribution to this book) prefers to regard the basic operation of finance as a *payment with built-in deferred return on payment.* However this may be, from this perspective it is more reasonable to regard finance as a sub-system of the economy than as a primary function system (cf. Schmidt 1998: 220; Strulik 2000: 137). Discussing the level of operations is suitable for the detection of processes of differentiation and de-coupling, but does not answer the question of finance's function. Baecker (1988), Schmidt (1998) and Strulik (2000) all agree in regarding finance's function as some kind of *compression* of the general function of the economy, constantly appointing the economic system's conditions of possibility to proceed.

I agree with this position but would like to complement it by applying it to the structural changes between economy and finance. Compared to the other primary subsystems, economy's autopoiesis – an autopoiesis of payments – has to be *anchored* by a regulation of the medium itself. Because the economy deals with lack and shortage, *its medium itself has to be kept short.* But what seems to differ historically is the mechanisms that realize the medium's shortage. In the early stages of the differentiation of the economic system, the natural properties of gold have served as such an anchor (as I stated above, this assumption is not identical with Marx's commodity theory of money). The operational closure and internal differentiation of the heterarchic system was limited by an external – and in this case even extra-social – point of reference. The system of Bretton Woods then can be understood as a first step towards the loosening of this external point of reference. As a functional equivalent of the natural properties of gold, political decisions such as the coordination of money via monetary policy still anchor the economic system's operational closure, but no longer with reference to an extra-social point of reference such as gold-quantities (the linking of the dollar to gold was more an ideal benchmark than a real limit. In fact, dollar's capacity to act as world-money itself served as a point of reference). The recent rise of financial markets might be interpreted as a further shift toward the autonomy of the economic system from society, because external points of reference that govern the shortage of the system's medium – whether political or extra-social – are increasingly offset by system-internal structures. The central role of today's financial markets results from their role as functional equivalents of functions once fulfilled system-externally. Although central banks still act as lenders of last resort, it seems to be the competition between at least two currencies to act as world-money that assures the shortage of the medium. Insomuch as these processes are left to market dynamics, the external anchors of the economic system's monetary autopoiesis are partly substituted by a system-internal form of center/periphery-differentiation: Financial markets do not govern or control the economic system hierarchically, but play nevertheless a central role in the system's autopoiesis because of their central position within the heterarchic system. By regulating the price of money, they generate criteria and norms (e.g. shareholder value) that benchmark and determine the conditions of the whole system.

5. Conclusions

It was the aim of this paper to present theoretical investigations for a deeper and more theoretical understanding of the recent phenomena of the cataclysmic dynamics of finance and the economy. Starting from the neglect of money in neoclassical orthodoxy as well as in traditional economic sociology, our search for alternative points of view has tended to stress the similarities between Luhmann and Marx and it is up to those who disagree with the reading of Marx and Luhmann presented in this paper to offer alternatives. My approach is based on the assumption that in the comparison of different theoretical traditions and approaches, the two most common procedures are both regularly unsatisfactory: It is unsatisfactory to criticize one theoretical program somewhat externally by an unquestioned acceptance of the position of the other. It is no less unsatisfactory to mix up theoretical keystones from one theory with those from the other without taking into account the prevailing epistemological backgrounds. What seems to me more suitable on theoretical grounds is to detect points of difference and similarity and to stimulate mutual irritations and suggestions. Concerning empirical affairs both theories might serve best if used as complementary conceptual strategies to decrypt the secrets of money. As an example of the latter concern I want to come back briefly to the initial question about an uncoupling or decoupling of global finance and discuss this question with reference to Luhmann and Marx. Although my reconstruction of Marx and Luhmann has no doubt left open many questions, it should be possible nevertheless to make some critical comments on the recent debate on the financial sphere's nebulosity.

According to Marx, the objectivity of value stems from the indirectly social character of capitalist reproduction (cf. Reichelt 1970; Campbell 2002). This is a point that cannot be grasped within an action-theoretical framework because it does not refer to the qualities of single commodities but belongs to a systemic level. Value, however, is no metaphysical entity embodied in a commodity – as traditional *pancake-labour-theories of value* suggest – it is a principle, a movement, a fact that readings of Marx by eco_nomists have failed to come to grips with. Separating Hegel from Marx as if they were removing a tumour, they usually made a hash of Marx. For example, Joan Robinson, a student and assistant of Keynes, asked in her *Open Letter to a Marxist* of 1953 »what business had Hegel putting his nose in between her and Ricardo« (cf. Arthur 1996: 897). It was Hegel's business to provide a *system of logic* that Marx could develop in order to decipher the *logic of a system.* Capitalist reproduction is at the same time private and social. It is *social synthesis through the neglect of social synthesis* (Alfred Sohn-Rethel). We can regard the *system of economic categories* to be an outcome as well as a form of mediation of the twofold character that society's metabolism with nature has adopted in modernity. Marx described this mediation as a processing contradiction (Luhmann would probably have described it as the unfolding of a paradox): Although the economic categories allow this contradiction to proceed, they do not remove it. These categories originally emerge as by-products of intentional agency (simple circulation) and than take off on their own as soon as they constitute cycles of positive feedback (mediated circulation) and become the »*nexus rerum*« (Marx 1973: 223) of symbolic and material reproduction. In this respect, »credit money is just as much a thing as gold money« (Campbell 2002: 226). This makes clear that economic categories, such as money's basic functions and its reflexive forms (e.g. interest), are more than mere heuristic categories used by economics but produce post-hermeneutic states of affair. We cannot understand their logic by following the paths of traditional economics. This is why Marx added to the original economic problem of the content and size of value »the further problem of its ›deranged form‹, in order to give a coherent solution to the former« (Backhaus 1992: 81). Form-analysis is an attempt to understand what is non-understandable by reconstructing the genesis of emergent forms, which is where, according to Marx, labour comes into play. The critique of political economy shows value to be a social relation, it unfolds that economic forms are historically specific forms of human practice (cf. Bonefeld 1995). Expecting finance on the basis of Luhmann's theory of social systems to have differentiated from the economy and to have reconfigured as an operationally closed system should not be confused with the statements of a hyperreality of finance mentioned in the introduction. The concept of hyperreality stems from Jean Baudrillard's postmodern philosophy. As far as I know Luhmann never dealt with Baudrillard's concept of hyperreality and referencelessness in a detailed way, but we can refer to an interview of 1992 (Breyer, Werber 1992: 47, translation H.P.) where Luhmann simply stated: »I don't believe in Baudrillard. I hope my bank account is not simulated«. Leaving polemics aside, the crucial point here seems to be that systems-theory neither pleads for an ontology of social affairs nor for a postmodern state of referencelessness. Instead, it regards *reference* as an internal construction and outcome of systemic operations and asks for the prevailing system of elements (cf. Piel 2003). Both traditional approaches and postmodern epistemologies often work with under-complex basic decisions that deny the possibility of an adequate modelling of the problems under consideration. *In the field of economics and finance it seems that hyperreality is merely the other extreme of the neglect of money in mainstream-economics. Following our assumptions, the point is not to opt for one side or the other, but to question the validity of the distinction itself.* To take just one basic example: Luhmann's conception of the economy's autopoiesis stands orthogonal to the above-mentioned differentiation. Albeit the fulfilment of needs is external reference for the economic system this does not imply that needs do not matter at all. They do of course matter, but system-internally they are visible only in the language of the prices. As was demonstrated above: Closeness and openness should not be regarded as opposite conditions but as conditions of mutual amplification. In this resect, a further decoupling of financial affairs from the so-called real economy increases interactions and repulsions between both realms, although these cannot be grasped as causal interferences.

References

Alexander, Jeffrey C. (1984),: »The Modern Reconstruction of Classical Thought: Talcott Parsons«. *Theoretical Logic in Sociology*. Vol. 4. London.

Arthur, Christopher J. (1996), »Capital: A Compulsive-Neurotic Subject« http://www.psa.ac.uk/cps/1996%5Carth.pdf

— (1998), »The Fluidity of Capital and the Logic of the Concept«, in: Christopher J. Arthur and Geert Reuten (eds), *The Circulation of Capital. Essays on Volume Two of Marx's Capital.* Basingstoke, 95–128.

Backhaus, Hans-Georg (1992), »Between Philosophy and Science: Marxian Social Economy as Critical Theory«, in: Werner Bonefeld, Richard Gunn and Kosmas Psychopedis (eds), *Open Marxism,* Vol.1. London, Boulder, 54–92.

— (1996), »Die Irrtümer der nationalökonomischen Marx-Kritik als Grundmängel der nationalökonomischen Theoriebildung«, in: Helmut Brentel (ed.), *Gegensätze. Elemente kritischer Theorie. Festschrift für Jürgen Ritsert.* Frankfurt a.M., 31–47.

Baecker, Dirk (1998), »Guter Geist ist trocken – und Systeme sind unzuverlaessig. Nachruf auf Niklas Luhmann (8.12.1927–6.11.1998)«, in: *Berliner Zeitung,* November 12th 1998, 11.

— (2001), »Kapital als strukturelle Kopplung«, in: *Soziale Systeme,* Vol. 7, 313–327.

Beckert, Jens (1997), *Grenzen des Marktes. Die sozialen Grundlagen wirtschaftlicher Effizienz.* Frankfurt a.M.

Bonefeld, Werner (1995), »Money, Equality and Exploitation: An Interpretation of Marx's Treatment of Money«, in: Werner Bonefeld and John Holloway (eds), *Global Capital, National State and the Politics of Money.* Houndsmills, 178–209.

Breyer, Gerald/Werber, Niels (1992), »Die Systemtheorie zwischen Involution und Normativität. Ein Interview mit Niklas Luhmann«, in: *Symptome. Zeitschrift für epistemologische Baustellen.* Vol.10, 46–56.

Bruegger, Urs/Knorr-Cetina, Karin (2002), »Global Microstructures: The Virtual Societies of Financial Markets«, in: *American Journal of Sociology,* Vol. 4, 905–950.

Campbell, Martha (2002), »The Credit System«, in: Martha Campbell and Geert Reuten (eds): *The Culmination of Capital. Essays on Volume III of Marx's Capital.* New York, 212–227.

Castells, Manuel (2001), *Der Aufstieg der Netzwerkgesellschaft. Das Informationszeitalter 1.* Opladen.

Deutschmann, Christoph (2001), *Die Verheißung des absoluten Reichtums. Zur religiösen Natur des Kapitalismus.* Frankfurt a.M.

Dodd, Nigel (1994), *The Sociology of Money. Economics, Reason and Contemporary Society.* Cambridge.

Foley, Duncan (2005), »Marx's Theory of Money in Historical Perspective«, in: Fred Moseley (ed.), *Marx's Theory of Money. Modern Appraisals.* New York, 36–49.

Froud, Julie/Haslim, Colin/Johal, Sukhdev/Williams, Karel (2000), »Shareholder Value and Financialization: Consultancy Promises, Management Moves«, in: *Economy and Society,* Vol. 1, 80–110.

Ganßmann, Heiner (1996), *Geld und Arbeit.* Frankfurt a.M.

Giddens, Anthony (1990), *The Consequences of Modernity.* Cambridge.

Girschner, Christian (2001), *Falsche Kategorien oder verkehrte Welt? Eine Kritik des Dienstleistungsbegriffs und der Außenhandelskategorien am Beispiel der Globalisierungsdiskussion.* Bremen.

Guttmann, Robert (n.d.), »Internationale Regulierung als letzter Ausweg? Strategien zur Rückgewinnung politischer Gestaltungskompetenz auf Finanz- und Kapitalmärkten«, URL http://www.hbs-hessen.de/pol/guttman.htm.

Habermas, Jürgen (1979), »Handlung und System. Bemerkungen zu Parsons' Medientheorie«, in: Wolfgang Schluchter (ed.), *Verhalten, Handeln und System. Talcott Parsons' Beitrag zur Entwicklung der Sozialwissenschaften.* Frankfurt a.M., 68–105.

— (1981), *Theorie des kommunikativen Handelns.* Frankfurt a.M.

— (1986), »Entgegnung«, in: Axel Honneth and Hans Joas (eds), *Kommunikatives Handeln. Beiträge zu Jürgen Habermas' »Theorie des kommunikativen Handelns«.* Frankfurt a.M., 327–405.

Heinrich, Michael (2001), *Die Wissenschaft vom Wert.* Münster.

— (2004), *Kritik der politischen Ökonomie. Eine Einführung.* Stuttgart.

Heinsohn, Gunnar/Steiger, Otto (2002), *Eigentumstheorie des Wirtschaftens versus Wirtschaftstheorie ohne Eigentum.* Marburg.

Hessling, Alexandra/Pahl, Hanno (2006), »The Global System of Finance: Scanning Niklas Luhmann and Talcott Parsons for Theoretical Keystones«, in: *American Journal of Economics and Sociology. Special edition on Talcott Parsons.*

Ingham, Geoffrey (2004), »The Nature of Money«, in: *Economic Sociology*, Vol. 5, 18–28.

Itoh, Makoto/Lapavitsas, Costas (1999), *Political Economy of Money and Finance.* London.

Krätke, Michael R. (2000), »Geld, Kredit und verrückte Formen«, in: *MEGA-Studien*, Vol. 1, 64–99.

Luhmann, Niklas (1976), »Generalized Media and the Problem of Contingency«, in: Jan J. Loubser, Rainer C. Baum, Andrew Effrat, Victor Meyer Lidz (eds), *Explorations in General Theory in Social Sciences.* Vol. 2, New York, 507–532.

— (1977), »Differentiation of Society«, in: *Canadian Journal of Sociology*, Vol. 2, 29–52.

— (1986), *Ökologische Kommunikation. Kann die moderne Gesellschaft sich auf ökologische Gefährdungen einstellen?.* Wiesbaden.

— (1988), *Die Wirtschaft der Gesellschaft.* Frankfurt a.M.

— (1995), *Das Recht der Gesellschaft.* Frankfurt a.M.

— (1997), *Die Gesellschaft der Gesellschaft.* Frankfurt a.M.

MacKenzie, Donald (2002), »Opening the Black Boxes of Global Finance«, Paper presented at the workshop ›Approaches to Global Finance«, University of Warwick, December 6 and 7, 2002.

Marx, Karl (1973), *Grundrisse. Foundations of the Critique of Political Economy* (Rough Draft). London.

— (1976), »The Commodity. Chapter One, Volume One of the first edition of Capital«, in: Albert Dragstedt (ed.), *Value: Studies by Karl Marx.* London, 1–40.

Maturana, Humberto R./Varela, Francisco J. (1980), *Autopoiesis and Cognition: The Realization of the Living.* Dordrecht.

Meyer, Lars (2005), *Absoluter Wert und allgemeiner Wille. Zur Selbstbegründung einer dialektischen Gesellschaftstheorie.* Bielefeld.

Murray, Patrick (1998), »Beyond the ›Commerce and Industry‹ Picture of Capital«, in: Christopher J. Arthur and Geert Reuten (eds), *The Circulation of Capital. Essays on Volume Two of Marx's Capital.* Basingstoke, 33–66.

Nassehi, Armin (2004), »The Two Worlds of Functional Differentiation and Social Stratification«. http://www.lrz-muenchen.de/ls_nassehi/nassehi/rginequal. pdf

Pahl, Hanno (2004), »Die Realität gesellschaftlicher Einheit. Anmerkungen zum ontologischen und epistemologischen Status gesellschaftlicher Einheit am Beispiel eines Vergleichs der Systembegriffe bei Karl Marx und Jürgen Habermas«, in: Christine Kirchhoff, Lars Meyer, Hanno Pahl, Judith Heckel, Christoph Engemann (eds), *Gesellschaft als Verkehrung. Perspektive einer neuen Marx-Lektüre.* Freiburg, 195–217.

Parsons, Talcott (1968), »Social Systems«, in: D. Sills (ed.), *International Encyclopedia of the Social Sciences.* Vol. 7. New York, 458–473.

Parsons, Talcott/Smelser, Neil J. (1956), *Economy and Society. A Study in the Integration of Economic and Social Theory.* London.

Paul, Axel T. (2004), *Die Gesellschaft des Geldes. Entwurf einer monetären Theorie der Moderne.* Wiesbaden.

Piel, Konstanze (2003), *Ökonomie des Nichtwissens. Aktienhype und Vertrauenskrise im Neuen Markt.* Frankfurt a.M.

Reichelt, Helmut (1970), *Zur logischen Struktur des Kapitalbegriffs bei Karl Marx.* Frankfurt a.M.

— (1996), *Kritik der politischen Ökonomie als Konstitutionstheorie des Werts.* Unpublished Manuscript. Bremen.

— (1997), *Werttheorie und Quantifizierbarkeit.* Unpublished Manuscript. Bremen.

— (1998), »Geldmedium und Rechtsform als Konstrukte«, in: Christoph Görg and Roland Roth (eds): *Kein Staat zu machen. Zur Kritik der Sozialwissenschaften.* Münster, 372–392.

Reusswig, Fritz (1993), *Natur und Geist: Grundlinien einer ökologischen Sittlichkeit.* Frankfurt a.M.

Riese, Hajo (2000), »Geld – die unverstandene Kategorie der Nationalökonomie«, in: *Ethik und Sozialwissenschaften. Streitforum für Erwägungskultur,* Vol. 4, 487–497.

Schimank, Uwe (2002), »Social Differentiation«, in: N. Smelser and P. Baltes (eds), *International Encyclopedia of the Social and Behavioral Sciences.* Oxford, 3663–3686.

Schinckus, Christophe (2005), »The Financial Simulacrum. The Consequences of the Symbolic and Technological Virtualization of the Financial Market«. Paper presented at the Alternatives Perspectives on Finance Conference, Kilkenny, Ireland, August 14–16, 2005.

Schmidt, Tobias (1998), *Grundlagen einer Systemtheorie des Finanzsektors.* Göttingen.

Spahn, Heinz-Peter (2002), »Die Ordnung der Gesellschaft als Zahlungswirtschaft«, in: Christoph Deutschmann (ed.), *Die gesellschaftliche Macht des Geldes.* Leviathan-Sonderheft 21. Wiesbaden, 47–72.

Strulik, Torsten (2000), *Risikomanagement globaler Finanzmärkte. Herausforderungen und Initiativen im Kontext der Bankenregulierung.* Frankfurt a.M.

Willke, Helmut (1993), *Systemtheorie.* Stuttgart/Jena.

— (1998), *Laterale Weltsysteme.* Manuscript. Bielefeld 1998.

— (2000), »Die Gesellschaft der Systemtheorie«, in: *Ethik und Sozialwissenschaften. Streitforum für Erwägungskultur,* Vol. 2, 195–208.

— (2001), *Atopia. Studien zur atopischen Gesellschaft.* Frankfurt a.M.

— (2003), *Heterotopia. Studien zur Krisis der Ordnung moderner Gesellschaften.* Frankfurt a.M.

Abbreviations

Volume I: Marx, Karl (1867; 1967): *Capital. A Critique of Political Economy.* Volume 1: The *Process of Capitalist Production.* New York (International Publishers).

Volume II: Marx, Karl (1885; 1967): *Capital. A Critique of Political Economy.* Volume 2: *The Process of Circulation of Capital.* New York (International Publishers).

Volume III: Marx, Karl (1894; 1967): Capital. *A Critique of Political Economy.* Volume 3: *The Process of Capitalist Production as a Whole.* New York (International Publishers).

MECW40: Marx, Karl/Engels, Friedrich (1983): *Collected Works.* Volume 40. New York (International Publishers).

An Institutional Approach to the Politics of Global Finance

Timothy J. Sinclair

1. Introduction

Globalization has created an unprecedented degree of volatility in socio-economic life.[1] One response to this development has been to separate central bank monetary policy from legislative and executive intervention. A second response has been to establish legislative constraints that impose discipline on fiscal matters. Less visible has been a shift in emphasis between what have come to be called ›fire alarm‹ and ›police patrol‹-type regulation forms (McCubbins/Schwartz 1987: 427). The fire alarm metaphor suggests a problem-focused, episodic approach to governance. Like municipal fire departments, problems – like fires – only receive attention when they have been identified and called-in by non-specialists. A framework is established – that fires will be reported by those who see them – which only requires occasional ›enforcement‹. Inspections are infrequent

1 An earlier version of this chapter was presented at a conference at the University of Sussex, May 2005. The author thanks participants at the Sussex and Bielefeld conferences for useful comments.

(perhaps annually) and the emphasis is on self-regulation in self-interest. In the case of police patrols, a much more aggressive process of looking for law-breaking is characteristic. The idea here is that many problems never mature into crises because of surveillance and early intervention. Although fire alarm approaches may be cheaper in cost-benefit terms, police patrol surveillance is attractive when the immediate costs of ›disgovernance‹ are very high, and consequent losses likely to be »lumpy«. Paradoxically, while public institutions seem to be increasingly moving from the police patrol to the fire alarm approach under fiscal and competitive pressures in a context of globalization, a tightening of governance is developing in the private realm, as institutions with the capacity for governance seek to compensate for the risks and opportunities created by change. Bond rating agencies are an example of this form of emerging private authority.

Understanding these emerging institutions of governance is challenging. Finance tends to be thought of as something modern in nature. Like bridges, airplanes and computers, finance is understood to be subject to all the methods that positivist knowledge can deploy. Like the study of security, academic consideration of the politics of global finance has been dominated by rationalist understandings of how the world works. In ratioalism, finance is understood as akin to the great forests, mountains or other brute facts of our world. Perhaps this conception seemed adequate when states and their interaction were the only major actors to be considered, even in investigations of global finance. But this hardly describes the situation in a globalizing world.

What if, like the state and other institutions, finance is not a brute or natural fact at all, but a social structure for which positivist methods, premised on the neutrality of the observer, get the way finance works quite wrong. This chapter explores this question, and suggests the analysis of finance must start instead with cognitive or social facts. This perspective on finance implies very different behavioral expectations about finance, ones better suited to the volatile world of global finance. Increasingly, we need to consider a new ontology and understanding of how actors behave. Structure, in global finance, cannot be understood as invariant, unaffected by the meaning attributed to the situation by participants. This realisation has immense implications for efforts to govern global finance. This chapter makes use of ideas in my recently published monograph to make a case for a constructivist (and economic sociology) understanding of global finance (Sinclair 2005). I start with some key conceptual points. Part two offers some brief empirical illustrations before I turn to the implications for the governance of global finance in the third part.

2. Conceptual Considerations

The New Masters of Capital is a study of specific institutions and associated »micro-practices« at the core of contemporary capitalism, including the effect of these institutions and practices on global economic and political life within states (Ruggie 1998: 27). Natural science seeks to establish universal laws, and considers specific events in terms of these laws. The objective in this case is always generalization. Many social scientists have also followed this path. The constructivist study of global finance has a different purpose. The objective here is similar to the »process tracing« discussed by Jepperson, Wendt and Katzenstein, in which they and their fellow contributors examine the historical development of interpretive frames used by actors to understand the world (Jepperson/Wendt/Katzenstein 1996: 67). A constructivist approach to the politics of global finance examines the distinctiveness of particular events, institutions and ways of thinking, and seeks to interpret and demonstrate their significance. The focus on undertanding the particular – rather than positing universal laws about the politics of global finance ›in general‹ – means that research design tends to be »reaistic«, and inductive, and does not aspire to the »hypothetico-deductive mode of theory construction« that dominates much of social science (Ruggie 1998: 34).

Substantively, *The New Masters of Capital* investigates the veracity of different approaches, or general theoretical orientations, to motivation and action that are the subject of contemporary debate in the field of international political economy (IPE) (Katzenstein et al. 1998: 646). These general theoretical orientations offer heuristics, in the form of relevant variables and causal patterns, which provide guidelines for research (ibid.). IPE has been dominated by rationalist approaches, especially realism and liberalism, informed by economics, in which the heuristic is the struggle between rational actors with fixed preferences, over scarce resources. This heuristic can be applied to any number of problems as a guiding set of assumptions about what is likely to be motivating the action (ibid.). In *The New Masters*, the dominant rationalist lens is compared and contrasted with a very different general theoretical orientation.

This second approach draws on economic and organizational sociology, and the social sciences other than economics, as its inspiration. It does not adopt the assumption that there is a one-to-one match between imputed material interests and social action. The constructivist approach can complement the instrumental cause-effect focus of rationalism. The constructivist heuristic focuses on the processes through which the preferences and subsequent strategies of actors (such as corporations and states) are socially constructed, as features of intersubjective orders, which vary over time and space, and define the identity or nature of the actors in relation to others (ibid.: 681–682). The norms, identity, knowledge and culture that comprise intersubjective structures – things held constant in Rationalism – are amongst the things that constitute or regulate actors in this theoretical orientation (ibid.: 679–680; Katzenstein 1996: 5–6). Both rationalism and constructivism are, *The New Masters* seeks to demonstrate, essential for understanding specific institutions. The constructivist lens has, however, so far been neglected in international political economy to the detriment of our full understanding of many problems, including the politics of global finance.[2] In part, *The New Masters* is an effort to correct that omission and to demonstrate the analytical contribution a critical constructivist social science can make to the understanding of global finance.

International political economy emerged in the late 1960s as the study of foreign economic policy, mainly of the United States and the European powers. These origins have led to IPE being dominated by the idea that markets and exchange are very different things from the typical institutionalized manifestations of politics, like political parties and legislatures. Unlike most economists, many IPE scholars have been interested in the interaction of the economic and political spheres (understood as different motivations), which scholars as diverse as Susan Strange and Robert Gilpin both thought were neglected. Only through an analysis of this interaction could an understanding of international economic relations be formed, one that included more variables than those identified by economists. This work has contributed much to our understanding of change in international relations since World War II, especially of the creation and decay of the Bretton Woods regime. However, as both global markets have developed and states have changed in form and behavior during the three decades since the end of the Bretton Woods regime, the strict separation

2 A pioneering effort to utilise a constructivist lens, and to link this to rationalist understandings, are the essays in Kirshner 2003.

of the subject matter of international political economy into the ›states‹ category on the one hand, and ›markets‹ on the other has become problematic. Increasingly, IPE scholars have been concerned with intermediary institutions that are neither states nor markets, but interact with both (Cutler et al. 1999; Hall/Biersteker 2002). Some IPE scholars have also decided to look into the economists' sphere itself, and have sought to reappraise the inherited notions of what markets are and how they work (Smith 1981; Abolfia 1996; Smith 1996, 1999).

Economic sociology offers an alternative theoretical source for IPE scholars looking for analytical insight.[3] The prime benefit it offers in abstract terms is to ground the agent-centric understanding (of states, of companies, of individuals) implicit in traditional IPE in a sense of structure emerging from social relations. Waltz and international relations Neorealism offered a sense of structure, but this did not encompass market relations, and tended to minimise the role of actors other than states, even if the formal account of the approach gave space to other agents.[4] By contrast with the Neorealist vision of an anarchy of self-regarding units, the notion of »embeddedness« identified by Granovetter, a key concept in economic sociology, sought to link institutions to the social relations in which they exist (Granovetter 1992: 53). In this understanding, economic life is not separate from society like a free-standing machine, but linked to historical and cultural circumstances, and therefore variable over time and space (Dobbin 1994). Change is linked to pervasive mental frameworks, which legitimate specific organizational forms (and negate others). Mental or intersubjective frameworks are just as consequential as other social structures. As W. I. Thomas noted in 1928, »If men [sic] define situations as real, they are real in their consequences«.[5] Thomas was suggesting that people respond not just to objective things like mountains and automobile accidents, »but also, and often mainly«, to their collective attribution of meaning to a social situation (Coser 1977: 521). As Coser suggests, if people think witches are real, »such beliefs have tangible consequences« (ibid.).

The importance of mental frameworks is reflected within institutions. Meyer and Rowan argue organizations and how they are structured reflect not the efficient undertaking of their function but myths, or mental frameworks, that depict a public story about what the organization is supposed

3 For an introduction, see Smelser/Swedberg 1994.

4 On Waltz and Neorealism, see Keohane 1989.

5 Thomas/Thomas 1928, cited by Coser 1977: 521.

to be about (Meyer/Rowan 1977: 340–363). Internal rules and organizational forms within institutions reflect »the prescriptions of myths« (ibid.: 349). These rules and organizational forms demonstrate that the organization is acting »in a proper and adequate manner« (ibid.). By conforming to the myth, the organization protects itself from interrogation (ibid.). For the organization, the key process is identifying the »societally legitimated rationalized elements«, and then reconfiguring the organization around them (ibid.: 352). Organizations, Meyer and Rowan suggest, typically face dilemmas between the prescriptions of these elements and their own internal shared sense of what they are really supposed to be about, and also between diverse competing rationalized elements coming from different parts of society, such as government, interest groups, market associations and so forth (ibid.: 355).

Professional judgment and analysis – and public expectations about its development and standards – is a key socially legitimated rationalized element of the mental framework of the rating agencies. One conception of how the rating mental framework can be understood in its wider social context is through what Peter Haas and his fellow contributors have called epistemic communities (Haas 1992). Haas defines epistemic communities as »networks of knowledge-based experts« that address complex, seemingly technical problems (ibid.: 2). Haas observes that the »recognized expertise and competence« of these professionals give them an authoritative claim to be offering good advice (ibid.: 3). The control of expertise, he notes, is »an important dimension of power« (ibid.: 2). Haas suggests four features of epistemic communities: (1) a shared set of normative and principled beliefs; (2) shared causal beliefs; (3) shared notions of validity in the area of expertise; and (4) a »common policy enterprise«, connected to enhancing human welfare (ibid.: 3). What epistemic communities do is neither guess nor produce data. Instead, epistemic communities interpret phenomena (ibid.: 4). The major role of epistemic communities lies in ostensibly »less politically motivated cases«, where they introduce a range of policy alternatives (ibid.: 16). Epistemic communities differ from the concept of profession in that epistemic communities share normative commitments. Epistemic communities may, however, form within professions (such as the subset of economists that are concerned with economic inequalities). Haas argues that epistemic communities do not behave as rational choice or principle-agent theory would predict, because of the central role attributed to their beliefs (ibid.: 20). Epistemic communities, Haas argues, are important in themselves. They are not epiphenomenal. They »convey new patterns of reasoning« to policy-makers, and »encourage them to pursue new paths of policymaking« with unpredictable outcomes (ibid.: 21).

There is much in the concept of epistemic communities that has relevance for *The New Masters of Capital.* The focus on patterns of reasoning, on the low politics of technical expertise, on the power that emanates from knowledge are all important to the arguments pursued in *The New Masters.* Although raters may indeed share a common policy enterprise, where *The New Masters* parts company with epistemic communities is in the key concept of normative beliefs. Although a subset of raters may share a conscious commitment to such beliefs, this conscious commitment to normative belief is a defining element of epistemic communities. An alternative concept, embedded knowledge networks, is elaborated below.

3. Empirical Observations

I have organized the following comments into two sections. The first examines the origins of rating ›power‹ and what rating ›power‹ means. The second considers challenges to that power and how raters respond to these problems.

Sources of Power

Embedded knowledge networks are analytical and judgmental systems that in principle remain at arms length from market transactions. ›Embedded‹ does not imply that embedded knowledge networks are locked-in or institutionalized in finance, and thus simply resistant to change. ›Embedded‹ does not suggest inertia, path-dependency or vested interests. Instead, it specifies that actors view embedded knowledge networks as endogenous rather than exogenous to financial globalization. Embedded knowledge networks are, therefore, generally considered legitimate rather than imposed entities by market participants. How embedded knowledge networks construct and reinforce this collective understanding of themselves is of great interest. Where institutions that are embedded knowledge networks in one society attempt to transplant themselves into others, they risk losing their embedded status, unless they recognise the necessity of getting the market actors in these other places to recognise their endogeneity. To return to the discussion of myth and mental frameworks, rating agencies must adapt themselves to public expectations of what they should be doing, as they expand from their American home base. But achieving endogeneity, and hence legitimacy, has been easier in some places than others for the major US bond rating agencies.

The role of knowledge in investment decision-making is at the heart of embedded knowledge network activity. Market actors are overwhelmed with data about prices, business activity and political risk. A typical form of knowledge output is some sort of recommendation, ranking or rating, which claims to condense these forms of knowledge. This knowledge output becomes a benchmark around which market players subsequently organize their affairs. Market actors can and do depart from benchmarks, but these still set the standard for the work of other actors, providing a measure of market success or failure. In this way, embedded knowledge network outputs play a crucial role in constructing markets in a context of less than perfect information and considerable uncertainty about the future. Rating agencies, acting as embedded knowledge networks, can be thought to adjust the ›ground rules‹ inside international capital markets and thereby shape the internal organization and behavior of institutions seeking funds. Their views on what is acceptable shape the actions of those seeking positive responses from them. This anticipation effect, or structural power, is reflected in the minds of capital market participants in terms of their understandings of the views and expectations of the agencies. In turn this acts as a base point from which business and policy initiatives are developed.

The views about rating that circulate in financial markets can be gleaned from many different sources, including newspapers and other media, and from surveys of market participants.[6] Bond traders and pension fund managers have seemingly contradictory views on rating agencies. They are at times critical of the work of the rating agencies. As Scott suggests in his research on the public roles played by the powerful and the powerless, in addition to a positive public discourse about the dominant, there is typically a »hidden transcript«, a critique of power which exists as a sort of back-chat, spoken out of sight of the dominant (Scott 1990: 12). Back-chat only

6 For example, the surveys of market opinion of the rating agencies undertaken by Cantwell and Company since 1997. Interview with Joseph E. Cantwell, New York City, March 2000. For further details, see www.askcantwell.com.

becomes public, suggests Scott, in times of crisis or unusual stress. But back-chat is just that. Financial market actors take the rating agencies seriously. Market participants usually treat the rating agencies and their views as matters of considerable interest. Rating agencies, especially Moody's and Standard & Poor's, have worked hard at creating their reputation for impartiality over the last century or so. In some situations where people surrender their own powers of judgment to an institution or to a group, the surrender may be quite fragile, as in the case of a fad or fashion (Bikchandani et al. 1992: 1016). The circumstances, including the longevity of the rating agencies, make their particular authoritative niche more resilient than that of most other non-state institutions. Their position within the capital markets provides them with considerable resources.

In addition to the respect for the reputation of the agencies, there is also an awareness of the market influence of the rating agencies.[7] As Gary Jenkins, head of credit research at Barclays Capital, London, observed, »Love them or loathe them, if they did not exist, we would have to invent them«.[8] Even if a trader or bond issuer does not respect a particular judgment of the rating agencies, they might anticipate the effect the judgment will have on others, and may act on that expectation, rather than their own views of the actual quality of the judgment itself. The intersubjective process described here is sometimes termed »Keynes' beauty contest«, after J.M. Keynes' discussion of the similarities between financial market behavior and the tabloid newspaper beauty contests of the 1930s. In these competitions, the objective was not to guess who was the most attractive young woman, but to approximate best who was generally thought to be the prettiest by all competition entrants. With professional investment, Keynes argued, »We have reached the third degree where we devote our intelligences to anticipating what average opinion expects the average opinion to be« (Keynes 1936: 156).

Rating agency outputs comprise an important part of the infrastructure of capital markets. They are key benchmarks in the cognitive life of these markets: features of the marketplace, which form the basis for subsequent decision-making by participants. In this sense, rating agencies are impor-

---

7 A confirmation of the growing importance of ratings can be found in the Japan Center for International Finance's 2001 survey on attitudes to bond rating, »Characteristics and Appraisal of Major Rating Companies« (2001 Edition), p. 1. See www.jcif.or.jp/e_index.htm

8 Jenkins quoted in Charles Batchelor, »Companies and Regulators Go On Offensive in the Global Ratings Game«, Financial Times, July 5, 2003, p. 3.

tant not so much for any particular rating they produce, but for the fact that they are a part of the internal organization of the market itself. So, we find that traders may refer to a company as an ›AA company‹, or some other rating category, as if this were a fact, an agreed and uncontroversial way of describing and distinguishing companies, municipalities or countries.[9]

A rationalist way to think about what rating agencies do is to see them as serving a ›function‹ in the economic system. In this view, rating agencies solve a problem in markets that develops when banks no longer sit at the center of the borrowing process.[10] Rating agencies serve as what Gourevitch calls »reputational intermediaries« like accountants, analysts, and lawyers, who are »essential to the functioning of the system«, monitoring managers through a »constant flow of short-term snapshots«.[11] Another way to think about the function of the agencies is to suggest rating agencies establish psychological »rules of thumb« which make market decisions less costly for participants (Heisler 1994: 78; Beckert 1996: 803–840). A functionalist historical analogy can be drawn with the Law Merchant, that dispensed commercial law in medieval times. The Law Merchant developed as a way of enforcing contracts by making judgments on trade disputes, and keeping records of these actions available for scrutiny by those engaging in intra-European trade. This mechanism backed-up the reputation of traders when their names were not well known to potential new trade partners in geographically distant places, enabling, for example, a Burgundian trader in ribbons to sell to a Catalan haberdasher. Rating agencies share the information-provision and disciplinary characteristics of the Law Merchant. They too can be interpreted as part of a system that keeps an eye on who is violating the prevailing norms of financial and commercial practice (Milgrom et al. 1990; Cutler 1998, 2003).

As I argue in *The New Masters*, the rating agencies have a strong interest in developing and preserving their eminence as sources of judgment. While this gives the agencies incentives to be as helpful as possible to investors, paradoxically it also means they have an interest in avoiding full disclosure of their information sources and ways of forming judgments. The agencies

---

9 In a 1992 interview, President Leo O'Neill of Standard & Poor's explained how bond traders would, on the one hand, dispute particular ratings with S&P, and on the other, refer to companies unproblematically as AA, A and so on. Ratings were the commonsense of the markets.

10 See, for example, Wilson 1987: 321–359. Also see Wakeman 1997: 25–28.

11 Gourevitch 2002: 1 and 11. Available at www.siswo.uva.nl/ES. Accessed June 12, 2002.

seem to be intent on preserving a sense of mystery surrounding the rating process in general, and any rating in particular, so as to reinforce their role in the capital markets (Scharfstein/Stein 1990: 465).

But purely functional explanations for the existence of rating agencies are potentially deceptive. Attempts to verify (or refute) the idea that rating agencies must exist because they serve a purpose, have proven inconclusive. Rating agencies have to be considered important actors because people view them as important, and act on the basis of that understanding in markets, even if it proves impossible for analysts to actually isolate the specific benefits the agencies generate for these market actors. Investors often mimic other investors, »ignoring substantive private information«.[12] The fact that people may collectively view rating agencies as important – irrespective of what ›function‹ the agencies are thought to serve in the scholarly literature – means that markets and debt issuers have strong incentives to act as if participants in the markets take the rating agencies seriously. In other words, the significance of rating is not to be estimated like a mountain or national population, as a ›brute‹ fact which is true (or not) irrespective of shared beliefs about its existence, nor is the meaning of rating determined by the ›subjective‹ facts of individual perception (Ruggie 1998: 12–13).[13] What is central to the status and consequentiality of rating agencies is what people believe about them, and act on collectively – even if those beliefs are demonstratably false. Indeed, the beliefs may be quite strange to the observer, but if people use them as a guide to action (or inaction) they are significant. Dismissing such collective beliefs, as structural Marxists once did, as ›false consciousness‹ misses the fact that actors must take account of the existence of social facts in considering their own action. Reflection about the nature and direction of social facts is characteristic of financial markets on a day-to-day basis. Rating agencies are important in investment most immediately because there is a collective belief that says the agencies are important, which people act upon in markets, as if it were true. Whether rating agencies actually add new information to the process does not negate their significance, understood in these terms.

12 Scharfstein and Stein 1990: 465.

13 Ruggie draws on Searle 1995. See also Berger/Luckmann 1966.

Challenges to Power

Three main types of challenge to the power and authority of rating agencies can be identified. The first challenge – problems in rating organization – is the public discussion of problems that market actors (including government officials and financial reporters) see in how the agencies are organized, and in how they do their business. The two key elements are perceived conflicts of interest in how ratings are paid for, and the question of unsolicited ratings. The second sort of challenge – performance issues – is a more serious challenge than the organizational problems. The major issues here concern the lagging nature of rating, specific concerns about ›split‹ ratings, and the lack of probabalistic quantitative analysis models in the rating process. The last sort of challenge to the power and authority of rating – rating crises – emerge from a series of high-profile failures to predict sudden bankruptcies or collapses of credit quality. Three are investigated in *The New Masters*: Orange County's financial problems of the mid-1990s, the Asian Financial Crisis of 1997/98, and the Enron collapse of 2001/2002.

At the heart of all these challenges lies the key reality of the rating process: reputation cannot be bought off the shelf. Instead, the reputation of Moody's and S&P has been constructed over time through a combination of serving a need by offering to solve the information problem between buyers and sellers, and by providing that information in a reliable way, thus generating epistemic authority. Given that the reputational assets of the rating agencies are not natural, but reflect a process of construction, the question of the deconstruction or degrading of those assets is of vital importance. In what ways is this reputation susceptible to attack? Is rating reputation vulnerable to falling apart, or does it decline incrementally? The view offered here is that the rating agencies, as embedded knowledge networks, have a robustness which makes them resilient in the face of problems, issues and crises in rating, but that for the rating agencies, a constant program of reinforcement by a variety of means makes good sense in an increasingly volatile world.

One of the commonplaces of the rating world, repeated in newspaper and magazine articles wherever the raters are a presence, is that work of the rating agencies is compromised by a conflict of interest inherent in charging the issuers of bonds for the rating work undertaken by the agencies. The problem inherent in issuer fees is that issuers are not actually the principals in rating. The principals – those for whom the rating work is done – are investors. So making issuers pay introduces the potential for issuers to influence the judgments of the agencies and undermine their commitment to giving a true account to investors.

The problem with making investors pay for ratings is that ratings are public goods like the news. Once a rating is released by an agency there is no way for the creator to prevent investors or intermediaries like banks who have not paid for the rating, from free riding on the rating. This makes it difficult for the agencies to get investors to pay for the full costs of rating. The dilemma for the agencies is the reconciliation of the public-good character of ratings with their need to earn revenue and make an appropriate return, while minimising the potential for perceived conflicts of interest that degrade the reputation of the agencies.[14] The solution they arrived at was to charge issuers, because investors will free ride. But the agencies have to make sure issuers do not shape the rating process, which would destroy the reputational value of ratings (and thus the rating franchise).

The major agencies have been very successful in managing this dilemma. Smith and Walter suggest that internal operating procedures, and analysts compensation policies that avoid linkage between salary and revenue streams, are designed to avoid conflict (Smith/Walter 2001: 43–44). If the agencies were to give in to the conflict of interest inherent in their situation, where issuers pay for their own rating, they would find that their status as embedded knowledge networks would be seriously impaired. The evidence for the viability of this position is the lack of any scandal related to conflict of interest, despite frequent comment in the financial and mainstream press about the issue. However, a more dynamic view of the rating industry suggests that conflicts of interest may become harder to manage in future if rating competition increases, driven by opportunities in emerging markets and by stock market sentiment about the agencies themselves (The Economist, December 4, 2001).

Things moved slowly as far as rating innovation was concerned in the era of rating conservatism that followed World War II. The biggest development was the introduction of issuer fees during the late 1960s by S&P (1968) and Moody's (1970) (The Bond Buyer, February 26, 1993, page 5). Even then, however, as former S&P president Brenton W. Harries noted, congressmen did discuss the performance of the agencies and questioned rating officials about their work (ibid.). Raters were never left alone to

14 For an excellent discussion of the conflicts of interest problem, see Smith and Walter 2001.

enjoy a sinecure. The ›hidden transcript‹ may have been more hidden during these years, but it was still there, and raters knew about it then too. Today, near continuous expressions of concern about rating performance – about how good the rating agencies are at their business – have become normal. Newspapers, magazines or online sites talk about the performance of the agencies and their failings.[15]

Three things are central to understanding the significance of this discourse of discontent. First, because there is a discourse at all, we have further confirmation of the importance of the agencies' role in financial globalization. The expression of the discourse of discontent happens because agencies cannot be ignored. The role of the agencies has a certain logic. They ›fit‹ in the capital markets, even if they have made that place for themselves. Perceived failings in their work are too important to be ignored. Second, the rating discourse is very much framed within this logic of function. It is about improvement to the agencies, rather than their replacement. Third, the agencies have to deal with these expressions of the hidden transcript, but can fall back on the logic of their role to stiffen their resolve, especially versus issuers, who seem constantly to be engaged in an effort to become the principals in their relationship with the agencies.

A common criticism suggests that the rating agencies are too slow, and apply the lessons of the past to the present, a bit like a general re-fighting the wars of his youth, even though technology and tactics have moved on substantially in the subsequent years. Market participants worry that the ratings they are looking at do not have much to do with the company whose balance sheet can move by billions in either direction in just a few hours. The traditional defense against this problem of timeliness was for the rating agencies to suggest they took a longer view, and wanted to offer ratings not just for today, but that would have some ability to withstand the normal business cycle. They would cite their track record on defaults of rated debt.[16] Increasingly, »event risk«, such as a merger or acquisition, came to be perceived as a vital ingredient in creditworthiness. More re-

15 A few of good examples from the last decade: Kilpatrick 1992: 1; The Economist, July 15, 1995, pp. 53–54; House 1995: 245–249; Richard Leftwich, »Survey – Mastering Finance 3: Evaluating the Bond-Rating Agencies«, Financial Times, May 27, 1997, p. 2; Sander Boley, Frederik von Dewall and Kees Hoekerd, »Rating May Be Overrated«, The Banker, May 2000, pp. 22–23; and Patience Wheatcroft, »Don't Give Raters Too Much Credit«, The Times, April 5, 2001, no page number, accessed from Lexis-Nexis, February 3, 2002.

16 For example, Historical Default Rates on Corporate Bond Issuers, 1920–1999 (New York: Moody's Investors Service 2000).

cently, the agencies have started to discuss the impact of market sentiment on issuers because of the Enron bankruptcy. For now, note that the agencies are exploring the contribution of sophisticated quantitative analysis to understanding this dimension of credit risk (The Economist, February 16, 2002: 69–70).

A less obvious, but interesting, performance issue arises when the agencies decide to treat specific financial instruments differently in their work, and where they split on rating an issuer.[17] In a world of increasingly sophisticated asset-backed securities and derivatives, having different views of the credit implications of these instruments calls into question one of the bedrock assumptions of the mental framework of rating orthodoxy: that there is a right way and a wrong way to understand specific economic and financial matters. Given that investment banks, regulators and other parties may also differ on how to understand financial innovation, perhaps this has less negative impact on the agencies than the situation in which the agencies give different ratings on the same issuer or bond issue.[18] Given how sensationally they are sometimes reported in the financial press, it might seem that split ratings are very rare. In fact, split ratings are quite common. According to Cantor, Packer and Cole, 50 percent of all corporate bonds had different ratings from Moody's and S&P when issued. Despite this observation, split ratings challenge the idea that there is a knowable rating universe out there that the agencies are trying to reflect in their work. There are only a few diviners of this knowledge, and if the agencies cannot ›get it right‹ with an accurate rating, what does this say about the quality of their staff or management? If some agencies are ›less strict‹ than others, do the less stringent agencies reduce the reputational assets for the rest?

Even if we grant that there is some static logic to the role of the agencies, financial globalization creates threats necessitating adaptability. As Strange noted in *Casino Capitalism* and subsequently in *Mad Money*, market volatility brings new risks for market institutions (Strange 1986, 1998). Like an aging sports champion eyeing up the competition, the agencies cannot predict when a new way of doing things will come along and steal their franchise. Nor do they know what failure or what accretion of perceived incompetence or mediocrity will be the thing that destroys the willingness

17 For an example of the differences of view between the agencies on financial innovation, see French 1998: 12.

18 On split ratings, see Cantor et al. 1997: 72–82.

of issuers to secure a rating from them.[19] Because they never know what will do it or when it will happen if ever, raters have to adjust their practices with a careful ear to what the market is saying and doing. Even if raters present themselves as stoical and unmoved by the turmoil of markets around them, they, like any purveyor of symbols or professional knowledge, must keep one eye on the audience at all times. In this regard, rating agencies are like an academic who has become recognised for expertise in some area, but who must always look over his or her shoulder anticipating the arrival of a new scholar determined to »go beyond« the work of the established professor. Like academics, there is an anxiety in rating agencies belied by the calm exterior.

4. Implications for the Governance of Global Finance

What are the implications of the increasing role of the rating agencies for the governance of global finance? In considering this question we need to recognise that governance has a specific political meaning. This is clear when we consider global governance, in which the governance of global finance is an element.[20] The first major statement that used the concept of global governance is found in the report of the Commission on Global Governance, published as *Our Global Neighborhood* in 1995 (Commission on Global Governance 1995). Stimulated by the end of the cold war and what the Commission termed a »heightened sense« of an »endangered future«, (Sinclair 2004: 19) the report asserted that governance »is the sum of the many ways individuals and institutions, public and private, manage their common affairs« (ibid.: 2). This is a management vision of global governance, one concerned with dealing with feasible, tractable problems, and definitely not broad issues of blame for poverty and exploitation, or adjustments to the prevailing world order.

A central feature of global governance, as articulated by the Commission was the role of private, non-state institutions in the creation and enforcement of governance. Economic integration, especially the growth of

---

19 How many errors like the one reported in the following item are needed to destroy a reputation? Julie Earle and Peter Thal Larsen, »S&P in Setback Over Calpine Error«, Financial Times, February 26, 2002, no page number, accessed from www.ft.com, March 4, 2002.

20 This discussion of global governance is based on Sinclair 2004: 1–7.

capital markets, has created a multitude of new actors, suggested the Commission. In some cases, the Commission suggested, governance will rely on markets and markets institutions, »perhaps with some institutional oversight« (ibid.: 5). The incorporation of private sources of governance such as NGOs, citizens' movements and MNCs was necessary now in order to acknowledge the broader scope of governance after the cold war. Previously, governance had primarily been understood as a consequence of intergovernmental relations. Accepting the role of private institutions in governance would, suggested the Commission, increase their effectiveness. But emphasis on these newly relevant private sources of governance fitted neatly into a more managerial vision of how to deal with global problems. The management focus of the global governance concept would be reinforced by the priority given to private agents, because private agents are not – in the commonsense understanding of the term – political. They are by nature, technical. Even if they are lobby groups like NGOs, their main focus is on practical projects, not political change. Rating agencies fit smoothly into this managerial agenda. Rating agencies help to depoliticise controversy by making policy decisions with significant distributional impacts seem technically necessary. Political actors can blame the agencies for pushing them to take these actions.

The new Basel Capital Accord (Basel II) proposals published for comment in January 2001 reflected this developing managerial role of the rating agencies.[21] Michael King and I were concerned that these proposals, which sought to integrate ratings into the risk weightings of banks, were negative for the governance of global finance in several ways. We suggested that rating agencies may make financial crises worse. The primary difficulty with basing the capital allocation of banks on credit ratings is that these same ratings have been pro-cyclical. A downturn in the business cycle will cause the ratings on firms to deteriorate, forcing banks to put aside greater capital at the worst possible time when the economy is heading into recession. Should ratings decline unexpectedly, as occurred in 1997 with Asian sovereigns, banks will not have the capital in place in advance of the event. Thus the trend-following behavior of ratings will exacerbate, not reduce, the risk of financial crisis and contagion.

King and I suggested rating agencies will increase the cost of capital in developing countries. The new capital adequacy framework will stunt the

21 Basel Committee 2001. The discussion of Basel II is adapted from King/Sinclair 2003: 345–362.

growth of firms in developing countries by raising their cost of capital relative to firms in the wealthy countries. The new framework raises the cost of capital in several ways. First, it allocates a higher risk weighting to non-rated assets than rated-assets. Most rated corporations and rated banks are located in OECD countries, and a higher per capita income is associated with higher ratings. By default, most firms in emerging markets are unrated and so loans to these borrowers will accrue a higher capital charge which will be passed on to the borrower.

There are no common rating standards or expectations for rating agencies. As a consequence, rating agencies are not liable for their own failures. Implicit in the idea of incorporating credit ratings into the system of global regulation is the view that these private agencies will be held accountable for their judgments and their mistakes. Ratings are actually incorporated into institutional regulation of the capital markets in Canada, the UK, France, Italy, and Japan. Despite this official role, no substantial public oversight of the rating agencies themselves actually exists. They have escaped democratic mechanisms of accountability despite playing an increasingly significant part in the operation of credit markets. The lack of a common standard makes it difficult for a regulatory agency or a court to establish an independent benchmark for measuring a rating agency's performance. However, even if the rating agencies were found liable for negligence in their duties, they would not have the resources available to settle such disputes without quickly going bankrupt.

The operation of rating agencies assumes good institutions. Weak institutions in developing countries will undermine ratings. The reputation of the global rating agencies depends on a track record built up in the US, where both market and non-market institutions have supported and enhanced their success. Can this track-record be repeated in the context of emerging markets where the judicial system, the supervision of banks, the sophistication of investors and the level of financial disclosure are far different from the industrialised countries?

More generally, King and I argued the multiplication of ratings for firms combined with the structure of Basel II will create incentives for ratings shopping. Studies of the existing rating agencies have shown that the smaller agencies tend to provide higher ratings than the global leaders. This problem will only worsen as banks seek out the highest ratings available on the market in order to reduce the capital charge on their loans. Any rating agency which does not want to lose market share will be forced to compete in this market.

Basel II may look good on paper, but in practice its implementation will be highly bureaucratic. The use of rating agencies is intended as a step towards the internal credit ratings approach where individual banks determine their capital allocation using their own analysis. No one doubts that building these risk models will be an expensive and time consuming endeavour, requiring the accumulation of credit risk expertise and vast investment of senior management time.

Finally, Michael King and I claimed that institutionalizing rating agencies in Basel II will – given the high barriers to entry – undermine the reputational constraint enforced by the ratings market. Any degrading of reputational enforcement will in turn loosen inhibitions on inflating ratings to satisfy issuers. Although rating agencies are a ›drop fit‹ into contemporary governance and internationally, into global governance, a close analysis of these institutions suggests a range of specific problems for the governance of global finance.

In broader terms, what are we to make of the role of these institutions? Rating agencies are nothing new in themselves. They have been around since before World War I, but things have changed in the wake of the re-emergence of international capital mobility. The policy autonomy of national governments and the choices of municipal governments and corporations have been significantly affected by this development. A process of change in how financial capital is organized has taken root. Increasingly, under the spur of financial globalization, banks look like expensive places in which to borrow money, spurring the growth of capital markets. In rationalist terms, these markets needed a way for lenders to obtain reliable information about borrowers. Considered through a constructivist lens, rating agencies do more than merely serve a function. They have become a significant instance of non-state authority in the post-bipolar world. Rating agencies now need to be incorporated into accounts of global governance, like the IMF or World Bank. Because they are ostensibly private, and operate in the commercial sphere of the capital markets, the power of rating agencies is more effectively camouflaged than these higher profile institutions, and therefore even more deserving of our attention.

Rating agencies do not replace the role of states, even though they represent the shape of newly emerging authority. This authority interacts with pre-existing powers. At times, rating agencies wield power against states, corporations and municipalities. At other times, the power of rating agencies is anticipated by these issuers. Political actors will use the rating agencies to show how effective they are at management, or to justify changes in public policy. National states, especially in emerging markets, enlist rating agencies in encouraging the development of their own capital markets, in order to increase transparency and cheapen the cost of lending. This national government-rating agency relationship is a paradoxical one. But in general, it is clear the role and influence attributable to rating agencies has grown in the conditions described.

Identifying rating agencies as powerful is difficult for thinkers from traditions in which power is only something that public entities such as sovereign governments can possess. Their view is that rating agencies do not exercise power. Power implies coercion to these critics, who see rating agencies merely as the functional agents of rational market actors. This position is unconvincing for three reasons. First, this is an impoverished view of power. Power does not merely imply coercion. Consent is also a key element of power. The power of rating agencies is certainly as much a product of the success of the rating agencies in generating consent, as it is derived from exercising coercion. Second, power is not limited to relational power, which is of a behavioral form. Structural power – involving the anticipation of the exercise of power in its relational form – is a feature of the rating world. This latent understanding of power must be deduced rather than counted. Third, any social behavior which has such potentially enormous consequences for hundreds of millions of people can hardly be considered apolitical. Because rating is so consequential it is not a private affair, just as General Motors, as Robert Dahl observed, »is as much a public enterprise as the US Post Office« (Dahl 1970: 120). Rating agencies are political in these terms, and they exercise power. As much as they would like to deny it, they cannot reasonably be fenced off from politics understood in this wider sense. What they do is simply too important.

A key feature of the new power of the agencies is dependence on reputation. Rating agencies sell the understanding that their judgments are important and accurate, or at the least, that others think so and act accordingly. Through a combination of providing a rationalist solution to the ›information problem‹ in disintermediated capital markets, and a long history of perceived accuracy, rating agencies have constructed for themselves the eminence of an epistemic authority like a judge, to the extent that what they say is not so much persuasive as it is widely perceived to be authoritative. The agencies are held to be worthy of being listened to, and in this context it takes a brave individual to go against their judgment. Once made, reputation is a very considerable resource at the disposal of the rating agencies. It seems to be resistant to strong assault. But rating agencies have to be careful they do not allow the basis of their power to be undermined, so precipitating a sudden, unexpected collapse of their epistemic authority. For this reason, rating agencies are attentive to what is said about them, and to presenting themselves in a strong self-confident way. They never know when the eminence they have established may be fatally weakened. As the former executives at Arthur Andersen know, financial globalization throws up more risks of this happening today than in the more sedate world of the 1940s and 1950s, when bond rating was institutionalized.

5. Conclusions

Rating agencies face many challenges. Newspapers often carry outraged headlines after a rating downgrade. The Japanese government has sought to undermine the system publicly as their creditworthiness deteriorated in the early 1990s. Rarely does this lead anywhere more threatening to the agencies. The downgraded, it seems, will always need to vent their anger. But what is it that actually corrodes the authority of the rating agencies? What is it that can destroy their franchise? In recent years, the rise of numerous providers of market intelligence and the much great availability of all manner of economic and financial data has raised the question of whether institutions can wield authority at all. People who possess heightened analytic skills, cannot be fooled, we are told. But ›fooling people‹ is not central to rating. The rules of thumb provided by the rating agencies become social facts of the market even the most highly skilled must take account. Are others using these ratings? If they are, then these ratings have a status in the markets, even if the analysis of the individual is divergent. They are part of the environment even the most skilled need to acknowledge, because they may be affecting the behavior of others, which in turn can change the market in which all bonds are priced. In other words, even if smart people do not ›believe‹ in bond ratings, they must incorporate them to the extent others do. An authority, even if wrong, will still give rise to all manner of social action because what it does (and how it relates to others) is a social fact.

What are some of the consequences of the power and authority of rating agencies? Rating agencies and the rating process provide a transmission belt for the delivery of policy and managerial orthodoxy to widely scattered governments and corporations, despite criticism and periodic rating crises such as Enron. The agencies promote convergence, »best practice« and »transparency« in the world. The most significant effect of rating agencies is not their immediate view of a particular budget deficit, but their implicit promotion of the norms of rating orthodoxy in relation to how all problems, including budget deficits, are to be assessed. It is this adjustment of the ›operating system‹, or mental schemata, that is the most consequential impact of the work of the agencies, and the least considered elsewhere.

A rationalist understanding of the politics of global finance is no longer adequate, if it ever was. This chapter has sought in a very brief and hesitant fashion to illustrate an alternative way of thinking about finance and the actors and processes that dominate it by examining the role of the major American bond rating agencies. Rather than focus on brute facts of an inescapable reality, I have sought to show, as I do in a much more developed manner in the monograph that forms much of the basis of this chapter, that intersubjectivity and meaning are vital for understanding how global finance works. Constructivism and economic sociology provide some useful tools for the pursuit of these concerns. Without these tools we can never really get at the identity of global finance in different times and places, and will always end up imputing motives to it we might see in our own behavior. Applying these tools should point the way to re-socializing our understanding of the politics of global finance and the creation of more effective governance mechanisms, some of which are explored at more length in *The New Masters of Capital.*

References

Abolafia, Mitchel Y. (1996), *Making Markets: Opportunism and Restraint on Wall Street.* Cambridge.

Basel Committee (2001), *Overview of the New Basel Capital Accord.* Basel.

Batchelor, Charles (2003), »Companies and Regulators Go On Offensive in the Global Ratings Game«, in: *Financial Times*, July 5, 3.

Beckert, Jens (1996), »What is Sociological about Economic Sociology? Uncertainty and the Embeddedness of Economic Action«, in: *Theory and Society*, Vol. 25, 803–840.

Berger, Peter L./Luckmann, Thomas (1966), *The Social Construction of Reality: A Treatise in the Sociology of Knowledge.* New York.

Bikhchandani, Sushil/Hirshleifer, David/Welch, Ivo (1992), »A Theory of Fads, Fashion, Custom, and Cultural Change as Informational Cascades«, in: *Journal of Political Economy*, Vol. 100, 992–1026.

Boley, Sander/von Dewall, Frederik/Hoekerd, Kees (2000), »Rating May Be Overrated«, in: *The Banker*, May 2000, 22–23.

Bond Buyer, The (1993), »Profits, Racism, Quality of Life, and Other Issues Facing Rating Agencies«, February 26, 5.

Cantor, Richard/Packer Frank/Cole Kevin (1997), »Split Ratings and the Pricing of Credit Risk«, in: *The Journal of Fixed Income*, Vol. 7, 72–82.

Commission on Global Governance (1995), *Our Global Neighborhood: The Report of the Commission on Global Governance.* Oxford.

Coser, Lewis A. (1977), *Masters of Sociological Thought: Ideas in Historical and Social Context*, 2nd edition. New York.

Cutler, A. Claire (1998), »Locating ›Authority‹ in the Global Political Economy«, in: *International Studies Quarterly*, Vol. 43, 59–81.

— (2003), *Private Power and Global Authority: Transnational Merchant Law in the Global Political Economy.* Cambridge.

Cutler, Claire/Haufler, Virginia/Porter, Tony (eds) (1999), *Private Authority and International Affairs.* Albany.

Dahl, Robert A. (1970), *After the Revolution? Authority in a Good Society.* New Haven.

Dobbin, Frank R. (1994), »Cultural Models of Organization: The Social Construction of Rational Organizing Principles«, in: Diana Crane (ed.) *The Sociology of Culture: Emerging Theoretical Perspectives.* Cambridge.

Earle, Julie/Larsen, Peter Thal (2002), »S&P in Setback Over Calpine Error«, in: *Financial Times*, February 26, no page No., accessed from www.ft.com, March 4.

Economist, The (1995), »Rating the Rating Agencies«, July 15, 53–54.

— (2001), »In Their Drive for New Revenues, Credit-Rating Agencies are Opening Themselves Up to Conflicts of Interest«. April 12, no page No., accessed from www.economist.co.uk, December 4.

French, Jeff (1998), »Securitization Wrinkle Complicates Ratings: Moody's, S&P Differ on Assets Not Transferred to Trusts«, in: *The Wall Street Journal Europe*, April 23, 12.

Gourevitch, Peter (2002), »Collective Action Problems in Monitoring Managers: The Enron case as a Systemic Problem«, in: *Economic Sociology – European Electronic Newsletter*, Vol. 3: 1 and 11. Available at www.siswo.uva.nl/ES. Accessed June 12.

Granovetter, Mark (1992), »Economic Action and Social Structure: The Problem of Embeddedness«, in: Mark Granovetter and Richard Swedberg (eds), *The Sociology of Economic Life.* Boulder.

Haas, Peter M. (1992), »Introduction: Epistemic Communities and International Policy Coordination«, in: *International Organization*, Vol. 46, 1–35.

Hall, Rodney Bruce/Biersteker, Thomas J. (eds) (2002), *The Emergence of Private Authority in Global Governance.* Cambridge.

Heisler, Jeffrey (1994), »Recent Research in Behavioral Finance«, in: *Financial Markets, Institutions and Instruments*, Vol. 3, 76–105.

House, Richard (1995), »Ratings Trouble«, in: *Institutional Investor*, October, 245–249.

Jepperson, Ronald L./Wendt, Alexander/Katzenstein, Peter J. (1996), »Norms, Identity, and Culture in National Security«, in: Peter J. Katzenstein (ed.), *The Culture of National Security: Norms and Identity in World Politics*. New York.

Katzenstein, Peter J. (1996), »Introduction: Alternative Perspectives on National Security«, in: Peter J. Katzenstein (ed.), *The Culture of National Security: Norms and Identity in World Politics*. New York.

Katzenstein, Peter J./Keohane, Robert O./Krasner, Stephen D. (1998), »International Organization and the Study of World Politics«, in: *International Organization*, Vol. 52, 645–68.

Keohane, Robert O. (ed.) (1989), *Neorealism and Its Critics*. New York.

Keynes, John Maynard (1936), *The General Theory of Employment Interest and Money*. London.

Kilpatrick, Lynne (1992), »Debt-Rating's Flaws«, in: *Financial Times of Canada*, March 30–April 5, 1.

King, Michael R./Sinclair, Timothy J. (2003), »Private Actors and Public Policy: A Requiem for the New Basel Capital Accord«, in: *International Political Science Review*, Vol. 24, 345–362.

Kirshner, Jonathan (ed.) (2003), *Monetary Orders: Ambiguous Economics, Ubiquitous Politics*. Ithaca.

Leftwich, Richard (1997), »Survey – Mastering Finance 3: Evaluating the Bond-Rating Agencies«, in: *Financial Times*, May 27, 2.

McCubbins, Matthew D./Schwartz, Thomas (1987), »Congressional Oversight Overlooked: Police Patrols versus Fire Alarms«, in: Mathew D. McCubbins and Terry Sullivan (eds), *Congress: Structure and Policy*. Cambridge.

Meyer, John W./Rowan, Brian (1977), »Institutionalized Organizations: Formal Structure as Myth and Ceremony«, In: *American Journal of Sociology*, Vol. 83, 340–363.

Milgrom, Paul R./North, Douglas C./Weingast, Barry R. (1990), »The Role of Institutions in the Revival of Trade: The Law Merchant, Private Judges, and the Champagne Fairs«, in: *Economics and Politics*, Vol. 2, 1–23.

Ruggie, John Gerard (1998), *Constructing the World Polity: Essays on International Institutionalization*. London.

— (1998), »Introduction: What Makes the World Hang Together? Neo-Utilitarianism and the Social Constructivist Challenge«, in: John Gerard Ruggie, *Constructing the World Polity: Essays on International Institutionalization*. London.

Scharfstein, David S./Stein, Jeremy C. (1990), »Herd Behavior and Investment«, in: *The American Economic Review*, Vol. 80, 465–479.

Scott, James (1990), *Domination and the Arts of Resistance: Hidden Transcripts*. New Haven.

Searle, John (1995), *The Construction of Social Reality*. New York.

Sinclair, Timothy J. (2004), »General Introduction«, in: Timothy J. Sinclair (ed.), *Global Governance: Critical Concepts in Political Science*, Vol. 1. London, 1–7.

— (2005), *The New Masters of Capital: American Bond Rating Agencies and the Politics of Creditworthiness.* Ithaca.

Smelser Neil J./Swedberg, Richard (1994), »The Sociological Perspective on the Economy«, in: Neil J. Smelser/Richard Swedberg (eds), *The Handbook of Economic Sociology.* Princeton.

Smith, Charles W. (1981), *The Mind of the Market: A Study of Stock Market Philosophies, Their Uses, and Their Implications.* Totawa, N.J.

— (1999), *Success and Survival on Wall Street: Understanding the Mind of the Market.* Lanham.

Smith, Roy C./Walter, Ingo (2001), »Rating Agencies: Is There an Agency Issue?«, in: *Stern School of Business,* New York University, February 18.

Strange, Susan (1986), *Casino Capitalism.* Oxford.

— (1998), *Mad Money: When Markets Outgrow Governments.* Ann Arbor, MI.

Thomas, W.I./Thomas, Dorothy Swaine (1928), *The Child in America.* New York.

Wakeman, L. Macdonald (1997), »The Real Function of Bond Rating Agencies«, in: Joel M. Stern and Donald H. Chew, Jr. (eds), *The Revolution in Corporate Finance,* 3rd edition. Oxford, 25–28.

Wheatcroft, Patience (2001), »Don't Give Raters Too Much Credit«, in: *The Times,* April 5, no page No., accessed from Lexis-Nexis, February 3, 2002.

Wilson, Richard S. (1987), *Corporate Senior Securities: Analysis and Evaluation of Bonds, Convertibles, and Preferreds.* Chicago.

Part 2

Cultures and Techniques of a Cognitive Mode

How Financial Numbers are Symptomatic

Hendrik Vollmer

1. A Government of Numbers?

The contributions in the present volume are united by a common interest in global finance and its contemporary mode of regulation. More specifically, the editors have taken great care to make the idea of a cognitive, learning-based mode of governance a recurrent theme. The case for a general role of knowledge and learning in financial governance might almost be a truism and there is an understandable lack of informants willing to volunteer evidence to the contrary. The case for »intelligent« regulation would be an entirely uninteresting topic were it not for the suspicion regulators' ideas of regulation, even if cunningly accumulated, will be utterly unlikely to present a comprehensive representation of actual regulatory processes. Behind carefully drafted displays of regulatory action and counter-action, across sophisticated forms of financial exchange, its standards, technologies and respective regulatory accommodations, still more complex social dynamics are at play, a fact the emerging sociology of finance is demonstrating more and more extensively (cf. MacKenzie 2006; Knorr Cetina/Preda 2005). The subsequent argument tries to focus more precisely on the difference between regulatory processes and their representation by individual and corporate, public and private agencies. To bring this difference into focus, it turns to the most elementary piece of information mobilized by the regulation of global finance: financial numbers.

How can the role of numbers in financial governance be initially characterized? Contemporary economic life is governed by financial numbers, while production, circulation and utilization of financial numbers themselves make up highly regulated forms of social conduct. There is a government *by* finance to which today's economy is subjected, and there is a government *of* finance in which a variety of organizations and professions try to establish, safeguard and manipulate ratified orders of financial transactions and markets, standards, technologies and, finally, numerical measures. Governing finance becomes both a privileged object and a prominent subject of regulatory endeavours. Regarding its various forms in organizations, markets and networks, it turns out to be a government of private and public authorities, a decentralized and often fragmented government, a government of experts and, finally and perhaps most generally, a government of numbers. Overall, an immense increase in the amount and significance of financial numbers mobilized for purposes of governing public and private economies stands to be diagnosed. The expansion of the »shifting sphere of the economic« (Hopwood 1992) goes along with a quantification and financialization of social life, and an escalating commitment to acting, reacting, inspecting and regulating by numbers. Some of the collective costs incurred through this escalating commitment are represented by the enormous efforts and institutional investments in safeguarding, standardizing and regulating the production and utilization of numerical signs. Such costs and efforts illustrate that financial numbers bear an apparent tendency of gradually turning from means into problems of government. What keeps this escalating commitment alive, therefore becomes a crucial question faced by attempts at understanding contemporary forms of governance.

This question calls for elaborating the observation that the escalating commitment to mobilizing and using financial numbers is associated with an escalating commitment to specific forms of regulation and government, and also – and this is what the following considerations would like to suggest – to a specific form of social exchange between regulators and regulated. The first association is well established within the contemporary literature. Many authors have demonstrated how contemporary assemblages of regulated and regulating financial activities can be reflected using Michel Foucault's notion of government. Alongside Foucault's analyses of the »governmentalization of the state« (Foucault 1991: 103), one might place analyses of the governmentalization of economic life, of which the ascending use of numerical information has become the pivotal expression (e. g. Miller/Rose 1990; Robson 1993; Kalpagam 2000). Governmentalization predicates the exercise of domination on the accumulation of knowledge about its objects, on a programmatic discourse fostering and continuously reformulating this knowledge, on technologies feeding information into its discourses, on establishing spaces of representation and intervention (cf. Rose/Miller 1992: 175–188; Miller/O'Leary 1996: 138–139; Dean 1999: 168–170). The proliferation of governmental discourses and technologies not only strengthens the exercise of its specific form of regulation, but raises the efficiency of this exercise through establishing a »numericized environment in which (...) free choosing actors may *govern themselves* by numbers« (Rose 1991: 691; emphasis added). Governmental programs then become particularly ambitious and reflexive in trying to exploit the readiness of individuals and organizations to deliberately conduct themselves through the use, provision and inspection of information, in attempts to decentralize and diffuse regulatory processes, and thus bring about a form of governance that is truly »economic« (cf. Vollmer 2003: 362–365).

The Foucauldian notion of government therefore resonates well with processes of regulation lacking a definitive center – a state or political system, if you will – from which governance is administrated, and thus with contemporary financial governance diffused over a whole range of public (state or inter-state) and private (professional, standard-setting or market-policing) agencies, business firms and even nonprofit organizations, down to individual investors, politicians, if not all »enterprising selves« (cf. Du Gay/Salaman 1992: 627–631). Yet as transparent as the prominent role of numerical information in this mode of regulation might appear, especially once it is placed within a more general history of government and power-knowledge formations (cf. Hoskin/Macve 1986; Townley 1993; Hoskin 1994: 71–73), one might doubt if arrangements of regulatory programs and technologies adequately represent the activities which they claim to regulate (cf. Armstrong 1994: 30–32). This skepticism suggests that more thorough investigations of the social dynamics bearing on the use of financial numbers are needed to fully grasp the inherent dynamics of governing by numbers (cf. Munro 1993: 267–268). Analysts should not to easily surrender to the somewhat idealized accounts regulatory discourses and technologies provide about themselves. A more differentiated understanding of the utilization of numerical signs in regulatory processes will be essential in developing some critical distance. The present paper takes what it terms the symptomatic qualities of financial numbers as a starting point.

The argument continues by briefly considering how symptomatic qualities of financial numbers are introduced into and maintained within social situations (2.). It then goes on to discuss how attempts of participants and audiences to regulate ongoing activity by numbers affect and gradually transform these situations (3.), and how numerical signs in turn acquire qualities which transcend any narrowly informational understanding of their use and significance (4.). The rising prominence of numbers and calculations can then be reconsidered as symptomatic of a more general information syndrome bedevilling the government of finance, if not of contemporary regulatory activity per se (5.). In conclusion, a sociological reconstruction of governing by numbers is offered (6.).

This reconstruction suggests that the escalating commitment to mobilizing and using financial numbers does not merely involve a belief in the value of a certain breed of information, but rests upon participants' willingness to sustain a *numericized form of social exchange*. If this kind of social exchange was to be recognized as a particularly responsive mechanism of collective regulation, a more intelligent notion of governance than the one presently trapped in a strangely one-dimensional fixation on accumulating and regulating information might eventually evolve.

2. Utilizing Numbers as Symptoms

In monetary economies, the meaning of financial numbers possesses an indisputable everyday anchoring in prices of tradable assets, and basic numeracy works as a most general demand placed upon participants of economic exchange. With progressive economic development, and especially once the organization of economic activity gains complexity, many transactions which do not involve an actual transfer of money come to be treated as transfers of financial capital as well, e.g. when enterprises take into account depreciation of fixed assets. The numerical value adopted by financial capital is then considered to be incorporated even in non-monetary assets, unpriced items, unpaid efforts or in actual or potential productivities of organizations or individuals. Trained observers equipped with the appropriate theories and tools of measurement will be able to extract financial information from just about every scrap of reality.

Surely, in everyday life some pragmatic ignorance about the actual or virtual financial implications of activities is mostly upheld. While there have been some notable efforts at expanding financial accounting in corporations to include intangible assets (Mouritsen et al. 2001) or environmental impacts (Power 1994), these have also been confined to small groups of expert reckoners and accountants. If one restricts the category of financial numbers to numbers representing prices and therefore, one might assume, valuations of goods and services, their overall significance for economic activity is, perhaps surprisingly, limited. If one broadens the category to include all numbers which have or may have a bearing on financial calculations, hardly any number though can be excluded. The category of financial numbers thus is itself malleable. Its delineation is sometimes a matter of professional dispute, for example between accountants, industrial engineers and lawyers (cf. Abbott 1988: 226–239), and often a mere function of the efforts participants are prepared to invest in trying to grasp the financial implications of what they confront. Sociological analysis is utterly unable to stipulate an adequate or average level of financial sensibility which might serve to normalize the category, yet it may offer some understanding of how numbers (be they explicitly »financial« or not) acquire meaning in social situations. To begin with, two basic kinds of qualities assumed by numbers can be identified.

Through calculative practice, participants might relate any number, any measure, any kind of numerical value to monetary measures, transactions or balances. In calculative practice all numbers are essentially equivalent, regardless of what empirical measure they represent. Through processes of measuring and counting, all kinds of initially non-quantitative observations may be mobilized for computation. This aspect of meaning may be called the *calculative quality* of numbers. But each number can also be taken to encapsulate more complex information about the value or quality of traded goods and services, about the profitability of an investment, about productivities, accomplishments or underachievements, in fact about any aspect of reality. This aspect of meaning defines *symptomatic qualities* of financial numbers – their potential of being read as symptoms of some share of the world (cf. Vollmer 2006).

Regardless of how narrowly or broadly the category of financial numbers is defined, their calculative and symptomatic qualities often appear to reinforce each other. To the extent numbers result from more complex calculations and measurements (calculative quality), treating them as being correlated to more complex realities is warranted (symptomatic qualities); to the extent numbers are taken as symptomatic, participants will try to relate them to other numbers and observations. Taken together, the calculative and symptomatic qualities of financial numbers often diffuse financial meaning over a whole population of numerical signs in an almost infectious manner (»time is money« etc.), with calculative qualities relating numbers to other numbers, symptomatic qualities relating them to realities. Yet both kinds of relations, and accordingly both kinds of qualities, are not provided for by some intrinsic nature of numerical signs, but need to be brought into existence through the collective efforts of participants involved in the use of numbers.[1] What kind of efforts are thus called for?

The calculative quality of numbers results from the institutionalization of a single set of norms for handling numbers in computations all across society, safeguarding participants will always and everywhere find a fair deal of social support for getting »4« as a result of »2+2« (Bloor 1994; Barnes et al. 1996: 169–187). Sophisticated rule-scepticism aside (cf. Wittgenstein 1956; Kripke 1982), usually that is the end of the story: one institutionalized set of rules protecting computation effectively against deviance in all kinds of social contexts. Symptomatic qualities of numbers, on the other hand, appear much harder to police, since referring numbers to realities calls for more arbitrary sense-making activities which turn out differ across participants and settings.

One category of social settings in which symptomatic qualities of numerical signs are generated and maintained on a regular basis is constituted by networks in which numbers routinely circulate across social situations. In such networks, numbers come to work as inscriptions (cf. Latour 1999: 306–307; Robson 1992), which, produced at one place (e.g. a factory floor, an inventory, a terminal), can be mobilized by other parts of the network to be accumulated, analyzed and computed in centers of calculation (cf.

1 Comprehensive evidence for the social origins of both the calculative and symptomatic qualities of numbers has been collected by social studies of mathematical practice (e.g. Bloor 1991; Livingston 1986; Heintz 2003). While insights and methods from the sociology of science have recently been increasingly brought to bear on the field of finance and vice versa (e.g. Porter 1995a; MacKenzie 2001; Preda 2004), the sociology of mathematics has remarkably had just a marginal impact.

Latour 1987: 237–241). This puts participants at centers of calculation, located in offices of managers, investors or tax authorities, to act on peripheries at a distance, without ever leaving the center (Robson 1992: 689–692). Participants at centers treat the numbers which are fed back to them as symptomatic for realities they try to act upon, and for effects their actions subsequently put forth, to then develop models of intervention continuously recalibrated and improved by fresh numerical inscriptions.

A general tendency to read numbers as symptoms may be promoted by the mere separation of social situations embedded in networks across which numbers circulate, especially once they become the primary source of information about settings for which more direct form of observation or access are not at hand. This tendency though does not settle *how* numbers will be interpreted and construed as symptoms by participants aiming to observe and act at a distance. Symptomatic meaning in this specific sense has to be established by frameworks referring the interpretation of numbers to broader sets of meaning. Regarding financial numbers, such frameworks are usually mobilized from management discourse, participants' understanding of accounting systems, or from financial economics (cf. Callon 1998; Abolafia 2005). One might call these frameworks *frames of consumption*, since they regulate the use of numerical signs by participants which take the position of consumers with respect to signs the value of which is established through these sets of frames (Vollmer 2006). Consumers of numerical information might be managers trying to calculate their way around costs, investors scrutinizing financial statements, or customers wondering what the price of a product might indicate. Frames of consumption, if of professional, corporate, scientific, or more mundane origins, help participants transform numbers into symptoms by establishing the significance of measures, providing categories, standards, margins, and other ways of comparing one number with another.

In short, symptomatic qualities of numbers emerge from the embedding of activity in a circulation of numerical signs across social settings and these qualities might be established and ratified on a collective level if institutionalized frames of consumption orient the utilization of numbers as indicators of realities. The dynamics of interaction which result from participants taking each other's use of numbers as symptoms into account though can still be seen to quickly evolve ambiguous, complex and duplicitous patterns of sign use, even if observations remain restricted to simple asymmetric forms of circulating numbers between centers of calculation and peripheries.

3. The Circulation of Numbers and the Unfolding of Regulatory Drama

Symptomatic qualities of financial numbers so far have appeared to derive from a kind of consumer's perspective on signs as indicators of something he or she would like to know more about, e.g. from a regulator's perspective on distant activity, or a politician's concerns about national economic productivity or competitiveness etc. (cf. Tomlinson 1994; Miller/O'Leary 1996: 126–130). However, in networks of circulation numbers are not only received, inspected and interpreted, they also need to be produced and processed. If the use of numbers as symptoms is on the one hand a response to the embedding of activity in networks of circulation, this response is, on the other hand, likely to be anticipated by participants with vested interests in the registration and provision of numbers and their evaluation by others. One might think of foremen collaborating with workers in accommodating data (Zuboff 1988: 352–355) and certainly of all forms of creative accounting (Shah 1996; McBarnet/Whelan 1999).

Across almost any network over which financial numbers are circulated, behavior directed at their manipulation can be observed (e.g. Johnson/Kaplan 1987: 73–74; O'Connell 2004: 737). Using numbers as symptoms thus affects not just the informational but also the behavioral resources available to participants, and this may systematically transform how a situation is defined and consecutively enacted. Situations focussed on manufacturing goods or services, for example, might become refocussed on bringing about or »beating« numbers. Attempts to regulate activity by the numbers do not forestall such transformations, but motivate them through establishing structured opportunities and defining resources for fabricating appearances in which the provision of numbers substitutes other forms of providing goods, services or evidence (cf. McBarnet/Whelan 1997: 137–157; Macintosh et al. 2000: 31–33). More specifically, the symptomatic use of financial numbers and its collective anticipation by participants may induce a pattern of activity which takes on the form of a scripted drama.

The structural prerequisite of turning regulatory processes into regulatory drama is a differentiation between audiences and performers. A spatial segregation of performers and audiences is established by the distance travelled by numerical information from one party to the other. Role differentiation between performers and audiences comes to pass once the first group of participants specializes on producing strips of activity furnished for purposes of expression and inspection on numerical displays, while the complimentary group comes to be primarily concerned with receiving and assessing the numbers. While similar divisions of labour between performers and audiences are at play in all kinds of staged performances, some aspects unique to regulatory drama executed through the use of numbers are worth singling out.

In numericized regulatory drama, audiences for which performances are staged are not present in person, and feedback between performer activity and audience response is mediated and delayed by the circulation of numerical signs. This combines with a persistent aspiration of the audience to intervene into performances. While the audience will scan performances given in numerical form for opportunities of intervention, performers will for their part try to selectively avoid or manufacture respective numerical expressions. The display of numerical signs connecting performers and audience monopolizes both parties' attention to the extent of turning sets and sequences of numerical displays into *the* stage on which regulatory drama unfolds. By focussing their attention in this way, participants of regulatory drama cooperatively foster the impression that the numbers are where the action is.

Given some bifurcation of partisan interests, which in most contexts of regulation might be assumed to prevail, the plot of regulatory drama often takes the form of an expression game. Erving Goffman offers the following description:

»There will be situations where an observer is dependent on what he can learn from a subject, there being no sufficient alternate sources of information, and the subject will be oriented to frustrate this assessment or facilitate it under difficult circumstances. Under these conditions gamelike considerations develop even though very serious matters may be at stake. A contest over assessment occurs. Information becomes strategic and expression games occur.« (Goffman 1969: 10)

Financial reporting and auditing clearly are cases in point (Pentland/Carlile 1996). Performers turning numbers in will be unwilling to fully surrender their activity to external observation and regulation. They come to treat the display of numbers (accounts, balance sheets) as an expressive front which they need to safeguard and manipulate in order to retain some measure of control over their domain of activity. The audience of regulators in turn will know performers to likely be involved in respective backstage preparations (cf. Goffman 1959: 114–135) and try to successively establish more sophisticated means of measurement in struggles to improve the resolution of numerical displays and make technologies mobilized for the accumulation and inspection of data more tamper-proof, introducing, for example, statistical sampling into the audit process (Power 1992).

Yet despite some contrarian interests and role obligations of performers and audiences, numericized regulatory drama is unlikely to become fully antagonistic. Maintaining a segregation of domains of activity defines a common interest of both parties and thus an incentive for cross-party cooperation. Regulators are acting at a distance and either cannot or will not want to enter in person the setting or activity which they are trying to regulate. Performers whose activity is regulated from afar will for their part not want to provoke regulators to work out more immediate forms of supervision and intervention. Although intelligence regarding the possibility and likelihood of fabrication within the provision of numerical displays will often be available to both parties, they might very probably keep up regulatory appearances. Regulators and regulated may choose to tacitly agree to accept numerical displays as temporary playing fields for their struggle over control of activities, while accepting each other's backstage autonomies. Regulatory drama then involves both parties in a kind of normalcy show, »a show in which all participants have the task of acting unfurtively« (Goffman 1971: 331).

In this sense, the social dynamics inherent in staging regulatory drama are quite different from strategic interaction of a more immediate kind, e.g. expression games between police interrogators and suspects. The theatrical character of regulatory drama derives from the segregation and numerically mediated coupling of performer and audience domains, from a degree of collaboration among audiences and performers in sustaining the impression that realities staged by the numbers actually yield to regulatory efforts, and finally, from the scripted character of performances, which turn expression games from adversarial contests into ritualized shows (as when corporations present annual statements to their shareholders). Keeping up regulatory appearances requires a degree of coordination across segregated teams of participants who often are unlikely to ever meet, and this coordination is accomplished by staging activities and their regulation according to scripts provided by regulatory discourses and technologies (management discourse, accounting standards etc.).

Financial numbers are then treated as symptomatic despite being understood by regulators and regulated alike to be expressions intentionally fabricated rather than expressions just given off (cf. Goffman 1959: 14–16), and such hypocrisy is an essential precondition for keeping this discursively scripted and dramatized form of regulation alive. If the credibility of numerical displays collapses, the audience will not be able to maintain its willing suspension of disbelief. The symptomatic qualities of numerical signs will need to be reaffirmed, standards and technologies will need to be refurnished, participants will need to commit to novel scriptings. While such adaptations might reinstate symptomatic qualities of numbers by updating ratified frames of consumption, they also reaffirm the use of numbers as »expressive equipment of a standard kind« (Goffman 1959: 32). Behind the scenes, financial numbers will again gradually come to be treated not as symptoms, but as facades.

4. How Numbers are Existential

These observations call for some further clarification about how numbers in general, and financial numbers in particular, acquire meaning. While symptomatic qualities of numbers are essential for staging regulation by numbers, they should be recognized as representing neither the full range of problems participants are trying to come to terms with through mobilizing numerical signs, nor the full range of problems this mobilization of numbers in turn confronts them with. Treating numbers as symptoms means focussing on the information they contain or should contain, employing them in calculations allows for accumulating, dissecting and reassembling such information, but for performers in regulatory drama, number are not merely of a symptomatic and calculative, but also of expressive and instrumental value.

In regulation at a distance, if not in all social situations in which participants depend on the use of numbers in bringing about and sustaining social interaction, numbers turn out to be mobilized not only to deal with problems of information, but to support a whole range of activities through which participants collaboratively work out the course of ongoing activity: establishing frames of references for ongoing activity, getting access to and distributing resources, supporting impression management. If numerical displays are put to work as primary references of ongoing activity, which with financial numbers suggests interpretations of events in terms of costs, prices, risks and rewards, if numbers regulate access to further resources (as do credit ratings, annual reports or piece-rates) or become primary means of impression management (projected earnings, benchmarks, ratings), they come to stand in for all those aspects of reality on which numbers are participants' monitors. Numerical signs in this way become symptoms, are used as windows on the world, but they also become the primary means for participants of *relating* to the world and to others. In this way, the symptomatic use of numbers is coupled with more expressive and instrumental uses that define broader *existential qualities* acquired by numbers in the course of social interaction.

Three distinct qualities of financial numbers therefore have to be put in perspective if one is to fully grasp how numerical signs are put to work in regulatory processes: a *calculative* quality realized through computation, *symptomatic* qualities realized through interpreting numbers as representations of broader aspects and elements of reality, and *existential* qualities realized through participants' efforts of situating their own activity and self, or that of some agency they represent (corporations, political authorities, interest groups), in broader social realities accessed, constructed and manipulated through numerical signs. While the calculative quality is based on relations of numbers to other numbers and symptomatic qualities derive from the relation of numbers to non-numerical realities, existential qualities of numbers emanate from sign-to-user relations.

One might be tempted to treat existential qualities as effects of a primarily psychological or emotional attachment would they not so decisively impinge upon the functions of numbers in economic activity and its regulation. One cannot well speak of »calculating selves« (Miller 1992) without assuming a distinct form of involvement in the use of numbers among participants, nor could numerical displays work as stages of regulatory drama without assuming a disciplined form of attentiveness. The discourses, technologies and dramas of regulation are all based on the premise that numbers are first and foremost discrete carriers of information, and this presupposes quite specific forms of involvement among participants inspecting or providing them. But how could one assume such narrow forms of involvement to prevail across participants which have clear and present stakes in the production, articulation and interpretation of numerical sign?

What is calling for sociological explanation is not that phenomena like creative accounting, fraudulent financial reporting, or biassed ratings do in fact occur, but that despite common knowledge of participants' interested involvement in the production and use of numbers, a front appearance of regulatory activity is upheld across discourses, technologies and dramas in which numerical signs are treated as mechanical reflections of realities. Numbers are treated as symptoms despite the likelihood their existential might gradually undermine their symptomatic qualities, and despite the fact respective erosions regularly, and often quite spectacularly surface (Enron, Parmalat etc.). Even momentous damages cause regulators to question the symptomatic qualities of numbers only accidentally. In the end, the demand is likely to be for more, rather than less numbers, resulting in more rather than less trust in numbers as symptoms. The focus of regulatory activity on symptomatic qualities of financial numbers might therefore in itself be taken as a symptom of a strangely perseverant fixation of regulatory discourses and technologies.

5. The Information Syndrome of Government

The obsession of contemporary governmentality on exercising regulation through mobilizing information is reflected in a financial government of economic activity fixated on treating financial numbers as symptoms of economic realities. The symptomatic use of financial numbers thus itself might be considered symptomatic of a general state of government characterized by a chronic fixation, an information syndrome. Some elicitors of this syndrome are easily identified. Economic activity has become embedded in ever broader, and finally global contexts of production, investment, supervision and inspection, which has been shifting the execution of government toward action at a distance by multiple public and private authorities, predicating regulatory efforts on the circulation of information across various regulating and regulated settings. Participants of economic activity, regardless of their roles in multi-layered regulatory processes, come to depend on numbers to find out about the world or letting the world find out about themselves in responding to the enhanced embedding, consequentiality and risk of sustaining economic activity in globalizing social settings.

However, this increasing dependence on numerical signs is not a mere function of their informational value. It confers upon numerical signs symptomatic and calculative, but also existential qualities. These qualities amplify certain risks of using numbers as carriers of information. While numbers will often be participants' prime resources for embedding their activity in wider contexts (e. g. corporate cash-flows, capital markets), these resources might have been tampered with throughout to systematically affect this embedding or the activity to which it gives access (e. g. investment decisions, tax assessments). Because existential qualities of numbers go along with their use as symptoms, mobilizing numbers, rather than reducing the intrinsic uncertainties of economic decisions and actions, presents them with additional risks, which in turn will just again reinforce the demand for numerical information. While efforts to mobilize numerical information may superficially present perfectly reasonable moves by participants trying to act economically at a distance, participants simultaneously become exposed to the *risk of over-investing in the circulation of numerical information.* Appreciating this risk asks for a more comprehensive understanding of regulatory processes to take into account the circulation of numbers not merely as an exchange of information, but as a more general trade of social resources.

Before elaborating this change of perspective, some comments about the retention of information syndrome within regulatory processes are in order. As the dynamics of regulatory drama have illustrated, escalating commitment to numerical information precipitates escalating efforts at information engineering. Regulatory agencies are of course well aware of this and the lesson for the assessment of numerical information is obvious: »The very fact that the observer finds himself looking to a particular bit of evidence as an incorruptible check on what is or might be corrupted is the very reason why he should be suspicious of this evidence; *for the best evidence for him is also the best evidence (...) to tamper with.*« (Goffman 1969: 62–63; emphasis ibid.) A life cycle of measures is involved here, leading from events to measurements, to the circulation of measures, and finally their gradual disqualification as symptoms (cf. Goffman 1969: 69–70). An active information syndrome is borne out once participants tend to respond to the disqualification of information by scaling up investments in the search and capitalization of further, alternative, more reliable and in any case: additional sources of information. This tendency is evident even in cases in which regulatory discourse and programs claim to demand not more, but simply »better« or more »qualitative« information. When infrastructures of expert inspections and »personal« evaluations take the place of more mechanical calculative procedures they neither reduce the amount of resources committed to producing information (effectively making it more costly), nor bring they down the inherent contingency of information and its susceptibility to exploitive fabrications (just wait for the next big corporate scandal). In other words, there are different ways of committing resources to mobilizing, accumulating and controlling numerical information, and different techniques for black-boxing the inherent vulnerability of any of these processes, but the route to a substantial demobilizations appears to be blocked.

Maybe, eminent causes of these commitments are to be found in the fact most participation units in the regulation of contemporary economic activity are organizational actors (business firms, tax authorities, institutional investors etc.). As Feldman and March have famously argued, the gathering of information by organizations provides ritualistic assurances for their internal and external stakeholders that appropriate attitudes about decision-making are being groomed (Feldman/March 1981: 177). The command and display of information enhances the perceived competence of organizational actors, interweaving symbolic and instrumental aspects of information use to the extent they become practically inseparable (cf. Feldman/March 1981: 180–182). Organizations define positions to which responsibility for decision-making can more or less unambiguously be attributed, and participants inhabiting such positions invest an excess amount of time and energy in preparing for eventually being made to account for the choice of alternatives. This motivates asking, and being seen to ask for, struggling, and being seen to struggle for, critically inspecting, and being seen to critically inspect all the information that might possibly be of relevance now (when a decision is to be made) and later (when it might have be defended). For most organizations, financial numbers define a category of information better not left in any sense unattended.

The obvious alternative to a government based on the »trust in numbers« (Porter 1995b) would be a government executed through trusted intermediaries, be they persons, organizations or professions. Although one might think regulatory depth and efficacy would be qualitatively improved by positioning agents of regulation within situated activities to be regulated rather than trying to act at them from a distance, replacing trust in numbers by trust in persons or professional agencies merely delegates the problem of regulation. Participants aspiring to regulate the stakes of embedded economic activity through their own devices will still be left with the choice of either doing a lot of travelling, visiting and inspecting for themselves, while giving up the opportunity to inspect many places at once by the numbers (Latour 1999: 38), or of making use of signs which might circulate at high rates and velocities, which are handily inspected, experimented with, elaborated and redirected, or, finally, of giving up both and trust somebody else who is to subsequently face the same kind of problem. Even institutionalizing personal meetings between regulators and regulated does not establish a radically different alternative to these options, but just embroils and focusses them on a single social situation, reducing neither the efforts invested in collecting, accumulating and presenting information, nor the dramaturgical aspects of the regulatory process with which the circulation of information comes to be associated (cf. Roberts et al. 2006: 290–292).

Perhaps the most powerful rationalization of the information syndrome of government is the idea that information gives actors a degree of control over ongoing activity beyond their immediate perceptual and behavioral reach. Withdrawing regulatory involvements in the circulation of numerical information then is usually just an episodic fancy until the next collapse of numerical displays is experienced, and the call for »transparency« induces a new wave of investments in standards and technologies of financial calculation and evaluation. Rather than lamenting this state of affairs, preaching conceptual blueprints of »qualitative« remedies, or falling for regulators' claims that they already found some by themselves, social scientist would do well to concentrate on understanding better the self-supporting aspects of the syndrome with which they are confronted. An intrinsic part of the self-supporting dynamic is participants' perception control is and will be gained by mobilizing numerical information – if this claim is possibly wrong, why do participants, regulators and regulated alike, tend to stick to it?

6. Governing by Numbers as Trading for Social Capital

Regulatory drama is easily be denounced by exposing the artistic and superficial, if not often hypocritical aspects of its cross-party productions. Yet these aspects are also authentic expressions of participants' efforts at establishing and preserving common grounds for negotiating and collaboratively sustaining economic activities across spatially and temporally segregated social situations. As argued above, numericized regulatory drama apparently »pays off« for both regulators and regulated – but just what do they trade?

The varieties of goods and services which participants might directly or indirectly want to secure by taking part in regulatory drama are potentially unlimited and subject to individual and organizational preferences. Among regulators, controlling assets and investments, planning and evaluating interventions are generically claimed desires; among regulated, accessing resources (investments, markets, licenses) and prevailing over peers in assessment contests (gradings, ratings, evaluations) are legitimately confessed motivations. One however needs to take into account that overt motives are unlikely to be accurate descriptions of what the parties are actually acquiring. More critically, if numbers are expression deliberately put on display, they can no longer be naively treated as symptoms (i.e. as expressions just given off), and this depreciation of informational value affects the potential stakes of both regulators and regulated. Regulators might not effectively act at a distance, regulated might not be effectively graded. All parties of regulatory drama, despite their confessed motivations, are aware of this, yet they keep on participating. The kind of trade which is going on therefore needs to be reconstructed either as somewhat callous to the depreciation of numerical information or as bearing some intrinsic defense mechanism against it.

One can advance in this general direction by hypothesizing regulators and regulated involved in governing by numbers to trade *control of information* for *recognition of social status*. Control of information is what regulators are willing to give up in order to be recognized as participants entitled to evaluate performances. Recognition of higher social status is what regulated parties are willing to grant in order to gain a measure of control over information accumulated and used by regulators. With respect to the control of information, the trade therefore is just the opposite of what regulatory discourses and technologies claim to bring about. Regulators do not get, they give up control of information – dramatizing control is simply an effort to symbolize the social status regulators obtain in return. The incurred loss of control over information thus is usually articulated only to the extent to which it serves treating numbers as providing objective, i.e. innocent and potentially unwanted information. The control of information gained by those who stand to be regulated can as well benefit them only if the information proves to be robust enough to support regulatory employments. They also need to cultivate a more specific understanding of how information they control will later be used. Control of information forwarded to and utilized by others can after all only be of value if one knows who the others are and how they are likely to employ the information they receive. Providing numerical expression is a form of paying deference and this makes it more likely the one addressed in this way will also be the ones with the status required to act on what information they receive.

Now, why might such an exchange-based reconstruction of governing by numbers, as briefly as it can only be outlined here, offer a promising approach towards analyzing contemporary forms of financial governance?

1. It avoids taking individuals and organizations to be naive about the use of numerical signs. Readiness to take the informational value of numbers for granted may be common among observers innocent of involvement in regulatory drama. But such readiness would neither suit participants of regulatory processes well, nor does it in fact appear to be common among them. Seasoned participants of governing by numbers rather take the objective, reflective or symptomatic quality of numerical signs as something in need of deliberate crafting and catering for – just to the extent regulatory exchanges require to continue. This fact has amply been reflected by studies of financial and accounting practice (cf. Morgan 1988; Lukka 1990; Montagna 1990: 248–249).

2. Instead of implying effective technological fixes to the vulnerability of numerical expressions would actually exist, this reconstruction points to certain self-regulating dynamics which limit the depreciation of numerical information. Not solely the regulators, but also the regulated have a vested interest in preventing numerical expressions from becoming deconstructed. They will therefore usually abandon opportunities for exploitive fabrications which are likely to be exposed. Technically speaking (cf. Coleman 1990: 131–136), the system of exchange will tend towards a relative equilibrium in which regulators do not overly burden the regulated with intrusive interventions and the regulated show some restraint in exercising control of information, thus establishing an exchange rate relatively favorable to the party that is going to be regulated (a good deal of information control for showing little deference). If fabrications do surface, heavier intrusions are likely to be waged against the regulated, which threatens them with a rise in costs. Some »Foucauldian« discipline might therefore be market based.[2]

3. This reconstruction reiterates the social functions of regulatory discourse which have been visible in the brief analysis of numericized regulatory drama. While regulatory discourse often claims to describe reality as it is or should become, in the first place it establishes *frames and scripts* for cooperatively maintaining front displays of regulatory processes across

---

2 The working of this self-regulatory mechanism though assumes that a change of transaction partners is not an immediate option. In the production of financial statements, and particularly once the role of regulators is taken by audit firms which are contracted by those they are supposed to inspect, such an option is often manifest.

regulators and regulated. Regulatory discourse affords an anticipation of the value and use of numerical information by broadcasting frames of consumption. It also accommodates reasons for cross-party contacts, offering a cover for initiating transactions (e.g. cross-party backstage preparations for staging regulatory activity, as common in auditing). The discursive description of appropriate regulatory appearances supports individuals and organizations in their frontstage performances and helps cultivating talk as a separate domain of activity from which action might gradually be decoupled (Brunsson 1989; Meyer/Rowan 1991). Regulatory discourse therefore defines opportunities for social exchange, facilitates cross-party coordination, and presents a source of legitimacy.

4. These considerations also open up an analytical perspective on the *accumulation of social capital in emerging forms of governance*. Governing by number has often been assumed as starting with existing authority relations between regulators and regulators (management accounting practices are the most obvious example). Formal authority surely does not equal social status, but the connection is not completely mistaken. The opportunity for the kind of exchange under review is established by the mere fact regulators hold control over certain goods and services of interest to the regulated (like performance rewards or sanctions, investment capital etc.), while the disposal of these goods and services may be influenced by providing or withholding information. Regulators' ability to trade information control is thus usually a result of executing control over something more substantial and authority positions are a special kind of access to such control. In the global financial system, multiple parties control impressive amounts of resources, and most of them will strive for social status to be able, for example, to marginalize competitors, influence terms of trade, take part in the setting of standards, etc. (cf. Blau 1964: 132–140). The general problem is to translate control of resources into social status, to transform economic into social capital (cf. Lin 2001: 78–98). In governing global finance, the influence of formal authority is increasingly thrust aside by private or semi-private agencies like accounting firms, rating agencies or banking networks. Is it a coincidence that those which appear to be experts at assembling social capital are also experts at assembling numerical signs?

5. Finally, elaborating this perspective might help to *recontextualize regulatory efforts*. What makes governing by numbers a responsive form of governance is not the amount of information that is circulated across situations, but the ability of the regulatory process, in its more and less drama-

tized forms, to absorb, process, and generate social complexity. In their conception of regulatory efforts agencies need not (and often simply cannot) match the overall social complexity of regulation, yet they need to be able to strategically respond to this complexity. On the one hand, trying to get the least spoiled information for regulatory purposes one possibly could might draw some short-term profits, since investing in the mechanization of circulating numbers, for example, keeps down regulators' expenditures in social exchange (i.e. the degree of information control they transfer). But given an exchange rate which cannot unilaterally be amended, such a strategy alone cannot safeguard returns – information technology does not at all mechanize the mobilization of social status. For the accumulation of social capital though, regulatory strategies have remained as underdeveloped as they have been underresearched. Maybe, past the market for information (Barker 1998), a market for social expertise might develop after all. Hopefully, it will not be a market devoid of sociologists.

References

Abbott, A. (1988), *The System of Professions: An Essay on the Division of Expert Labour.* Chicago.

Abolafia, M. Y. (2005), »Interpretive Politics at the Federal Reserve«, in: K. Knorr Cetina and A. Preda (eds), *The Sociology of Financial Markets.* Oxford, 207–228.

Armstrong, P. (1994), »The Influence of Michel Foucault on Accounting Research«, in: *Critical Perspectives on Accounting,* Vol. 5, 25–55.

Barker, R. G. (1998), »The Market for Information: Evidence from Finance Directors, Analysts and Fund Managers«, in: *Accounting and Business Research,* Vol. 29, 3–20.

Barnes, B./Bloor, D./Henry, J. (1996), *Scientific Knowledge: A Sociological Analysis.* London.

Blau, P. M. (1964), *Exchange and Power in Social Life.* New York.

Bloor, D. (1991), *Knowledge and Social Imagery.* 2nd edition. Chicago.

— (1994), »What Can the Sociologist of Knowledge Say About 2+2=4?«, in: P. Ernest (ed.), *Mathematics, Education and Philosophy: An International Perspective.* London, 21–32.

Brunsson, N. (1989), *The Organization of Hypocrisy.* Chichester.

Callon, M. (1998), »An Essay on Framing and Overflowing: Economic Externalities Revisited by Sociology«, in: M. Callon (ed.), *The Laws of the Markets.* Oxford, 244–269.

Coleman, J. S. (1990), *Foundations of Social Theory.* Cambridge, Mass.

Dean, M. (1999), *Governmentality: Power and Rule in Modern Society.* London.

Du Gay, P./Salaman, G. (1992), »The Cult(ure) of the Customer«, in: *Journal of Management Studies,* Vol. 29, 615–633.

Feldman, M. S./March, J. G. (1981), »Information as Signal and Symbol«, in: *Administrative Science Quarterly*, Vol. 26, 171–186.

Foucault, M. (1991), »Governmentality«, in: G. Burchell, C. Gordon, P. Miller (eds), *The Foucault Effect: Studies in Governmentality*. Chicago, 87–104.

Goffman, E. (1959), *The Presentation of Self in Everyday Life*. Garden City, N.Y.

— (1969), *Strategic Interaction*. Philadelphia.

— (1971), *Relations in Public. Microstudies of the Public Order*. London.

Heintz, B. (2003), »When is a Proof a Proof?«, in: *Social Studies of Science*, Vol. 33, 929–943.

Hopwood, A. G. (1992), »Accounting Calculation and the Shifting Sphere of the Economic«, in: *The European Accounting Review*, Vol. 1, 125–143.

Hoskin, K. (1994), »Boxing Clever: For, Against and Beyond Foucault in the Battle for Accouting Theory«, in: *Critical Perspectives on Accounting*, Vol. 5, 57–85.

Hoskin, K./Macve, R. (1986), »Accounting and the Examination: A Genealogy of Disciplinary Power«, in: *Accounting, Organizations and Society,* Vol. 11, 105–136.

Johnson, H. T./Kaplan, R. S. (1987), *Relevance Lost: The Rise and Fall of Management Accounting*. Boston.

Kalpagam, U. (2000), »Colonial Governmentality and the ›Economy‹«, in: *Economy and Society,* Vol. 29, 418–438.

Knorr Cetina, K./Preda, A. (eds) (2005), *The Sociology of Financial Markets*. Oxford.

Kripke, S. A. (1982), *Wittgenstein on Rules and Private Language: An Elementary Exposition*. Cambridge, Mass.

Latour, B. (1987), *Science in Action: How to Follow Scientists and Engineers Through Society*. Cambridge, Mass.

— (1999), *Pandora's Hope: Essays on the Reality of Science Studies*. Cambridge, Mass.

Lin, N. (2001), *Social Capital: A Theory of Social Structure and Action*. Cambridge.

Livingston, E. (1986), *The Ethnomethodological Foundations of Mathematics*. London.

Lukka, K. (1990), »Ontology and Accounting: The Concept of Profit«, in: *Critical Perspectives on Accounting*, Vol. 1, 239–261.

McBarnet, D./Whelan, C. (1999), *Creative Accounting and the Cross-Eyed Javelin Thrower*. Chichester.

Macintosh, N. B./Shearer, T./Thornton, D. B./Welker, M. (2000), »Accounting as Simulacrum and Hyperreality: Perspectives on Income and Capital«, in: *Accounting, Organizations and Society*, Vol. 25, 13–50.

MacKenzie, Donald (2001), »Physics and Finance: S-Terms and Modern Finance as a Topic for Science Studies«, in: *Science, Technology & Human Values*, Vol. 26, 115–144.

— (2006), *An Engine, Not a Camera: How Financial Models Shape Markets*. Cambridge, Mass.

Meyer, J. W./Rowan, B. (1991), »Institutionalized Organizations: Formal Structure as Myth and Ceremony«, in: P.J. DiMaggio and W.W. Powell (eds), *The New Institutionalism in Organizational Analysis*. Chicago, 41–62.

Miller, P. (1992), »Accounting and Objectivity: The Invention of Calculating Selves and Calculable Spaces«, in: *Annals of Scholarship*, Vol. 9, 61–86.

Miller, P./Rose, N. (1990), »Governing Economic Life«, in: *Economy and Society*, Vol. 19, 1–31.

Miller, P./O'Leary, T. (1996), »The Factory as Laboratory«, in: M. Power (ed.), *Accounting and Science: Natural Inquiry and Commercial Reason*. Cambridge, 120–150.

Montagna, P. (1990), »Accounting Rationality and Financial Legitimation«, in: S. Zukin and P. DiMaggio (eds), *Structures of Capital*. Cambridge, 227–260.

Morgan, G. (1988), »Accounting as Reality Construction: Towards a New Epistemology for Accounting Practice«, in: *Accounting, Organizations and Society*, Vol. 13, 477–485.

Mouritsen, J./Larsen, H. T./Bukh, P. N. D. (2001), »Intellectual Capital and the ›Capable Firm‹: Narrating, Visualizing and Numbering for Managing Knowledge«, in: *Accounting, Organizations and Society*, Vol. 26, 735–762.

Munro, R. (1993), »Just When You Thought It Safe to Enter the Water: Accountability, Language Games and Multiple Control Technologies«, in: *Accounting, Management & Information Technology*, Vol. 3, 249–271.

O'Connell, B. T. (2004), »Enron. Con: ›He That Filches From Me My Good Name ... Makes Me Poor Indeed‹«, in: *Critical Perspectives on Accounting*, Vol. 15, 733–749.

Pentland, B. T./Carlile, P. (1996), »Audit the Taxpayer, Not the Return: Tax Auditing as an Expression Game«, in: *Accounting, Organizations and Society*, Vol. 21, 269–287.

Porter, T. M. (1995a), »Information Cultures: A Review Essay«, in: *Accounting, Organizations and Society*, Vol. 20, 83–92.

— (1995b), *Trust in Numbers: The Pursuit of Objectivity in Science and Public Life*. Princeton, N.J.

Power, M. (1992), »From Common Sense to Expertise: Reflections on the Prehistory of Audit Sampling«, in: *Accounting, Organizations and Society*, Vol. 17, 37–62.

— (1994), »Constructing the Responsible Organization: Accounting and Environmental Representation«, in: G. Teubner, L. Farmer, D. Murphy (eds), *Environmental Law and Ecological Responsibility*. Chichester, 369–392.

Preda, A. (2004), »Informative Prices, Rational Investors: The Emergence of the Random Walk Hypothesis and the Nineteenth-Century ›Science of Financial Investments‹«, in: *History of Political Economy*, Vol. 36, 351–386.

Roberts, J./Sanderson, P./Barker, R./Hendry, J. (2006), »In the Mirror of the Market: The Disciplinary Effects of Company/Fund Manager Meetings«, in: *Accounting, Organizations and Society*, Vol. 31, 277–294.

Robson, K. (1992), »Accounting Numbers as ›Inscription‹: Action at a Distance and the Development of Accounting«, in: *Accounting, Organizations and Society*, Vol. 17, 685–708.

— (1993), »Governing Science and Economic Growth at a Distance: Accounting Representation and the Management of Research and Development«, in: *Economy and Society*, Vol. 22, 461–481.

Rose, N. (1991), »Governing By Numbers: Figuring Out Democracy«, in: *Accounting, Organizations and Society*, Vol. 16, 673–692.

Rose, N./Miller, P. (1992), »Political Power Beyond the State: Problematics of Government«, in: *British Journal of Sociology*, Vol. 43, 173–205.

Shah, A. K. (1996), »Creative Compliance in Financial Reporting«, in: *Accounting, Organizations and Society*, Vol. 21, 23–39.

Tomlinson, J. (1994), »The Politics of Economic Measurement: The Rise of the ›Productivity Problem‹ in the 1940s«, in: A.G. Hopwood, P. Miller (eds), *Accounting as Social and Institutional Practice*. Cambridge, 168–189.

Townley, B. (1993), »Foucault, Power/Knowledge and Its Relevance for Human Resource Management«, in: *Academy of Management Review*, Vol. 18, 518–545.

Vollmer, H. (2003), »Bookeeping, Accounting, Calculative Practice: The Sociological Suspense of Calculation«, in: *Critical Perspectives on Accounting*, Vol. 14, 353–381.

— (2006), »How To Do More With Numbers«, Paper presented at the 8th Interdisciplinary Perspectives on Accounting Conference (IPA), Cardiff, July 2006.

Wittgenstein, L. (1956), *Remarks on the Foundations of Mathematics*. Oxford.

Zuboff, S. (1988), *In the Age of the Smart Machine: The Future of Work and Power*. New York.

Cultures of Economic Calculation

Herbert Kalthoff

1. Introduction

A characteristic feature of modern societies is the calculation of a vast number of social phenomena. It is generally assumed that calculation is an appropriate and reliable means to achieve the control required by social and political fields which are shaped by global developments. In this sense it can be argued that modern societies are accounting societies; their basic trait is the assumed rationality of calculation. Historical studies demonstrated that this development started in the 18th century and lead to surveying land and property, measuring time and standardization of measures (e.g. Porter 1995; Desrosières 1993; Zerubavel 1982).

Until today sociology has neglected the role and importance of economic calculation; even in recent studies in economic sociology calculation is scarcely taken into further consideration. This immunization of sociology towards calculation goes back to Max Weber and Karl Mannheim. For Max Weber (1985: 3–4) the meaning of the formula »2 x 2 = 4« is an example of what he calls current or motivational understanding. We immediately understand the formula, that is to say we understand the rules of the formula and its correctness. Furthermore, we motivationally understand somebody performing this formula, that is to say we can rationally explain the meaning of such an action placing it in the context of its performance (»economic calculation«, »scientific demonstration«, »technical calculation«, Weber 1985: 4). Our understanding is thus tied to a divided knowledge which, as Wittgenstein argues (e.g. 1994: 243), is related to the training of a technique we experienced at school. For Karl Mannheim (1995) mathematical knowledge is free of social factors (such as interests) because of its relation to theoretical developments alone. Mathematical knowledge as well as scientific knowledge represents an independent form of knowledge. The paradigm for this socially independent knowledge is the formula »2 x 2 = 4« (Mannheim 1995: 251, 256). For, early sociologist calculation seems to constitute the core of rational practices with no social impact and effects. Weber's and Mannheim's positions intersect at one point: the use and performance of mathematical rules is of no interest for sociological research because there is no sociologically relevant core of calculation as calculation. Max Weber and Karl Mannheim hold the position of mathematical realism – also presented in the work of David Bloor (1973). Questions of the role and function of mathematics, of its object, the objects' ontology and their relatedness to empirical reality as well as criteria on how to decide about the truth of mathematical statements has been widely and controversially discussed and answered within the philosophy of mathematics. Mathematical realism (and its various forms), for instance, ascribes an existence to mathematical objects which is independent from time and space. They precede, in other words, social experience (cf. Brown 1999). Instead, an antirealistic position is hold by formalism: formalism states that mathematical objects are arbitrarily made abstractions and thus concepts based on conventions. Within the history of mathematics this position was articulated by David Hilbert with the aim to establish a theory of proof (cf. Rheinwald 1984). Intuitionism is a more radical anti-realistic position represented for example by Luitzen E. J. Brouwer. It is argued that mathematical objects are not discovered in reality ›out there‹ but created in and through mathematics and its procedures (cf. Mehrtens 1990). When it comes to logicism (represented by Bertrand Russel and Gottlob Frege) it restricts mathematical formulations to being analytical descriptions excluding the production of new knowledge. Accordingly, mathematics do not explain empirical objects but the way of speaking about them mathematically (cf. Shapiro 2000).

The positions briefly outlined underline several problems and questions. The realistic position has to explain how spacio-temporally independent entities can be dealt with by humans depending on time and space whereas formalism has to show how formal axiomatic, which is central to his theory of proof, can be established by optionally arranged axioms fulfilling the criteria of completeness and consistence. At the same time solutions to mathematical questions have been developed within disunity. For instance logicism: it contributed to the dissolution of the strong empirical position which holds that knowledge is based on empirical experience. Logicism instead shows that mathematical formulations understood as analytical formulations can be performed without empirical verification (cf. Kleinert 2002; Falkenburg 1994; Otte 1994; Heintz 1993; 2000).

Within the sociology of mathematics three main directions can be highlightened: (1) a sociology of knowledge-oriented research carried out by David Bloor, (2) ethnomethodological-oriented research carried out by Eric Livingston and (3) an approach-oriented one towards the sociology of scientific knowledge carried out by Bettina Heintz. It is a strategic decision which makes the difference between the research of Bloor and Livingston. Bloor (1973; 1987), on the one hand, anchors his work within the (traditional) sociology of knowledge and in doing so he explains inner-mathematical mechanisms (e.g. consensus formation) by underlining extra-mathematical factors (e.g. power, conventions). To privilege social factors means to reduce at the same time phenomena which are typical for mathematics (e.g. formal writing). Also excluded is the possibility of a special ontological position of mathematical science. Livingston (1986; 1993), on the other hand, explains the logics of mathematical demonstration und its power to generalization by an empirical analysis of the lived mathematical practice. Critical voices raise the question to what extent emphasizing inner-mathematical factors leads to a reification of mathematical practices and not to their sociological analysis (cf. Heintz 2000: 30–31). In her research Heintz (2000; 2003) takes a different approach. She analyzes mathematical research as an epistemic practice which is characterized by mediated objects, aesthetics of proof and ways of cooperation within which trust and writing play an import role. The sociology of mathematics encounters, following Heintz (2000: 233pp), two specific problems: first, the coherence of mathematical demonstration representing the epistemic position of mathematics as a proving discipline and, second, the form of problem solving. Sociological research has two possible points of departure: analysis of procedures and media of formalization on the one hand, analysis of communication as a technology of trust (Porter 1995) on the other side. This allows to sociologically analyze the logics and cunning of representation devices used in mathematics and thus the theoretical model implemented in them; it allows furthermore to grasp the coherence of procedural objectivity and at the same time to analyse the specific forms of consensus formation within mathematics as a proving discipline.

Sociological studies on economic calculation have been carried out within the field of accounting studies. An important part of these studies can be called critical accounting studies inspired by Foucault's (1977) model of panoptism and its disciplinary force and by Actor Network Theory with the model of inscription of reality through its translation (e.g. Latour 1999). Central to these studies (cf. Hopwood/Miller 1994; Miller 1992; Power 1997) is among other things the theorem of visibility: something hidden is made visible by calculation and what is made visible by these translating procedures of inscription is subject to control over distance – a control which is performed by dominant actors (say, the management of an enterprise). To understand economic calculation as a regime of visibility which performs itself by a scopic technology involves more far reaching questions which have been neglected so far by accounting research. Just to open up this discussion I would highlight two aspects:

To speak of a regime of visibility implies an analysis of the performativity and mediality of representation devices used for calculation procedures (e.g. tables, formulas, writing). How is ›reality out there‹ depicted, ordered and made visible in and through these devices? What are, following Austin (1992) or Butler (1997), the extra-representational effects of these representation devices?

To assume a regime of visibility implies, too, a theory of seeing. Nothing is made visible through calculation and its devices if there is not – in the sense of Foucault (1977) – a gaze endowed with knowledge and power. It is this independent mechanism coupled with the desire of seeing and recognizing economic practices, objects and (hidden) financial circumstances of a company within the ordered world of figures.[1]

---

1 One can assume that the desire of seeing is part of a new accentuation in philosophy: something which can be shown (the acroamatic) and is thus visible supersede something which can be heard. A connection of reason (logos) and the acroamatic appears and does not only establish a hierarchy of senses but causes also a strong connectivity between knowing (episteme) and seeing (cf. Riedel 1984). Transferred to modern calculus and mathematics this development indicates a detaching of mathematical signs on the one hand and what is represented from the world out there on the other. A formula or a calculus does not just represent or embody what mathematicians have cognitively in mind but mathematical

These dimensions lead the sociology of (economic) calculation to a broader concept of practices (e.g. Reckwitz 2002; Schatzki 1996). Accounting studies usually refer to social action as an intentional and goal-oriented doing of human actors; this kind of a realistic approach leaves untouched questions concerning the role of representational and technological devices and the involvement of the human body.

As far as cognition is concerned the paper deals with essential concepts of the cognitive »such as deciding, understanding, and seeing« (Woolgar 1989: 321) by proposing an empirical investigation of the production, use and effects of representation devices (such as economic ratios, maps, models, formulae, tables, lists, charts etc.) in economic contexts. The central aim of the paper, however, is not to analyse or conceptualise human agents' capacities of cognitive understanding, but to focus on the devices which frame their practices. This is not a detour but a concentration on the social realm in which cognition can be observed because cognition as such is not observable in any other way for sociology (cf. Coulter 1989). Thus, this paper proposes an empirical investigation of the infrastructure of economic practices. It does not follow those concepts in cognitivism which assume the existence of a mental plan (*Entwurf*) that actors just carry out in their (routine) activities as if they were following a rule. Instead, the paper treats these practices as framed by the situation in which they are performed and by the technologies which are part of the setting (e.g. Suchman 1987).

The importance of representation devices for cognition consists, first, in their ability to represent entities of the external world, to make them available as objects and to work upon them. Second, representation devices exert a performative force on their users, making the world objective in the way they represent it. These devices shape what is being perceived by human actors. This will be discussed later in the paper.[2] A crucial debate in science and technology studies has lead us to point out that these technologies do not operate in a neutral manner but are shaped by theoretical assumptions or models (cf. Harding 1976). That is to say that they structure, edit and format the information which they provide and produce. In economic theory and decision theory as well the concept of information is generally used to designate an interpretation-free depiction of reality which produces a transparent world and allows for rational action and decision-

notation system and cognitive objects are interdependently linked. In this sense mathematical notations constitute what they represent (cf. Krämer 1997a: 112–114).

2 For a sociological account on the social use of maps in banking cf. Kalthoff (2002).

making. From this point of view it is assumed that as soon as one disposes of information, one disposes of the world of economic exchange. This paper argues instead that information is itself shaped by its production and representation. Concerning information, Heidegger (1991: 124) notes: »Yet while information in-forms, that is, apprises, it at the same forms, that means, arranges and sets straight. As an appraisal, information is also the arrangement that sets humans, all objects and stuffs in a form […]«.[3] One can, in this sense, state that economic actors are ›being set‹ by the representation devices which they work with in order to be informed for their transactions and decisions.

A related observation concerning representation devices is that they are themselves subject to change. Concerning economic ratios one can even speak of an accounting industry which continuously overwrites old concepts with new ones; old ratios such as Return on Investment are replaced by new ones such as Raroc (or Rorac), old formulae (e.g. the Black and Scholes model) are replaced (or at least transformed) by new ones (e.g. the Cox Ross Rubinstein model). This process only knows an end in itself: the promise of a ›better‹ understanding and handling of risk, return and transaction techniques and thus an endless reworking of calculation devices for the process' own sake.

The aim of this paper is to outline a research program for a sociology of calculation which takes questions of representation, performativity and the desire of seeing/interpretation into consideration. In doing so it takes an empirical and cultural theory perspective on knowledge production within banking and finance. It challenges sociological understanding insofar as it argues for a shift from mathematical realism to a constitution theory perspective. Mathematical realism – as outlined above – assumes that (economic) objects exist independently from their calculation; mathematical signs just depict as they are ›out there‹.

Economic Objects → Mathematical Operation/Calculation

3 The translation has been changed in two places.

A constitution theory perspective argues instead that economic objects are produced by the written and oral procedures of mathematical operations. In other words: objects, such as, cash flow, risk or profit exist only in and through economic calculation.

Mathematical Operation/Calculation → Economic Objects

Thus, such a perspective gives up the ontological pre-eminence which mathematical realism ascribes to the world of economic objects. What is at stake and what has to be analyzed is the role of economic representation as well as the relation between economic representation and practices (cf. Kalthoff et al. 2000). A constitution theory perspective, which can be traced back to Heidegger's work on technology (cf. Heidegger 1997; Dreyfus 2002; Drefus/Spinosa 1997), assumes that economic objects once brought into existence through calculation contribute to a reconfiguration of economic practices. The paper now analyzes more theoretical questions concerning representation devices used for calculation (2). In a second step it analyzes some empirical data which shows the will to knowledge and the desire of seeing embodied within practices of interpretation (3). The examples used derived from ethnographic fieldwork taken place in the risk management department of two big international banks (cf. Kalthoff 2005; 2006).

2. Outline for an Empirical Sociology of Calculation

In what follows, the paper will describe three dimensions of an empirical research program on economic calculation: the use and function of operative modes of writing within banking units designed for the development and stabilization of formulae (1), the performativity of representation devices and thus the relation between economic representation and practices (2) and social practices of interpretation in which the will to knowledge and the desire of seeing are materialized (3). The implementation of formulae into software programs used in finance and banking is not taken into further consideration here.

Operative Modes of Writing

The first dimension refers to the media of expression or devices of representation in which calculation appears. If one tries to find an answer to the question of what economic actors do while carrying out a calculation, the answer will be: among other things, they write using writing, mathematical symbols and representation devices (such as lists, tables, diagrams and even choropleth maps). That is to say, economic actors produce written documents which are structured by an information design developed within the organization which allows them to be recognisable while circulating through the (international) organization.

In general, sociological research on writing follows a pragmatic view – stating three functions of writing: the preservation function, the relief function and the transportation function. First, the preservation function: social practices or activities documented in writing function as memory anchors because that what would otherwise be forgotten is made to endure in written form; second, the relief function: with the record as memory support, forgetting becomes possible: risk analysts or financial analysts thus do not only write things down because they would forget them otherwise, but in order to be able to forget them; third, the transportation function: the places of preservation (tables, files, notes, etc.) in which events, practices or negotiations etc. as well as their performance endure in written form are portable documents by definition.

This pragmatic view has been criticized by very different authors such as Luhmann or Derrida. Luhmann (1995; 1998: 249pp) reminds sociology that writing does not just store knowledge and keeps it at one's disposal but that a text documents what he calls »non-updated options« (»nichtaktualisierte Möglichkeiten«, Luhmann, 1995, 106; my translation). These options lead to decisions whether a text (and its information) will be used or not. Every text thus portrays an »unmarked realm of the excluded« (»unmarkierte[r] Bereich des Ausgeschlossenen«, Luhmann, 1995: 107; my translation). In this sense, texts perform their own contingencies, which calls for re-reading and re-decision. Derrida (1984) takes a different stance against the pragmatic view. He criticizes two aspects: firstly, a phonocentrism, which he considers to be deeply rooted in occidental philosophical tradition; and secondly, the unreflected notion that writing cancels out the spatio-temporal limitation of orality, leaving it untouched, however, in the process.

Both critiques are interesting for a sociology of economic calculation. Luhmann points out to the fact that decisions which underline every written document can be deconstructed und that this deconstruction is informed by the written document itself. As far as Derrida's criticism is concerned, it was taken up by Krämer (1996) in suggesting an extended notion of writing which permits a view of other forms of written symbols as equally included in the writing concept (for instance, the *Dupont Formula* or the *Option Pricing-Model*; cf. MacKenzie 2003). The argument goes as follows: it hardly makes sense to restrict writing to spoken language or to the written form of language; conceptually, writing should include other modes of notation as well. Her predominant concerns are *operative modes of writing*. Operative modes of writing »do not emerge from writing down phonetic language, but are graphic systems sui generis which might at best then be rendered in spoken form. What is specific to this mode of writing is that is does not refer to spoken sounds, but to cognitive objects« (Krämer 1997b, 115; my translation). If it is possible to assign theoretical objects to mathematical signs in such a way that every possible mathematical expression represents a ›true‹ part of these objects, then complex cognitive operations can be performed using visible symbols on paper (or the computer screen). This means: what is at stake is not a nexus between natural objects and mathematical expressions (or calculus), but the correspondence between non-visible (theoretical) entities and their formal mathematical expression. These (theoretical) entities are thus brought into existence and made calculable by operative writing.

Operative modes of writing thus assume a double function as symbolic machines: they represent objects (such as economic figures) and at the same time permit operations with these objects while being indifferent towards the symbols' meanings. Characteristics of this operation are, firstly, a decoupling of construction and interpretation, of access and understanding – understanding and interpretation only set in later; and, secondly, a shift from truth to correctness: for a symbolic operation all that is relevant is a procedure according to the rules and thus to internal plausibility (cf. Krämer 1997a; 1997b; Heintz 1993).

This is due to the fact that numeric symbols do not simply represent an object but an operation which is performed on them or whose result they are. Thus, formulae operate on two levels. They connect different entities and in doing so they bring reality into being; they organize the encounter of economic actors and economic objects and provide information, continually allowing operations with and upon them.

The first aim of a sociology of calculation is thus to investigate in more detail the development, invention and stabilization of formulae designed to be used in banking and finance and thus to empirically observe operative modes of writing, its social use and communication function in such contexts.

Performativity of Calculation Tools

Following Luhmann's famous statement on media, one can say that economic actors – like international banks – do know what they know (about markets, actors or institutions) through means of representation. Thus, the second dimension which has to be observed in more detail is the use actors make of calculation tools while carrying out a finance transaction. Recent studies in economic and financial sociology have underscored the important role computers play in the world of banking and finance. In some financial markets they are constantly updated with information about markets, actors and activities; in some banking departments (e.g. risk management) calculation tools are used to work upon written documents corporate clients provide to prove their creditworthiness. The technologies used in international banks or on financial markets for the representation of markets, enterprises or price movements differ one from another in a systematic way. The cash flow or ratio sheet which is central to risk management in corporate banking shows historical figures of a company, but these software programs are not designed for transaction purposes. They represent economic practices by using a certain rhetoric and thus indicate transactions.

Name, Domicile: *Investment AG,* K-Twon (Poland)		Industry Code, Busines: 71231000 Development and selling of real estate		
Account Manager: A/C Manager Not Assigned	Branch/Customer No: 5300090	999	Unit Risk Management	
Legal Status: AG	Group	Currency: T PLN		
Type of Statement		Annual	Annual	Annual
Date		31.12.1999	31.12.1998	31.12.1997
Earnings before Tax	*540*	*61,872,000*	*46,988,000*	*28,587,000*
Net depriciation	341B441	0	297,000	525,000
Change in pension provisions	♠ 256	0	0	0
Change in special reserves (tangible assets) ...	♠ 262	0	0	0
Extraordinary Cash Items	346B446	4,032,000	1,261,000	B446,000
Interest	332	11,196,000	4,555,000	9,086,000
EBITDA		*77,100,000*	*54,978,000*	*23,496,000*
Interest	332	B11,196,000	B4,555,000	B9,086,000
Repayment of CPLTD	219 t-1	B1,603,000	0	0
Taxes current	348	B19,258,000	B14,622,000	B7,456,000
Changes in provisions for taxes	♠ 223	1,630,000	1,290,000	1,442,000
Cash Flow I (Cash available...)		*46,673,000*	*37,091,000*	*8,396,000*
...	...	...	...	...

Table 1: Technology of Objectivation – The Cash Flow Sheet

Information systems used on financial markets represent the market and at the same time allow carrying out transactions which in turn are displayed in the price movements. To give a simple example: the German share index (DAX) is, on the basis of 30 shares, calculated minute by minute. The calculation is carried out by a statistical index formula developed by Laspeyres which measures the development of the share value in correspondence to time variation (cf. Janßen/Rudolph 1992). This calculation has two effects: on the one hand it effects the stock exchange – thus the calculation effects exactly the entity which it has calculated; on the other hand the DAX is, in the sense of constitution theory perspective, brought into existence in and through the index formula. In other words: representation devices implemented in software programs shape the market and in doing so they take an active part in producing and sustaining it. Furthermore, these technologies create different lifeworlds within banking and financial markets because they both presuppose and create different forms of communication and decision processes.

The overall question – are these technological artefacts just tools in the hands of human actors or is it possible to assume that technological artefacts do act in their own right? – has been tackled by different schools in Science and Technology Studies. Actor Network Theory argues that non-human entities act and that these action frames human action. The core of human agency is thus a technically framed and performed interaction (cf. Latour 1999). The main purpose of this approach is to decenter the human subject and its role in sociological accounts, but one may doubt whether the semiotic notion Actor Network Theory makes use of is able to grasp all relevant elements of social practices. Furthermore, one may ask whether the separation of human and non-human worlds is not a too clear cut. For instance: in his conception of the embeddedness of economies into economics Callon (1998) proposes two separate worlds which are linked by the notion of »performation« (Callon 1998: 23), meaning the privilege of one world (economics) to act upon another (market economies). With this perspective Callon (1998) shifts sociological research on the realization of economic models and on the analysis of the role of cognitive instruments for economic practices.

Differently from Actor Network Theory, social constructionism in science and technology studies (e.g. Bijker et al. 1989) stresses the process of interpretation and stabilisation of technical artefacts and the social use humans make of non-human entities. The autonomy of technical artefacts is confronted with the actors' knowledge of how to act. It is stated that even though human actors may be framed by technical artefacts, they dispose of, produce, and invent them. In this sense one can speak of a turn from non-human to human actors, focussing (again) on human agency, taking into account the material reconfiguration of their lifeworlds as well as their human bodies in which their practices are grounded (cf. Pickering 1995; Rammert/Schulz-Schaeffer 2002).

For a sociology of calculation as outlined here the question to be taken into consideration is the status of economic representations and thus their frame of reference. In this respect it is possible to take an objectivist or realistic standpoint arguing for a strong correspondence between representation and reality. The problem – as already mentioned – is that the fact that economic figures and economic objects are rooted in calculating procedures is neglected. Neglected is furthermore the force which is exercised by representation devices themselves. Drawing for instance on Rheinberger's work on molecular biology (cf. Rheinberger 2001), it is argued that, through their performative function, economic representations have a constitutive effect on economic objects. The use of lists, tables or even maps makes use of the performative force of these devices. But these devices or models do not make things just visible; for a sociology of calculation it is far more interesting to conceive of these devices as a work upon economic representation that produces those economic objects which they represent. As I have shown elsewhere (e.g. Kalthoff 2002), representation devices are by no means neutral devices; they do not just depict reality ›out there‹ but represent them in a specific way and offering a specific view upon them. The second aim of a sociology of calculation is thus to investigate these performatives of economic representation and their relation to economic practices in more detail. Important, too, is to empirically investigate the constructivity of figures and thus to show how human actors produce economic figures in interaction with computer-related calculation tools.

Interpretation and Knowledge Generation

The third component to be studied are communication or negotiation processes within which the desire of seeing can be observed. So far, calculation has been treated as an example of operative writing. Referring to Heidegger one can state that calculation is not limited to operations with numbers: ›Computing in a broader, more essential sense means: to calculate with something. That means to take into consideration, to count on something, i.e. set into expectation‹ (Heidegger, 1954: 54; my translation). It also means: to form a judgement with something upon something – activities, in which images, categories and distinctions are involved. In his discussion of the ›world picture‹

Heidegger (1977: 129) underlines the empirical relevance of cognitive presentation (*Vorstellung*), arguing that getting a picture of something is equivalent to being in the picture, which in turn means to produce or to build something. To conceive of calculation as related to expectations or pictures widens the perspective on these practices. In other words: the technical calculation of numbers (e.g. economic ratios) is not the end of the story but rather the starting point of the process of ›calculating with something‹. Thus, following Heidegger, calculation can be understood as a form the desire of seeing can take on.

As I will show later by some examples, actors negotiate the figures they have calculated. They exchange different views on these figures, they try to figure out what the meaning of these figures might be and they develop a picture upon which they can agree. These situations are of interest for sociological research because what is said and what is written overlaps. In their sayings actors constantly make reference to written documents. With gestures and remarks they point out to what they are going to say, and they say what they read. For ethnomethodologists as well as system theorists, such collectivity – risk management-as-interaction – is not primarily integrated by shared beliefs but by shared procedures of doing or achieving things (e.g. taking a decision on a transaction). That is to say that the stories or sayings are not only »locally accomplished« (as a micro sociologist would argue), not only the outcome of a turn-by-turn exchange of co-present participants. Their stories are also the result of distributed and configured practices which are part of the overall procedures. The arguments they use enters the situation as a repetition or as a fabricated artefact: something which has been prepared long before enters the stage of these negotiations.

A strict differentiation between writing/literacy on the one hand and speech/orality on the other hand raises the question whether the production and social use of economic representation refers to a technology of writing or to a technology of talk. The third aim of a sociology of calculation consists in empirical research on how these two technologies constitute each other under these circumstances of seeing and interpreting economic figures.

3. Empirical Insights

The paper now turns to a more empirical part using research on lending business in international banks as an example (cf. Kalthoff 2006). The overall problem corporate banking departments are faced with is the economic time of the corporation and thus of the investment which makes the bank a player within the corporation. Banks are confronted with this knowledge problem, and related to it is the infrastructure of knowledge practices. Although direct observations are carried out in corporate banking and in investment banking as well, central to the knowledge practices of risk management are written documents (e.g. balance sheets, profit-loss accounts, market reports). In and through these written documents economic lifeworlds are represented.

Central to the work on and the production of economic representations is an infrastructure including the following elements: first, the technical tools of the production process. A global network of computer und software programs which supplies data, calculation tools and keep the data mobile. Second, the formats in which data are represented, ordered and assigned (e.g. tables, lists, maps). Third, a system of economic ratios (for instance »Return on Equity« or »Working Capital«). These categories classify economic practices and arrange them in groups. Fourth, procedures of calculation and economic models by which ratios and other economic values are calculated. These models exist themselves in a specific medium (»operative writing«, Krämer 1997a; 1997b). Fifth, the risk analysts themselves. As human actors they make use of technology, formats of representation and categories to figure out the economic time of markets, companies and the like. Their aim is to legitimate their investment decision in and through a coherent and plausible written representation.

The written documents local risk analysts produce are intended for in-house documentations called, for instance, ›credit proposal‹. These lay down the conditions of the corporate loan (e.g. amount, terms, covenants and clauses, securities offered), document the pros and cons of the loan, the economic situation of the company and the industrial sector involved, and further document the internal rating and its results, out of which the risk and the price of the loan are classified. The documents basically fulfil the function of making communication between the participants possible. This has two implications: firstly, the banking-driven documents are necessary in order for the participants to communicate at all. Negotiations are made possible through these written documents, which thus serve as a prosthesis of the oral. Secondly, the documents frame the standpoints maintained by the speaker within the context of negotiations because they are prepared, investigated, discussed and documented (see above). Thus, the speaker is not only an autonomous entity as it is conceived by a situationist approach but also a speaker who is cognitively adjust and prepared through practices of oral and written documentation which, in turn, are fabricated within the graded field of a bank. Furthermore, the negotiations are the social place where the interpretation of figures are stabilized and the business – and with it the risk – is constructed. A divided evaluation is made available and documented through recalculations, observations and anticipation; at the same time, the participants are always travelling on the fringes of what is predictable and therefore available as banking knowledge.

The problem risk analysts face is that their interpretation of calculated figures might fail due to, for instance, unforeseen economic changes. Therefore, agreements on risk are not final decisions, but they are monitored and left open for corrections and interventions, which are also partly regulated in the contract (the so-called covenants). At this point I will concentrate on negotiations, which subsequently take place between risk analysts of the subsidiaries (SU) and risk analysts at headquarters (HQ), who have to approve the credit proposal if the corporate loan exceeds the credit authority of the subsidiary. Risk analysts (headquarters) very often start conversation by questioning the quality and the plausibility of the documents received. In this respect they clarify the status of the documents. Headquarters doubt if they can trust the figures they read. Sometimes even the possibility of mirroring practices through economic representations is doubted. One example:

Extract 1

HQ1: ... You know we fear that the income statement doesn't give us the real picture.

SU1: You know the situation here in Poland is such that there is still some uncertainty how to properly set these figures up. We know from other companies also active in that field that they have similar or even equal statements. ...

HQ2: Yeah, but this financial statement was also qualified.

SU1: No, that is not true. That is not true ...

HQ2: Okay, you're right …

In this sequence headquarters explain that it seems impossible to get an adequate impression of the company's situation. This discomfort results from the fact that, firstly, the legal framework concerning accounting practices for leasing companies was not fixed at that time. Secondly, the audit firm made a remark on the tax situation of that company that was interpreted as a so-called ›qualified statement‹. In its reply the subsidiary argues with a practice of representation, which is common in this particular economic field. Furthermore, they successfully clear up the objection raised by headquarters against the financial situation of the company (›qualified statement‹). As local experts they explain how these figures are to be understood and how accounting practices are regulated.

After having clarified the documents' status, headquarters ask for further information about specific ratios, the company, the economic sector, the management and the technical procedures of the loan. One example:

Extract 2

HQ: ... In July there was an IPO and you mention in your credit report that there were international investors. Do you have a clue which are they? Some background about them? Is that a big Western European or US company ... or is it widely spread?

SU1: They are widely spread. We don't have any information that a big part of the shares belongs to one company.

HQ: Is it possible that the owner sells more of its shares? ... You know, it was not a substantial IPO. They sold only forty percent of the shares. And is it possible that the owner reduces his portion again?...

SU1: I think a few will be a major ownership of the shares. As we know he will not sell the majority of his shares.

SU2: He wants to keep it (to SU 1)

SU1: He wants to keep it.

HQ: You mentioned in the rating that ...

In this example headquarters are trying to figure out the management and the future ownership structure of the company. What motivates the questions is the wish to know with whom the bank will have to co-operate in the (near) future. Even if the subsidiary is sometimes suspected of withholding further information about the real situation of the company, in this case the participants only add a more or less vague assumption. Further questions concern, for instance, important items in the annual statement. After this clarification of questions concerning information and more technical aspects, the conference call shifts to the interpretation of the figures.

Extract 3

HQ: ... I also worried that the total credit line is quite high in relation to the company's equity.

SU1: Do you really think so? Do you really think so? When we look at other leasing companies, too, I don't think that's too much leverage.

SU2: We didn't agree with the statement that equity is low in this company.

HQ: Yeah, I am not saying it's low. What I'm saying is that if you look at the total credit lines it comes to about fourteen percent of the equity...

In this example headquarters express an argument which the participants classify as ›deal breaker‹. The credit policy of the bank group fixes the relation between the company's own equity and borrowed capital at ten percent. Later, in the course of further telephone conversations it emerged that the debt/equity ratio was about eighteen percent. A company leveraged too highly entails the risk of debt coverage. Reactions on the subsidiary side show that the question of leverage is an important and perhaps decisive point in the negotiations.

Finally, risk analysts negotiate the overall credit exposure the bank has with the company. This is an important point for every negotiation because credit stands for the bank's investment in a company. Since the credit exposure makes the bank a player in the company involved, the question is to what degree the bank will be committing itself. In this respect the function of headquarters is to control the involvement of the bank in a risky economic context. An example:

Extract 4

HQ: ... Is there anything we can do in the existing syndicated loan exposure? Can we reduce it? Can we sell it to another participant?

SU: Well, we can try at least from what I know. Well, we could do it of course. Yes. It's of course not such a big portion. Well, yes we could do that.

HQ: I mean, you know, just sell some of it off.

SU: Uhuh.

HQ: Is that market developing at all in Hungary or not? I don't have any idea.

SU: Well, not to the degree you're used to probably.

HQ: Right. So there is the ability to do it.

SU: Well, we could give it a try ...

In this case headquarters suggest a reduction of the current exposure – a portion of a syndicated loan – in order to approve the new credit facility. Even if the subsidiary is unsure whether it should agree to this or not, it is obliged to follow headquarters' suggestion because the ›ability to do it‹ is established. In their written report headquarters will lay down this suggestion as a condition for the new credit exposure. In this case, after the bank's portion of the syndicated loan has been sold on a debt equity market, the new commitment is fixed.

The problems the participants try to solve are encoded in these conversations. The subsidiary side tries to gain acceptance for its credit exposure which it has constructed and documented. It also defends its position against more general arguments coming from headquarters' side. As far as headquarters are concerned, they use the written documents to gain an impression of the company, the market, and the credit construction. To locate the possible blindness of the subsidiary they ask for more and more information, which they assume the subsidiary possesses. Also typical for such negotiations are reciprocally structured identifications: the subsidiary, for instance, is identified with the interests of the company and with an economic horizon which runs counter to the bank's policy. Headquarters are identified with general strategies which run counter to the local market and their potential.

What has been shown by these short examples so far supposes the dissolution of the traditional notion of a loan. What is not at stake is that a bank lends money to be put at the company's disposal, but that it undertakes economic co-operation by investment. The bank's credit process is, of course, structured by the distinction between the company and the bank. But this distinction is necessary in order to be able to perform the credit process at all. In this sense the notion of the credit process is a category of the field which establishes the capacity to act. With it the search for players is framed and the conditions of the game are encoded. This means that there is an assessment of an enterprise (the economic object) and a restructuring of the enterprise by the banks' investment, which makes the bank a player within the company. In this process numbers undertake the role of reducing complexity: they shorten, in other words, the decision-making process for the investment. However, as depicted they are not hard facts but rather ambivalent. In this context the function of the risk management department is not to avoid economic risk at all but to document it und to transform it into economic benefits for the bank.

4. Conclusion

The paper outlined an empirical research program for a sociology of calculation backed with a cultural and practice theory perspective. To speak of practices of calculation in this sense means to take into account the infrastructure of calculation (e.g. table, list, maps and their performative force), its technological embeddedness (e.g. computers, software programs and their theoretical model) and negotiations guided by interests, experience, bodily expressions and conversational moves. From such a sociological research one can expect, among other things, analytical insights into three important realms of economic practice: first, the use of writing to represent an internal relation of economic circumstances and processes of consensus formation within the community of the developer; second the accomplishment of calculation as a symbolic practice which allows to perform rationality and correctness of decisions as a play taking place within the interaction of the actors involved; third, the impact of representation devices and thus the logics of how these media represent economic objects and how their internal structure leave track on what is represented.

The aim is thus to understand these processes and activities as a social practice, its forms and materiality. It has not yet been determined how best to deal with the concepts of knowledge and practice themselves. Recent efforts (see Reckwitz 2003; Schatzki et al. 2001) suggest a range of possibilities. Included are poststructuralist approaches analysing systems of signs. They focus on how »things« are brought into a meaningful existence by ascribing signification to them. These approaches carrying out a relativization (known as ›decentring‹) of the social status of human beings to whom phenomenology and phenomenological sociology (cf. Husserl 1992; Schütz/Luckmann 1979; 1984) ascribe the competence of meaningful understanding. The constitution of meaning or signification is thus bound to individuals understood as subjects of everyday life. Posthumanist approaches, instead, argue while following Heidegger (2001) that the constitution of meaning is embedded in the bodily performed practice. Thus, social practices are placed within the context of socialities or activities mediated materially (for instance Garfinkel 1967; Pickering 1995). There are similarities to post-Wittgensteinian research (cf. Taylor 1995: 61pp), which embeds knowledge in the execution of practice, thus de-individualising it: knowledge is not known but rather produced, manifested and recalled within the framework of practices (cf. Coulter 1989). There thus exists a number of potential ways to build theoretically upon the sociology of economic knowledge-practices outlined here and to work with it empirically.

This article has placed emphasis on theory driven empirical research. Within the context of sociology of calculation outlined above empirical work means first of all qualitative research performing ethnographic fieldwork in calculating and developing organizations (1), conversation analysis of the professional everyday talk concerning »operative writing« (2) or discourse and rhetorical analysis following French or Anglo-Saxon schools of texts documenting economic calculation or representation in general (3). Empirical research carried out this way contributes, of course, to a sociological understanding of different local cultures working upon and with quantifying procedures. To open up empirical insights into these worlds of figures constituting a lifeworld in its own right is one important contribution of this research. Another important contribution concerns sociological theory on calculation which has to be further developed including the possibility to extend this research towards a sociology of economic quantification. This would imply a shift from the use of quantification procedures as a resource of inquiry to a topic of sociological research.

References

Austin, John L. (1992), *How to do Things with Words*. New York [1962].

Bijker, Wiebe E./Hughes, Thomas, P./Pinch, Trevor J. (eds) (1989), *The Social Construction of Technological Systems. New Directions in the Sociology and History of Technology*. Cambridge.

Bloor, David (1973), »Wittgenstein and Mannheim on the Sociology of Mathematics«, in: *Studies in History and Philosophy of Science*, Vol. 4, 173–191.

— (1987), »The Living Foundations of Mathematics«, in: *Social Studies of Science*, Vol. 17, 337–358.

Brown, James R. (1999), *Philosophy of mathematics. An introduction to the world of proofs and pictures*. London.

Butler, Judith (1997), *Excitable Speech. A Politics of the Performative*. New York.

Callon, Michel (1998), »Introduction: The embeddedness of economic markets in economics«, in: Michel Callon (ed.), *The Laws of the Markets*. Oxford, 1–57.

Coulter, Jeff (1989), *Mind in Action*. Cambridge.

Derrida, Jacques (1984), *Of Grammatology*. Baltimore.

Desrosières, Alain (1993), *La politique des grands nombres. Histoire de la raison statistique*. Paris.

Dreyfus, Hubert L. (2002), »Heidegger on Gaining a Free Relation to Technology«, in: Hubert Dreyfus and Mark Wrathall (eds), *Heidegger Reexamined. Vol 3. Art, Poetry, and Technology*. New York, 163–173.

Dreyfus, Hubert L./Spinosa, Charles (1997), »Highway bridges and feasts: Heidegger and Borgmann on how to affirm technology«, in: *Man and World*, Vol. 30, 150–177.

Falkenburg, Brigitte (ed.) (1994), *Naturalismus in der Philosophie der Mathematik*. Hamburg.

Foucault, Michel (1977), *Discipline and Punish: The Birth of the Prison*. New York [1975].

Harding, Sandra G. (1976), *Can Theories be Refuted? Essays on the Duhem-Quine-Thesis*. Dordrecht.

Heidegger, Martin (1991), *The Principle of Reason*. Bloomington. (*Der Satz vom Grund*, Stuttgart 1997) [1957].

— (1997), *The Question Concerning Technology and Other Essays*. New York.

— (2000), Vorträge und Aufsätze. Stuttgart [1954].

Heintz, Bettina (1993), *Die Herrschaft der Regel. Zur Grundlagengeschichte des Computers*. Frankfurt a.M.

— (2000), *Die Innenwelt der Mathematik. Zur Kultur und Praxis einer beweisenden Disziplin*. Wien.

— (2003), »When is a proof a proof?«, in: *Social Studies of Science*, Vol. 33, 929–943.

Hopwood, Anthony G./Miller, Peter (eds) (1994), *Accounting as a social and institutional practice*. Cambridge.

Janßen, Birgit/Rudolph, Bernd (1992), *Der Deutsche Aktienindex DAX – Konstruktion und Anwendungsmöglichkeiten*. Frankfurt a.M.

Kalthoff, Herbert (2002) »Geographic Space, Banking Knowledge, and Transformation«, in: Mihaela Kelemen and Monika Kostera (eds), *Critical Management Research in Eastern Europe. Managing the Transition*. London, 13–37.

— (2005), »Practices of calculation. Economic representation and risk management«, in: *Theory, Culture & Society*, Vol. 22, 69–97.

— (2006), *Zahlenwelten. Studien zur Praxis bankwirtschaftlichen Wissens*. Stuttgart (forthcoming).

Kalthoff, Herbert/Rottenburg, Richard/Wagener, Hans-Jürgen (eds) (2000), *Facts and figures. Economic representations and practices.* Marburg.

Kleinert, Ernst (2002), *Beiträge zu einer Philosophie der Mathematik.* Leipzig.

Krämer, Sybille (1996), »Sprache und Schrift oder: Ist Schrift verschriftete Sprache?«, in: *Zeitschrift für Sprachwissenschaft,* Vol. 15, 92–112.

— (1997a), »Schrift und Episteme am Beispiel Descartes'«, in: Peter Koch and Sybille Krämer (eds), *Schrift, Medien, Kognition.* Tübingen, 105–126.

— (1997b), »Kalküle als Repräsentation. Zur Genese des operativen Symbolismus in der Neuzeit«, in: Hans-Jörg Rheinberger, Michael Hagner, Bettina Wahrig-Schmidt (eds), *Räume des Wissens.* Berlin, 111–122.

Latour, Bruno (1999), *Pandora's Hope. Essays on the Reality of Science Studies.* Cambridge.

Livingston, Eric (1986), *The Ethnomethodological Foundations of Mathematics.* London.

— (1993), »The Disciplinarity of Knowledge at the Mathematics-Physics Interface«, in: Ellen Messer-Davidow, David R. Shumway, David J. Sylvan (eds), *Knowledges: Historical and Critical Studies in Disciplinarity.* Charlottesville, 368–393.

Luhmann, Niklas (1995), »Metamorphosen des Staates«, in: Niklas Luhmann, *Gesellschaftsstruktur und Semantik,* Vol 4. Frankfurt a.M., 101–139.

— (1998), *Die Gesellschaft der Gesellschaft,* Vol. 1. Frankfurt a.M.

MacKenzie, Donald (2003), »An Equation and its Worlds: Bricolage, Exemplars, Disunity and Performativity in Financial Economics«, in: *Social Studies of Science,* Vol. 33, 831–868.

Mannheim, Karl (1995), *Ideologie und Utopie.* Frankfurt a.M. [1931] (Ideology and utopia. London, 1968).

Mehrtens, Herbert (1990), *Moderne Sprache Mathematik. Eine Geschichte des Streits um die Grundlagen der Disziplin und des Subjekts formaler Systeme.* Frankfurt a.M.

Miller, Peter (1992), »Accounting and Objectivity: The Invention of Calculating Selves and Calculable Spaces«, in: *Annals of Scholarship,* Vol. 9, 61–85.

Otte, Michael (1994), *Das Formale, das Soziale und das Subjektive: Eine Einführung in die Philosophie und Didaktik der Mathematik.* Frankfurt a.M.

Pickering, Andrew (1995), *The Mangle of Practice. Time, Agency, and Science.* Chicago.

Porter, Theodore M. (1995), *Trust in numbers. The pursuit of objectivity in science and public life.* Princeton.

Power, Michael (1997), *The audit society. Rituals of verification.* Oxford.

Rammert, Werner/Schulz-Schaeffer, Ingo (eds) (2002), *Können Maschinen handeln? Soziologische Beiträge zum Verhältnis von Mensch und Technik.* Frankfurt a.M..

Reckwitz, Andreas (2002), »Toward a Theory of Social Practices. A Development in Culturalist Theorizing«, in: *European Journal of Social Theory,* Vol. 5, 245–265.

Rheinwald, Rosemarie (1984), *Der Formalismus und seine Grenzen.* Königsstein.

Riedel, Manfred (1984), »Logik und Akroamatik. Vom zweifachen Anfang der Philosophie«, in: *Philosophisches Jahrbuch,* Vol. 91, 225–237.

Schatzki, Theodore R. (1996), *Social Practices. A Wittgensteinian Approach to Human Activity and the Social.* Cambridge.

Shapiro, Stewart (2000), *Thinking about mathematics. The philosophy of mathematics.* Oxford.

Suchman, Lucy A. (1987), *Plans and situated actions. The problem of human-machine communication.* Cambridge.

Taylor, Charles (1985), *Human Agency and Language.* Cambridge.

Weber, Max (1985), *Wirtschaft und Gesellschaft. Grundriss der verstehenden Soziologie.* Tübingen [1922] (Economy and Society: An outline of interpretive sociology. Berkeley, 1978).

Wittgenstein, Ludwig (1994), *Bemerkungen über die Grundlage der Mathematik.* Frankfurt a.M. [1956] (Remarks on the foundation of mathematics. Cambridge, 1996).

Woolgar, Steve (1989), »Reconstructing Man and Machine: A Note on Sociological Critiques of Cognitivism«, in: Wiebe E. Bijker, Thomas P. Hughes, Trevor J. Pinch (eds), *The Social Construction of Technological Systems. New Directions in the Sociology and History of Technology.* Cambridge, 311–328.

Zerubavel, Eviatar (1982), »The standardization of time. A sociohistorical perspective«, in: *American Journal of Sociology*, Vol. 88, 1–23.

Cognitive Shifts in Regulation: The Role of Ignorance in the Regulatory Field of Accounting

Alexandra Hessling

1. Introduction

One of the core assumptions of positive accounting theory is that economic reality exists independently from financial accounting practices and that, vice versa, financial accounting provides scientific observations of the real world (Watts/Zimmerman 1986). Many scholars have convincingly questioned this understanding of unbiased accounting representations in recent years. Among these, many authors have assumed that the presented reality is a product of ongoing constructive and interpretative acts and that accounting numbers rather constitute than reflect economic reality. Following these critical comments on the traditional epistemology of representationism, this article focuses on accounting as a Janus-faced practice of revealing and concealing the world. It seeks to explore the paradoxical phenomenon that accounting involves on the one hand the construction of selective and contingent visibilities which facilitates a distinctive mode of cooperation and coordination, and that these constructions are on the other hand highly ambiguous. Even where organizational self-presentations comply with the rules, the relationship between financial statements and economic reality remains vague.

There has been a lively discussion on this issue in the social sciences[1], which long ago made its way into political and public opinion, particularly since the time when sophisticated accounting practices were developed and spread among business organizations. So why – from a sociological point of view – is the ambiguous nature of accounting once more worthy of taking note of? Through the lens of sociological systems theory, reassessing the ambiguous nature of accounting may clarify some basic dynamics of producing and handling knowledge and ignorance in the regulatory field of accounting. On this conceptual basis, the article aims firstly to explore regulatory problems that are arising from an increasing ignorance and knowledge-orientation. Secondly, it discusses the question: to what extent the regulatory field of accounting is open to cognitive modifications and is able to learn on a cognitive basis, and whether or not normative expectations are still needed to keep the regulatory frameworks from systematic enquiry. And it thirdly seeks to apply some basic theoretical concepts to empirically explore the peculiarities of ignorance and knowledge and the resulting regulatory issues in the field of accounting.

The article is hence divided into two sections. The first section concerns the *ignorance of accounting* from a conceptual perspective. Looking at various contributions to the critical accounting discourse, I will discuss how accounting constitutes social and organizational relations, and how it creates ambiguities at the same time (Section 2.1.). On these grounds, I will take a second look at the paradoxical phenomenon of accounting's certainties and ambiguities through the lens of sociological systems theory. Taking a counter position to the traditional epistemology of representationism, the dynamics of accounting knowledge and ignorance are being discussed from an operational constructivist point of view. From this theoretical perspective we can see that accounting not only creates specific patterns of visibility, but, due to its ambiguous nature, also causes regulatory problems which accountants, auditors and investors have to cope with (Section 2.2.). The second section sheds light on these *regulatory issues* from

1 The sociological discussion on this issue started with Frank Knight's and Daniel Ellberg's general contributions to uncertainty, risk and ambiguity. See Frank H. Knight 1921; Daniel Ellsberg 1961 and for critical comments Kenneth J. Arrow 1951. James March 1987, Bruce G. Carruthers 1995, Shanta Davie 2000, Ruth Hines 1991, Brendan McSweeny 1997, Richard C. Baker and Rick Hayes 2004, William H. Simon 2004.

different angles: Firstly, I will introduce a *de-centered understanding* of regulation that is inspired by some basic assumptions which are anchored in systems theory. These notions add up to a conception of accounting that is based on self-regulation and interdependencies of social actors, systems or networks. Then I will take a closer look at how social systems and regulatory frameworks are counterfactually closed according to their specific normative ideals and constructions of reality, but cognitively open to information, which is then translated into the language of the system (Section 3.1.). The following three sections are concerned with different regulatory shifts within the field of accounting. One example – *usable ignorance* – illustrates how cognitive efforts of accounting professionals and other experts in the field to specify this or that regulatory problem lead to adjustments of and additions to the conventional financial reporting systems. Here, one may think of the reporting gap between financial information and non-financial information and attempts to bridge this gap through intellectual capital statements (Section 3.2.). The second example directs attention to the *exploitation of ignorance* and sheds some light onto the complex interactions between regulations and the regulated. At this point, evasive accounting and management practices like ›income smoothing‹ or ›earnings management‹ come to the fore. Their appearance can be understood as a concomitant phenomenon rather than as an anomaly of accounting regulation. Here, dialectical forces between regulation and avoidance seem to be pervasive (Section 3.3.). However, the way regulatory bodies deal with these issues is being discussed in the next step. Auditors as well as accountants seem to soothe the ambiguities of accounting, and stabilize the normative ideal of a true and fair view in order to keep regulatory frameworks from systematic enquiry. Consequently, the ambiguities of accounting remain latent, unless accounting scandals cast doubt upon accounting numbers (*latent ignorance*) (Section 3.4.).

2. The Role of Ignorance in the Regulatory Field of Accounting

The critical accounting discourse has already provided intriguing insights into the paradoxical phenomenon of accounting's capacity to generate both order and ambiguity at the same time. The subsequent section brings some of the old arguments into recollection, and on these descriptive grounds, I will take a second look at the ambiguity of accounting through the lens of sociological systems theory. From this theoretical perspective, one can see the peculiarity that accounting's technical specificity and exactness enables organizations to observe themselves and others. But this inevitably means drawing a distinction between what is revealed through accounting and what is ignored. From this two-sided perspective on accounting, it becomes obvious that accounting does more than bring order into the world. It may as well be another addition to the »ramshackle technologies of modern governmentality, the latest wheeze of modernism as it performs diversities and fragmentations while dreaming of an impossible order« (Law/Akrich 1994: 215).

Notions on the Ambiguous Nature of Accounting

The concept of accounting ambiguities[2] basically refers to the capacity of accounting to reduce and to produce uncertainty and ambiguities at the same time. In the first instance this idea is based on a *critique of the traditional epistemology of representationism* according to which data are assumed to correspond with the reality that they purport to present, and in which accounting is thought to be a set of neutral devices for recording economic transactions. This belief that financial statements do, or could reliably represent economic reality is regularly proclaimed throughout most of the regulatory frameworks for accounting. From a normative perspective, this means that financial statements are considered an information medium, which has to

2 The term ambiguity, as it is used in this analysis, indicates in the first instance a state or quality of being liable to more than one interpretation. For a more detailed description of ambiguity see Daniel Ellsberg 1961, who refers to situations where available information is scanty or unreliable or highly conflicting. To clarify the link between ambiguity and decision-making see James March 1987. At this point one may also think of Karl Weick, who sees the organization as a system taking in equivocal information from its environment and trying to make sense of that information. According to Weick sense-making is an attempt to reduce multiple meanings (equivocality) and handle the complex informational data, used by the people in an organization. See ibid. 1995. Even though Karl Weick's *equivocality* might serve us as a term to describe the fuzziness of accounting in more detail, I prefer the term *ambiguity* – last but not least because the lively discussion on this issue more often than not carries the banner of ambiguity.

follow the overriding principle of a *true and fair view/fair presentation*[3] and has to have the primary qualities of *relevance* and *reliability*, which are thought to make accounting information useful for decision making.

The basic principle of a *true and fair presentation* is, for instance, described in IAS 1 – Presentation of Financial Statements – where it says:

»Financial statements shall present fairly the financial position, financial performance and cash flows of an entity. Fair presentation requires the faithful representation of the effects of transactions, other events and conditions in accordance with the definitions and recognition criteria for assets, liabilities, income and expenses set out in the Framework. The application of IFRSs, with additional disclosure when necessary, is presumed to result in financial statements that achieve a fair presentation« (IASB 2004: IAS1).

In comparison to the principles-based approach of the IASB, the FASB framework does not deal directly with such an overriding principle of *true and fair presentations*. But the FASB Concept Statement No 2 – Qualitative Characteristic of Accounting Information – recognizes relevance and reliability as the primary qualities that make accounting information useful for decision-making.[4] According to the Statement No. 2, the *quality of relevance* basically refers to accounting information that is capable of making a difference in decision-making by helping users to form predictions about the outcomes of past, present and future events or to confirm or correct prior expectations. The quality of *reliability,* however, is considered to have developed from two characteristics: representational faithfulness and verifiability. The corresponding definition within the conceptual framework explains this as follows:

3 While IAS 1 includes a *true and fair view* override, the FASB Concept Statement No. 2 does not provide the principle-based guidance necessary for making tradeoffs among the qualities of relevance and reliability and comparability and consistency. But the US equivalent to the IAS 1 can be found in Rule 203 of the AICPA Code of Professional Conduct, »which prohibits a member of the Institute from expressing an opinion that financial statements conform with GAAP if those statements contain a material departure from an accounting principle promulgated by the FASB, unless the member can demonstrate that because of unusual circumstances the financial statement otherwise would have been misleading.« See FASB 2003: 7

4 The IASB Framework identifies four qualitative characteristics that make the information provided in financial statements useful to users. The four principal characteristics are understandability, relevance, reliability and comparability. But the characteristics of relevance and reliability seem to be the primary ones in both frameworks IASB and FASB.

»The reliability of a measure rests on the faithfulness with which it represents what it purports to represent. [...] Reliability rests upon the extent to which the accounting description or measurement is verifiable and representational faithful [...]. Verifiability is a quality that may be demonstrated by securing a high degree of consensus among independent measurers using the same measurement methods. Representational faithfulness, on the other hand, refers to correspondence or agreement between the accounting numbers and the resources or events those numbers purport to present« (FASB 1980, Concept Statement No 2).

However, while most of the traditional accounting literature asserts that accounting is capable of successfully presenting the most truthful and fair views of reality, critical accounting scholars[5] have questioned this viewpoint. Instead, they assume a reflexive relationship between the two and claim that the presented reality is a product of ongoing constructive and interpretative acts.

But if – from an alternative standpoint – accounting is not thought to unambiguously reflect economic reality, how can we then understand *accounting's capacity to reduce ambiguity and produce ordering patterns of visibility*? In respect to the critical accounting discourse, I would argue that accounting reduces ambiguity by bringing ›order‹ 1) into business enterprises through its constitutive capacity of shaping social and organizational relations, and 2) into financial markets by facilitating coordination and cooperation between financial market actors: Within *business enterprises*, accounting seems to reduce ambiguities by »attributing financial values and rationales to a wide range of social practices, thereby according them a specific visibility, calculability and operational utility« (Miller 1990: 316). Accounting translates diverse activities and processes into a single figure and, at the same time, construes comparable entities – such as profit centers, cost centers, or strategic business units. »The labor efficiency variance, the return on investment of a division, and the net present value of an investment opportunity all share the elegance of the single figure. The objectivity and neutrality widely accorded to numbers achieves its most developed form« (Miller 2001: 2). Along these lines, accounting can be seen as a calculative apparatus that transforms business enterprises into what Latour calls ›centers of calculation‹, surrounded by a network of alliances (Latour 1987) These centers of

5 It may appear as an oversimplification to subsume the critical accounting literature without going into further details of different epistemological positions. But the purpose here is to draw a distinction between the traditional economic literature and the alternative or critical accounting research. For a review of the alternative accounting literature see Jane Baxter and Wai Fong Chua (2000).

calculation accumulate inscriptions that have been produced elsewhere in order to act upon sites of their production. Correspondingly, accounting numbers can be regarded as ›fabrications‹ that allow for ›action at a distance‹, linking the sites of their creation to places where they are accumulated and made subject to calculation Baxter/Chua 2003). In this regard, business enterprises are seen as sites of situated practices in which economic realities are actively created rather than just mechanically reflected on (Miller/O'Leary 1994b, Vollmer 2003). Within *financial markets* accounting standards reduce complexity and ambiguity by generating »a strong element of global order in the modern world, such as would be impossible without them« (Brunsson/Jacobsson 2001: 1). They seem to function as a normative mechanism that contributes to the achievement of a certain degree of conformity among standard-following organizations and to maintaining a broad consensus on the objectives of financial reporting. According to most of the conceptual frameworks, the objective of financial reporting is to provide information about the financial position, performance and changes in the financial position of a business enterprise that is useful to a wide range of users in making economic decisions. And indeed, accounting numbers provide financial analysts, bankers and brokers, specialized journalists, institutional and private investors, rating agencies and auditors with a basis upon which to observe, evaluate and compare organizations, branches of trade and even national economies. These options for quantification, surveillance and evaluation are inevitably linked to accounting's capacity to ensure comparability.

But accounting not only reduces ambiguities by bringing a certain degree of ›transparency‹ and order into our world. Accounting can at the same time be regarded as an *ambiguity-creating activity* because it is inevitably accompanied by the obscurity and indeterminacy of financial statements in several respects: On the one hand, financial accounting is linked to ambiguities because the elegance of the ›single financial figure‹ conceals the various and sometimes fraudulent ways and means of its creation, and thus, the underlying accounting and management practices. Accounting failures like Enron/Anderson or other fraudulent cases of earnings management exemplify that although investors and auditors carefully look for warning signals, it is beyond their power to draw the curtain of corporate disclosure. How business enterprises use their non-standardized freedom and how they use the legal form of transactions to obscure the economic substance remains opaque. Accounting can, on the other hand, become an ambiguity creating activity because it draws a distinction between what is accounted for and what is ignored. Financial accounting is strictly confined to financial information, while non-financial aspects like the firm's intellectual capital, the employee's knowledge or organizational competencies remain for the most part, invisible. According to this reporting gap between financial information and intangible assets, accounting engenders an interrelated problem – the paradox of visibility – insofar, as the pretence of true and fair view is inevitably accompanied by the obscurity and indeterminacy of financial statements. Aspects beyond the balance sheet such as organizational knowledge remain invisible, incalculable and incomparable. At first glance this might be seen as a trivial idea, but giving upon closer look one might agree with Shanta Davie who argued »it is such associations of accounting with multiplicity, manipulation and silence, that make the practice of accounting a fertile source of ambiguity« (Davie 2000: 316).

The Indifference of Money and the Role of Ignorance in Accounting

To put the paradoxical phenomenon of accounting ambiguities on theoretical grounds that direct the attention to basic dynamics of knowledge and ignorance as well as on the following regulatory problems, one might scan through various sociological theories. One rich source of essential ideas on the indifference of money – and thus the ignorance of accounting – is certainly Georg Simmels *Philosophy of Money*. In his final pages (Simmel 1900: 519pp) he finishes off with the statement that »there is no more striking symbol of the completely dynamic character of the world than money. [...] Money is nothing but the vehicle for a movement in which everything else that is not in motion is completely extinguished.«

But while Georg Simmel saw pure motion in money at this point, he located an absolute motionlessness in another instance:

> »As a tangible item, money is the most ephemeral thing in the external-practical world; yet its content is the most stable, since it stands at the point of indifference and balance between all other phenomena in the world.«

If we carry on these arguments and then assign them to the regulatory field of accounting, one can identify at least two sociological issues that are worthy of discussing further. One of Georg Simmel's lines of reasoning concerns the *dynamic character of money*, which from today's point of view is one of the most striking characteristics of financial markets. The growth of financial transactions »is close to 1500 trillion dollars a day, which is more than seventy times the daily volume of international trade of goods« is seemingly limitlessness (Goldfinger 2000: 72). And the economic landscape is obviously no longer shaped by physical flows of material goods and products but by streams of data, images and symbols. These, and other developments, that indicate a hyper growth and ubiquity of financial markets have triggered controversial debates on how to understand the revolutionary changes of financial markets, instruments and institutions. But what does sociology have to contribute to the discussion on the globality of finance? Anthony Giddens, for instance, perceives financial markets as a central aspect of what he calls the disembedding of social systems, a lifting out of social relations from local and national contexts (Giddens 1990: 21pp). In a similar way, Manuel Castells talks about spaces of flows in respect to the development of strong ties between social actors who are spatially divided (Castells 1989 and 1996). These spaces of flows bear similarities to Saskia Sassen's spatio-temporal configurations of the dematerialized/digital activities of finance, on the one hand, and materialized activities on the other (Sassen 1999). But while Saskia Sassen suggests overlapping spatial and temporal orders, advocates of post-modern approaches would disagree with this interaction based notion, and emphasize the uncoupling of financial markets from the ›real‹ economy (Heine 2001). At this point I could for instance continue with Skip McGoun's hyper-reality of global finance, or Karin Knorr Cetinas flow architecture of financial markets (McGoun 1997; Knorr Cetina 2003). Besides their different epistemological backgrounds, they basically share the idea of modern or global finance as a social reality sui generis. In terms of sociological systems theory, the emergence of this social reality has to be seen from an evolutionary perspective. Along with Niklas Luhmann's idea of society's functional differentiation (Luhmann 1977) into societal sub-systems such as economy, law, science etc., one may see finance as an autonomous system that has emerged from the evolutionary peculiarities of the economic system. Even though such attempts to conceive of global finance as an autopoietic system in its own right are being controversially discussed among advocates of systems theory, the obviously dynamic nature of money assigns modern finance its own systemic qualities.[6]

6 Cf. e.g. Alexandra Hessling and Hanno Pahl 2006; Helmut Willke 2006; Konstanze Piel 2003; Torsten Strulik 2003; T. Schmidt 1998. It must, however, be added here that the idea of money's systemic qualities is not new. It was Karl Marx who first provided insight into

Looking at the globality of finance from the angle of different sociological theories is one way to reconsider Georg Simmel's notions on the dynamic nature of money. The other is to put his notions on the *indifference of money* into more theoretically comprehensive terms. The indifference of money, in contrast toto all other phenomena in the world, is certainly one of the most striking characteristics of money. Through the lens of modern systems theory, one can clarify this idea with the help of Niklas Luhmann's concept of generalized media of communication. On the one hand, generalized media – like money, power or truth – render communication faster and more efficient. People are able to »join with others in a narrow world of common understandings, complementary expectations, and determinable issues« (Luhmann 1976: 512) because generalized media of communication are meaningful constellations of combined selectivity and thus make communication more likely to occur. On the other hand, the use of money as a medium of communication increases the degree of abstraction and generality. Its abstraction and generality takes monetary financial communication further and further away from the ›real‹ economy of things. And this makes money indifferent. It forces economic actors to present themselves exclusively in highly aggregated monetary figures, while any other aspect of economic and organizational life has inferior status. In this sense, money is the sýmbolon and the díabolon of the economic system. It mediates economic communication and distinguishes it from other phenomena in the world.[7]

It is in particular the self-referentiality of money and its capacity to distinguish between monetary issues and anything else in the world that accounts for the Janus-faced functioning of financial accounting. Financial accounting appears to follow the logic of money exactly: both money and accounting, it seems, feature a high degree of abstraction, generality and indifference. Both make monetary and financial communication more likely to occur, and, in regard to the diffusion of International Financial Reporting Standards, even on a global scale. And at the same time, both disregard anything other than monetary issues. The cost of this indifference is, however, that money and accounting deliberately abstain from all other forms of societal interaction. Other social phenomena are displaced

the shift from money as a means to an end towards money as an end in itself. According to Marx, money has to be understood in terms of self-moving abstractions and capital is thus to be seen as a self-actualizing whole. On this issue, see Hanno Pahl's article in this book.

7 See Helmut Willke's theoretical notions on money as a generalized medium of communication and as a symbolic system in this book.

in spheres, which are being ignored by money and accounting. This is why both are getting involved with zones of ignorance. Along with George Spencer Brown's *Laws of Form* one can trace similar two-sided forms back to the making of a distinction. Brown wrote, »Draw a distinction and a universe comes into being« (Spencer Brown 1969), and I would argue: so does financial accounting. [8] Financial Accounting draws a distinction between what is accounted for and what is ignored, it links up the visible and the invisible, transparency and obscurity. The peculiarity of accounting that it enables the organization to observe itself can be understood as taking a slice of the world, dividing the world into what is revealed and everything else. There is hence no complete and true picture of world that can be achieved through accounting.

Spheres of ignorance inevitably accompany every description of economic and social life. But these – once they are cognitively acknowledged – create the need for new accounting approaches, for instance intellectual capital reporting, and enable them to flourish. In this sense a certain kind of ignorance – »the express recognition of what is not yet known but needs to be known in order to lay the foundation for still more knowledge« (Merton 1971: 191) – may provide grounds for the need to specify this or that piece of ignorance and thus to revise the traditional accounting approaches. Robert K. Merton has called this kind of ignorance *specified ignorance* (Merton 1987), which in contrast to unspecified ignorance advances new forms of knowledge through disputes among experts or models of risk calculation.

knowledge		*ignorance*	
knowledge	specified ignorance	specified ignorance	unspecified ignorance
functional causality	dispute among experts	calculation of risk experts	catastrophe

Table 1: Forms of Knowledge and Ignorance. Source: Japp 1997: 304.

The concept of unspecified ignorance (Japp 1997), however, hints at other regulatory problems that are caused by an ignorance that can hardly be specified. They are the unmarked spaces of accounting or the incalculable

8 For critical comments on Niklas Luhmann's references to the Laws of form, see Boris Henning 2000.

risks investors are taking whenever they use publicly disclosed financial information. One important kind of accounting ignorance that may never be completely supplanted by its specification concerns the uncertainty whether or not and to what extent financial statements are decoupled from the actual organizational practice.

Formal structure has much more to do with the presentation of organizational-self than with how things actually transpire within the organization. Formal structure is mythical and ceremonial, a kind of symbolic window-dressing. Thus, much more effort is expended in devising official statements of procedures than in subsequently adhering to them (Carruthers 1995: 315).

A vivid illustration of substantial discrepancies between formal structure and organizational practice and even of how organizations use the legal form of transactions to obscure the economic substance underlying those transactions is, for instance, the spectacular Enron accounting debacle (Baker/Hayes 2004). This, and other accounting failures, show that although investors and auditors look carefully for warning signals, it is beyond their power to draw the curtain of corporate disclosure. How business enterprises use their non-standardized freedom remains unclear. Professional audiences, like trained accountants, may be the ones who can best handle the ambiguous and political nature of financial reporting. But still, the elegance of the single financial figure conceals the various ways and means of its creation, and thus, the underlying accounting and management practices.

3. New Forms of Regulation and Quandaries of Ignorance

The basic dynamics of accounting knowledge and ignorance, it seems, cause a whole range of regulatory problems. These may concern the ignorance of financial statements about intangible assets, the uncertainty about organizational strategies to exploit regulatory gaps, or general concerns about the quality of financial statements. The regulatory problems, however, basically arise from normative expectations such as a true and fair presentation and the related qualities of representational faithfulness and verifiability that are explained within the regulatory frameworks but which are, in principle, unattainable. No matter what accounting dilemma one may think of, organizations, accountants, auditors and investors have to cope with the fact that there is no such thing as a representation that mirrors the unbiased truth of economic life. All of the involved actors have to face the unmarked spaces of accounting, different kinds of specified ignorance or other areas of the not yet but must be known. Despite these uncertainties, there are different cognitive mechanism that stabilize the normative ideal of accounting and that enable accountants, auditors and investors to cope with the ignorance of accounting.

A De-Centered Perspective on Accounting Regulation

Today, the field of accounting is no longer regulated by the use of legal rules backed by sanctions. Command and control regulation, which assigned a particular role to the state, has been successively displaced by global accounting rules. It was when regulatory frameworks such as the IFRS and the US GAAP started to disseminate on a nearly global scale, if not before, that accounting regulation could no longer be regarded as governed by *the state*. Neither hierarchical forms of control, such as the iron fist of the state, nor the anarchical invisible hand of the market seem adequate for understanding the complex interactions among the different actors that are involved in the regulatory field. A concept that is instead more open for heterachical forms of co-ordination[9] – e.g. self-organization among mutually interdependent actors – seems better equipped to grasp how certain forms of control are exercised throughout society.

Generally inspired by basic assumptions of sociological systems theory, one may identify at least five keystones to specifying a such a de-centered and heterachical understanding of regulation:[10] 1) *Complexity of interactions:* In terms of complexity, a de-centered concept draws attention to

> »the dynamic interactions between actors and/or systems, and to the operations of forces which produce a constant tension between stability and change within a

9 Forms of heterarchy include inter-personal and inter-organizational networks as well as *de-centerd intersystemic context steering*. This basically involves efforts to regulate a social system by modifying the surroundings rather than through externally imposed directives. See Manfred Glasgow and Helmut Willke 1987 and Helmut Willke 1992.

10 At this point I follow Julia Black's *Critical Comments on Regulation* and her 5 essential elements that add up to a decenterd understanding of regulation. See ibid. 2002.

system (loosely defined). Those interactions are themselves complex and intricate, and actors are diverse in their goals, intensions, purposes, norms and powers.«[11]

2) *Fragmentation of knowledge and control*: From a de-centered perspective, it is not assumed that any actor within the regulatory field has all the information and instruments that are necessary to solve complex, diverse and dynamic regulatory issues. Instead, knowledge and control are dispersed to various actors and/or social systems and they construct images of their environment through their own cognitive frames. 3) *Autonomy and ungovernability:* A de-centered understanding of regulation refers to self-regulating, self-organization and self-reproduction of social systems which are normatively closed and cognitively open.[12] This means that no system can act directly upon another and any regulatory attempt will produce outcomes that are unintended. 4) *Interactions and interdependencies:* De-centered approaches claim that regulation is a product of interactions and interdependencies between all those involved in the regulatory process, and particular between regulator and regulated. These may very well extend beyond national territorial borders, especially in social spheres of global communication. In this sense, regulation is a two, three or four-way process rather than a unilateral procedure of command and control. 5) *Collapse of the public/private distinction:* In de-centered analyses the changed role of formal authority in regulation challenges the traditional distinction between public and private. The crucial point is that regulation now takes place in the absence of formal sanction under public law. Instead, the formal legal authority may be only one actor among others in a network or web of influence.

Together, all of these elements form an understanding of regulation that is based on self-regulation *and* interdependencies of social actors, sys-

11 See Julia Black 2002: 3. As to the interactions within the regulatory field of accounting one can identify the following actors: those involved in the regulatory frameworks of accounting such as the IFRS and US GAAP that convey the normative ideals of representational faithfulness, business organizations that have to comply with the accounting rules, the standards-setting institutions behind the regulatory frameworks e.g. the IASB or FASB, institutions of second-order-observation who control the compliance with the rules, and private or public investors as the main audience of corporate disclosure.

12 The traditional adaptation of Niklas Luhmann's theory of social systems suggests a relationship between the societal development and institutionalization of normative and cognitive expectations on the one hand and the differentiation of law and science on the other. At this point I would go one step further and apply the concept of normativity to other attempts at regulation than the one under public law. Here one might think of global finance as one social area where regulation is being exercised through a complex network of control.

tems and networks that solve complex, diverse and dynamic regulatory issues in quite different ways. But what does this perspective on regulation contribute to clarifying the question whether or not and to what extent the regulatory field of accounting is about to witness a shift towards a cognitive mode of regulation? Therefore one has to take a closer look at how regulatory frameworks and social systems are normatively closed according to their specific normative ideals and constructions of reality, but cognitively open to information, which is then translated into the language of the system.

From a systems theoretical standpoint, the function of accounting rules is based on the need for society to have *normative expectations*.[13] In regard to the field of accounting these have been institutionalized in regulatory frameworks such as the US GAAP or IFRS, which have been concretized in the form of explicit normative ideals such as a true and fair presentation and the related qualitative characteristics of accounting information. This mode of normative regulation has contributed to specific forms of social order and enabled coordination from a distance and among distant social systems. But the knowledge that is achieved through accounting ›representations‹ is at the same time merged with the ignorance of accounting. Especially in the course of increased social differentiation, specialization and knowledge-orientation in most social areas, the implications for accounting regulation include a higher degree of reflexivity and complexity. When confronting the obvious ignorance of accounting, the general normative principle is then influenced by processes of cognitivization and knowledge-orientation which may lead to a shift from normative to more combined normative and cognitive modes of regulation.

In today's economic landscape one can indeed find several examples for suchlike changes from normative expectations to forms of knowledge-based learning where both cognitive and normative elements are included. In the above illustration some examples for regulatory shifts at the boundaries of normatively closed expectations and externally decided dynamics are shown. The externally decided dynamics are assigned to three types of specified ignorance, which basically concern 1) disputes among accounting professionals, 2) possibilities of making profit from regulatory ambiguities, and 3) mechanism to keep ambiguities latent.

13 Normative expectations are peculiar because, unlike cognitive expectations, they are not modified when they are contradicted by events, while cognitive expectations are easily modified in the face of contrary experience.

	usable ignorance	*exploited ignorance*	*latent ignorance*
distinctive feature	disputes among experts and professionals	profit options from regulatory gaps	regulatory attempts to disguise ignorance
normative implications	specification of normative expectations	de-stabilization of normative expectations	stabilization of normative expectations
cognitive modifications	development of new accounting approaches adjustments within regulatory frameworks	regulatory dialectics of accounting regulatory trilemma	turning distrust into trust in numbers re-regulatory answers to accounting failures

Table 2: Forms of Specified Ignorance and Implicated Regulatory Changes

The first example – *usable ignorance* –[14] hints at the internal dynamics of accounting regulation which are closed to other normative principles than the ones a hand, but open to cognitive modifications at the level of actual authoritative statements on how particular types of transactions and other events should be reflected in financial statements. At this point, one may think of the current projects of the International Accounting Standards Board to improve and develop accounting standards for small and medium-sized entities, for business combinations or for financial instruments. These modifications are based on cognitive efforts of accounting professionals and other experts in the field to specify this or that regulatory problem, and thereby increase the internal complexity of accounting regulation. But the disputes among experts about how high-quality accounting standards must be assessed in order to attain transparent and comparable information do not only provide grounds for adjustments within the regulatory frameworks. They may also result in endeavors to develop additions to the conventional financial reporting which allow, for instance, certain non-financial aspects to be part of a firm's reporting system. However, beyond these forms of cognitive learning, the basis upon which the persistence of accounting is justified is still a normative one. Nonetheless, it seems that the quality of today's cognitive modifications differs considerably from previous processes of incremental adjustments. While there was always a certain degree of fuzziness within regulatory frameworks, the piling up of the architecture of knowledge and ignorance is intensifying the uncertainties of accounting regulation and enforcing more comprehensive regulatory changes.

14 The idea of usable ignorance traces back to Jerry Ravetz 1987.

A second basic field of combined normative and cognitive dynamics concerns the intricate interactions between regulation and the regulated – or more precisely: audited self-regulation – which is directed toward the *exploitation of ignorance*. The exploitation of ignorance has basically evolved from the dialectical dynamic of accounting regulation and evasive organizational practices such as ›earnings management‹, ›income smoothing‹ or ›selective disclosure‹. These organizational practices probably occur because accounting rules are necessarily applied under local conditions and are therefore subject to creative interpretation. Furthermore, regulatory gaps particularly seem to provide a gateway for organizational strategies of exploitation. But organizations do not only develop strategies of impression management (Clark 1995) by exploiting ambiguities within regulatory frameworks. They also seem to work out tactics for taking advantage of how they are being observed by others. Because they are able to observe how others observe them, organizations may find opportunities to exploit the unmarked spaces of external observation and thereby manipulate how they are being observed. These dynamics touch upon the options of second-order-observation and make clear what Niklas Luhmann has called ›skills of managing external observation‹[15]. Along these lines, one seriously has to think about whether and to what extent the existing regulatory frameworks provide incentives for evasive accounting practices. Re-regulative reforms that are being enforced in the course of such accounting failures must therefore have a cognitive basis which takes the complex interactions between regulation and the regulated into consideration if and when the regulatory field of accounting is able and willing to learn on a cognitive basis. Other attempts to directly influence the regulated may easily result in what Gunther Teubner has called the ›regulatory trilemma‹.[16]

The third example stresses the fact that accounting regulation still needs normative expectations that exist beyond the immediate forms of cognitive learning. In order to save the normative principles from systematic inquiry, regulatory adjustments are required that keep the ignorance of accounting latent. The *latency*[17] *of ignorance* plays a major role in the stabiliza-

---

15 In my own loose translation and in Niklas Luhmann's terms: »Geschick im Managen des Beobachtetwerdens«. Ibid. 2002:166

16 At its simplest the trilemma describes three types of problems than can arise in the relationship between regulation and the regulated: the regulatory model is either under-effective, over-effective or distorted vis-à-vis the ›target' system. See Gunther Teubner 1987.

17 According to Niklas Luhmann, latency is an important medium for securing social structures or even the latency of social structures. See ibid. 1984: chap. 8.

tion and protection of normative expectations (and normative expectations about normative expectations). Normative expectations may be counterfactual and may be disappointed, but will still go on to exist. But certain cognitive dynamics are needed to conceal and counterbalance the ignorance and Janus-faced functioning of accounting – especially in times of general concern about the quality of accounting numbers: One basic mechanism of transforming distrust in numbers into trust concerns the watchdog industry, which monitors and certifies the departure from or compliance with accounting standards. Another central mechanism for restoring trust in accounting numbers has to do with regulatory responses such as the Sarbanes-Oxley Act, which basically requires firms to consider and identify the limitations of their own disclosures. This trend towards the revelation of both the options and limits of information disclosure indicates that rulemaking is more and more oriented towards the self-handling of ignorance and ambiguity. This is not only to reduce the informational risks for the audience of financial statements, but also to put responsibility for regulatory failures on corporate managers. Even though it is quite conceivable that the audience of financial statements is involved in regulatory problems – do companies not try to meet or beat Wall Street earnings projections? – financial analysts and investment banks are usually exempted from harsh critique and discharged from accountability. Such dynamics, however, link accounting regulation much more closely to externally decided dynamics, which are subject to intricate mutual influences from time to time.

Usable Ignorance: The Knowledge Reporting Gap

From the angle of a second-order-observer and using a different language than accounting offers, one of the most striking examples of specifying ignorance is the sociological discussion on the emerging knowledge economy, where intangible assets are thought to be the main resource for value creation.[18] From this perspective, accounting technologies not only create

18 Due to an insurmountable plurality of different epistemological approaches, management theories and organizational studies, it seems extremely difficult to find an extensive definition of organizational knowledge, intellectual capital or intangible assets. Nevertheless, the concept of intellectual capital, as it is used in this paper, refers to three conceptual notions on knowledge: the difference between data, information and knowledge (Nonaka & Takeuchi 1995, Willke 1997b), the concept of ›knowledge work‹ (Drucker 1993, Reich 1992, Bell 1976), and the Hayekian idea of ›dispersed knowledge‹ (Hayek 1945).

visibility, they also entail a reporting gap between financial and non-financial information. As soon as accounting exclusively attributes financial values to a wider range of social practices, everything beyond the balance sheet inevitably remains vague. This perception of vague and inadequate financial information has not only encouraged practitioners and researchers to develop new accounting approaches to coping with the reporting gap.[19] It also has also mobilized political and public opinion in the cause of reform. In this vein, former SEC Chairman Arthur Levitt has declared:

»The dynamic nature of today's capital markets causes problems that increasingly move beyond the clear distinction between black and white. New industries, spurred by new services and new technologies, are creating new questions and challenges that must be addressed. Today, we are witnessing a broad shift from an industrial economy to a more service based one; a shift from bricks and mortar to technology and knowledge. This has important ramifications for our disclosure and financial reporting models. We have long had a good idea of how to value manufacturing inventory or assess what a factory is worth. But today, the value of R&D invested in a software program or the value of a user base of an Internet shopping site is a lot harder to quantify. As intangible assets continue to grow, in both size and scope, more and more people are questioning whether the true value – and the drivers of that value – is being reflected in a timely manner in publicly available disclosure« (Levitt 1999).

Although the importance of intangible assets and intellectual capital is largely recognized today, most of the conceptual frameworks still define intangible assets in a very restrictive way. According to the International Financial Reporting Standard IAS 38, for instance, an intangible asset should be recognized initially, at cost, in the financial statements, if, and only if: (a) the identifiable asset is controlled and clearly distinguishable from an enterprise's goodwill; (b) it is probable that the future economic benefits that are attributable to the asset will flow to the enterprise; and (c) the cost of the asset can be measured reliably. In a nutshell, the definition of intangible assets

19 In this instance one may think of the debate on developing new accounting approaches that started in the mid 1980s when Karl-Erik Sveiby introduced the concept of intangible assets to managers in Northern Europe and Scandinavia and one of the first models, which was designed to measure and manage intangibles – the *Skandia Navigator* – developed in the early 1990s by Leif Edvinsson when he acted as the company's Chief Knowledge Officer. See Edvinsson & Malone 1997. Apart from these models, there have been many other endeavours to make knowledge measurable and manageable. The liveliness of this debate among practitioners and researchers may in the end indicate that the ambiguity of accounting provides grounds for the need for new accounting approaches.

according to IAS 38 basically codifies the traditional accounting approach that excludes ›assets‹ that cannot be directly linked to revenue flows (Zambon et.al. 2003). The resulting reporting gap between financial and non-financial information – also referred to as the GAAP Gap (Litan/Wallison 2000) – is recurrently thought to be proven by the huge market-to-book ratios, which have increased dramatically in knowledge intensive organizations. These are based on the difference between the company's market value (stock market capitalization) and its net accounting value (financial statement), which is supposed to be equal to the intangible asset value.[20]

What does this commonly noticed GAAP gap tell us about the ignorance of accounting? It illustrates that the fabrication of accounting numbers is strictly confined to monetary forms of quantification, while intellectual capital can, due to its intangibility, be regarded as the ignored sphere of financial accounting. But the ignored sphere of accounting can, in parts, be specified. Looking at the emerging knowledge economy, qualitative new forms of production and work are coming to the fore such as information processing, symbolic analysis and expert systems which are successively taking priority over the traditional productive factors as land, labor and capital. And yet, the ignorance of accounting cannot be completely revealed. The specification of accounting's ignorance, in terms of a knowledge-reporting gap, is suffering under the same constraint. Thus, ignorance can not be replaced by additions to the conventional financial reporting which allow certain non-financial aspects to be part of a firm's reporting system. So neither financial accounting systems nor intellectual capital reporting systems provide for a more ›truthful‹ representation of economic reality. Instead, both engender specific patterns of visualization, narration and quantification – not in the sense of mirroring the unbiased truth of economic life but rather in the sense of constituting social and organizational relations. The lively discussion on additions to conventional financial reports must therefore not neglect one crucial point: the only way to pro-

20 In the same way the so-called »Q« method – »Q« stands for the ratio between the company's market value and the replacement cost of its intangible assets – developed by James Tobin claims to reveal the intellectual capital. Althoughthis and other methods to measure intellectual capital are offset by several problems associated with their use, they are widely accepted as evidence of on emerging knowledge economy where immaterial rather than material assets are the sources of value creation. See Stefano Zambon et al. 2003 and for the discussion on the emerging knowledge economy cf. Daniel Bell 1976, Peter F. Drucker 1993, Robert Reich 1991, Helmut Willke 1997.

duce data and information likely to be in accordance with the regulatory frameworks is to draw an incomplete picture of the world.

Exploited Ignorance: Dynamics between Regulation and the Regulated

Evasive accounting practices like »income smoothing« or »creative accounting« don't have to be seen as anomalies of accounting regulation. Since ambiguity in the interpretation of regulatory frameworks is unavoidable, accounting failures and regulatory adjustments may also be seen as a concomitant phenomenon of regulation. Along the same line, Michael Power argued, in his article *Standardization and Regulation of Management Control Practices,* that standardization projects are

»in constant movement and reform as local judgments, resistance, contingency and creative idiosyncrasy are both the conditions of possibility for any success in applying standards as well as the condition of their chronic failure. Standards, it seems, whether they claim their origins in national or international institutions, are necessarily applied in conditions which are irredeemably local and thereby subject to creative interpretation, bias, fraud and error« (Power 2002: 192–193).

Frank Clarke et al. even assert that the »departure of standards is, as often as not, the only way to produce data likely to accord with the financial facts« (Clark et al. 1997: 29). Whether departure from or compliance with accounting standards is the most usual case is not the discussion here, but rather the dialectical dynamic between regulation and innovation.

Earlier in this paper, it was argued that a substantial discrepancy between formal structure and organizational practice occurs when business enterprises use the legal form of transaction to obscure economic substance, even to the point of outright fraud – and once uncovered, the monetary losses can be staggering. The creativity of enterprises to exploit regulatory gaps has also been addressed by Arthur Levitt (1998) in his »Numbers Game« speech. He identifies a certain pressure that is imposed on business enterprises to meet earnings expectations and puts it as follows:

»While the problem of earning management is not new, it has swelled in a market that is unforgiving of companies that miss their estimates. I recently read of one major U.S. company, that failed to meet its so-called ›numbers‹ by one penny, and lost more than six percent of its stock value in one day. [...] This is the pattern earning management creates: companies try to meet or beat Wall Street earnings projections in order to grow market capitalization and increase the value of stock options. Their ability to do this depends on achieving the earning expectations of analysts. And analysts seek constant guidance from companies to frame those expectations.« (Levitt 1998: 3)

It thus seems that business enterprises use earning management techniques to ›smooth‹ earnings in order to meet internally or externally imposed earnings forecasts and analysts' expectations – a process that is usually rewarded on the stock market. »Managers engage in income smoothing activities because they know that volatile earnings streams typically lead to lower market valuations« (Maghrat & Weld 2002: 2).

However, this section does not aim to investigate the use of misleading accounting practices in more detail, but rather to draw attention to the dialectical dynamic of accounting regulation and evasive practices. This idea of dialectical forces between regulation and avoidance has already been described by Edward Kane:

»The tandem nature of regulation and avoidance is featured in a conceptual framework designed to dramatize the process of financial and regulatory innovation: the regulatory dialectic. *Dialectic* is philosopher's shorthand for a process driven by tension between a succession of paired opposites. [...] To apply dialectical thinking to the regulatory scene, the thesis and antithesis may be identified with *regulation* and *avoidance*, and the third stage renamed *reregulation*. In the dialectical view, all regulation becomes *re*-regulation, whose shape is determined by the precise history of prior regulatory problems« (Kane 1988: 332).

The model of regulatory dialectics suggests understanding creative accounting practices as reactions to regulation, and regulatory adjustments as countermovements to accounting pathologies. The strength of this dialectical version is the evolutionary perspective; it provides an explanation of how organizational strategies of avoidance work and how rule-setting bodies such as the IASB and the FASB, watchdog institutions such as the Security and Exchange Commission (SEC), or public opinion and public policy respond to these problems of regulation.

Latent Ignorance: The Role of Watchdog Institutions

Are the recent corporate scandals from Enron to WorldCom indicative of inadequate accounting rules? Are they evidence of corporate misgovernance, or rather warning signals of auditor incompetence? These and other issues are regularly raised in discussions on the three-way crisis in accounting, auditing and corporate governance. And it is very rapidly becoming apparent that the accounting failures in recent years may be the result of various interacting forces, and that complex interactions and interdependencies may be involved in regulatory adjustments. Those involved include: (a) processes of corporate governance, (b) laws and accounting rules, (c) internal and external auditors who determine that management follows the rules, (d) the SEC, self-regulatory bodies, and the stock exchanges that provide regulatory oversight and enforcement of the rules and laws governing disclosure and behavior, and (e) the outside rating agencies and financial analysts, who monitor and interpret financial performance (Financial Economists Roundtable 2002). To explore these issues in detail is definitely beyond the scope of this paper, but it would be interesting to discuss the Sarbanes-Oxley Act as a regulatory response to the problem of ambiguity and corporate fraud.

The Sarbanes-Oxley Act, which was signed into law in July 2002, is one of the most important pieces of legislation affecting corporate governance, financial disclosure and the practice of public accounting since the US securities laws of the early 1930s. The law's purpose was to rebuild public trust in America's corporate sector and, thus, to reduce uncertainty on financial markets. Basically, the Sarbanes-Oxley Act requires that publicly traded companies adhere to significant governance standards that give board members' broad roles in overseeing financial transactions and auditing procedures. Compared to the securities acts of 1933 and 1934, the Sarbanes-Oxley Act provisions are concerned with inducing internal controls. The CEO and CFO are required to confirm that »based on the officer's knowledge« they are not misleading, and then to take responsibility for designing »internal controls to ensure that material information relating to the issuer [...] is made known to such officers by others within these entities« (Sec. 302(a)(4)(B); 15 U.S.C. Quoted in Simon 2004: 40). While these provisions impose strong obligations on corporate managers, the older provisions appear to have assumed that external reporting obligations would induce the firms to arrange adequate internal information flows.

Concerning the provisions of the Sarbanes-Oxley Act Edward Kane (2004) assumes that SEC rulemaking has created asymmetry in obligations across the chain of information and disinformation production. According to Kane, the SEC has exempted the self-interested ethical codes of the auditing industry as well as the accounting profession from the actionable obligation to affirm the material economic accuracy of audited reports.

Other information producers – first and foremost corporate managers – have to face vastly stronger obligations. From this strong focus on corporate managers one could draw the conclusion, that the SEC makes a distinctive response to the problem of calculated ambiguity. It may be seen as a response to ambiguity, because it requires firms to consider and identify the limitations of their own disclosures. This point was made very clear by William H. Simon when he argued:

»Annual reports must now include an ›internal control report‹ that asses the ›effectiveness of the internal control structure and procedures of the issuer for financial reporting‹ [Sec. 404(a)]. They are specifically to identify ›all significant deficiencies in the design or operation of internal controls which could adversely affect‹ financial reporting [Sec. 302(a)(5)]. These demands to explicitly identify ambiguities and weakness may present a new stage in the evolution of disclosure law, one that resonates with the evolution of the modern business structure toward hyper-articulateness« (Simon 2004: 42).

This evolutionary perspective suggests that there is a major trend towards transparency and explicitness in both business and law. Dynamic businesses seem to emphasize practices of ›transparency‹ designed to inhibit ignorance and ambiguity, while rule making like the Sarbanes-Oxley Act strengthens duties of inquiry and clear articulation. If Simon is right with his diagnosis, technologies for creating visibility – such as accounting – will become more and more decisive and ubiquitous in today's economy and society.

4. Concluding Remarks

In this article I have reassessed the broadly discussed ambiguities of accounting on theoretical grounds other than those of the discussions in *Accounting, Organizations and Society* and *Critical Perspectives on Accounting.* Through the lens of sociological systems theory, I have explored accounting's peculiarity of mediating financial communication and distinguishing it from all other phenomena in the world. In order to clarify and conceive of the disregard for accounting representations concerning any other aspects than financial information, I have referred to Georg Simmel's *idea of indifference* and Robert K. Merton's *concept of specified ignorance.* Along these conceptual lines, any ›presentation‹ of economic and social life – and this also applies to financial accounting – develops spheres of ignorance that can, in part, be specified. The specification of ignorance – the recognition of what is not yet known but needs to be known – may then lay the foundation for adjustments within or developments beyond the regulatory framework. In a conceptual sense, I have added to the specification of ignorance its usage, exploitation and latency to designate multidimensional regulatory shifts within the field of accounting.

In doing so, I have posed one crucial question: Is the field of accounting about to witness a shift towards a cognitive mode of regulation? A simple positive or negative answer to this question would certainly be overhasty. By taking a closer look at how social systems and regulatory frameworks are closed according to their specific normative principles, but cognitively open to information from outside, I have identified combined dynamics. The field of accounting still relies on and will rely on normative expectations such as a true and fair view and a fair presentation, respectively. But today this mode of normative regulation is challenged and influenced by processes of cognitivization and knowledge-orientation. Processes of cognitivization can, for instance, involve the specification of regulatory gaps and in the following advancements of accounting knowledge as well as exploitative strategies on the part of business organizations. Whatever processes one may think of, they all indicate a shift towards combined normative and cognitive modes of regulation. As a counterbalance to these challenging dynamics the maintenance of the regulatory frameworks apparently requires a mechanism of stabilizing the normative expectations of accounting. In this sense, the latency of ignorance is essential to keeping the foundations of financial accounting from systematic inquiry. Here, I have argued that institutions of second-order-control and responses to regulatory failures play a major role in transforming distrust in numbers into trust.

With respect to the traditional research on regulation based on a state-centered approach this article suggests opening up the understanding of regulation towards including self-regulation and interdependencies among the involved social systems. The fact that the state is now considered one actor among others does not imply that accounting is perceived as a prime example for deregulation. On the contrary, my argument is that the field of accounting is a good illustration for de-centered regulation, which is based on mutual observations, normative expectations (and expectations about expectations) as well as about cognitive adjustments to the challenges of an emerging global knowledge economy. Forms of cognitive learning, however, seem to successively pervade the whole regulatory field. Whereas in the past, regulatory frameworks were developed on the level of the nation-state and oftentimes adjusted under public law, self-regulation and interdependencies – which are now global in scope – vitiate normative elements of accounting regulation. Particularly since dynamics of knowledge and ignorance permeate the field of accounting, cognitivization turns out to be the distinctive feature of change in global accounting regulation.

References

Arrow, Kenneth J. (1951), »Alternative Approaches to the Theory of Choice in Risk-taking Situations«, in: *Econometrica*, Vol. 19, 417–426.

Baker, C. Richard/Hayes, Rick (2004), »Reflecting form over substance: the case of Enron Corp«, in: *Critical Perspectives on Accounting*, Vol. 15, 767–785.

Baxter, Jane/Chua, Wai Fong (2003), »Alternative Management Accounting Research – Whence and Wither«, in: *Accounting, Organizations, and Society*, Vol. 28, 97–126.

Bell, Daniel (1976), *The Coming of Post-Industrial Society. A Venture in Social Forecasting.* New York (first edition 1973).

Black, Julia (2002), »Critical Reflections on Regulation«, *CARR Discussion Paper Series DP 4*, London.

Brunsson, Nils (1989), *The Organization of Hypocrisy – Talk, Decisions and Actions in Organizations.* Chichester.

— (1998), »Homogeneity and Heterogeneity in Organizational Forms as the Result of Cropping-up Processes«, in: Nils Brunsson and Johan Olsen (eds), *Organizing Organizations.* Copenhagen, 259–278.

Brunsson, Nils/Jacobsson, Bengt (2000), »The Contemporary Expansion of Standardization«, in: Nils Brunsson and Bengt Jacobsson (eds), *A World of Standards.* Oxford, 1–16.

Carruthers, Bruce G. (1995), »Accounting, Ambiguity, and the New Institutionalism«, in: *Accounting, Organizations and Society*, Vol. 20, 313–328.

Castells, M. (1989), *The Informational City. Information Technology, Economic Restructuring, and the Urban-Regional Process.* Oxford.

Chandler, Alfred D. (1977), *The Visible Hand: The Managerial Revolution in American Business.* Cambridge.

Clarke, Frank/Dean, Graeme/Oliver, Kyle (1997), *Corporate Collapse: Regulatory, Accounting and Ethical Failure.* Cambridge.

Clark, Timothy (1995), *Managing Consultants: Consultancy as the Management of Impressions.* Buckingham.

Covaleski, Mark A./Dirsmith, M.W. (1988), »An Institutional Perspective on the Rise, Social Transformation, and Fall of a University Budget Category«, in: *Administrative Science Quarterly*, Vol. 33, 562–587.

Davie, Shanta S. K. (2000), »The Significance of Ambiguity in Accounting and Everyday Life, The Self-Perpetuation of Accounting«, in: *Critical Perspectives on Accounting*, Vol. 11, 311–334.

Drucker, Peter F. (1993), *Post-Capitalist Society*. New York.

Edvinsson, L./Malone, M.S. (1997), *Intellectual Capital. Realizing your Company's true Value by Finding its Hidden Brainpower*. New York.

Ellsberg, Daniel (1961), »Ambiguity, and the Savage Axioms«, in: *Quarterly Journal of Economics*, Vol. 75, 643–669.

FASB (1980), *Statement of Financial Accounting Concepts No. 2: Qualitative Characteristics of Accounting Information*. Norwalk.

— (2003), »Proposal for a Principles-Based Approach to U.S. Standard Setting«, File Reference No. 1125–001. http://www.fasb.org/proposals/principles-based_approach.pdf.

Fligstein, Neil (1990), *The Transformation of Corporate Control*. Cambridge.

Giddens, Anthony (1990), *The Consequences of Modernity*. Cambridge.

Global Reporting Initiative (GRI) (2000), *Sustainability Reporting Guidelines on Economic, Environmental, and Social Performance*. Boston.

Goldfinger, C. (2000), »Intangible Economy and Financial Markets«, in: *Communications & Strategies*, Vol. 40, 59–89.

von Hayek, Friedrich A. (1945), »The Use of Knowledge in Society«, in: *American Economic Review*, Vol. 35, 519–530.

Heine, M. (2001), »Die Entkopplungsthese – eine kritische Würdigung«, in: Arne Heise (ed.), *Neue Weltwährungsarchitektur*. Marburg, 25–40.

Hennin, Boris (2000), »Luhmann und die Formale Mathematik«, in: Peter-Ulrich Merz-Benz/Gerhard Wagner (eds), *Die Logik der Systeme. Zur Kritik der systemtheoretischen Soziologie Niklas Luhmanns*. Konstanz.

Hessling, Alexandra/Pahl, Hanno (2006), »The Global System of Finance. Scanning Talcott Parsons and Niklas Luhmann for Theoretical Keystones«, in: *American Journal of Economics and Socioloy*, Vol. 65, 189–218.

Hines, Ruth D. (1991), »The FASB's conceptual framework, financial accounting and the maintenance of the social world«, in: *Accounting, Organizations and Society*, Vol. 16, 313–331.

IASB (2004), »IAS 1: Presentation of Financial Statements«, http://www.ifrs-portal.com/Standards_en_neu/IAS_01_en/index.htm.

Japp, Klaus P. (1997), »Die Beobachtung von Nichtwissen«, in: *Soziale Systeme*, Vol. 3, 289–312.

Johnson, H. Thomas/Kaplan, Robert S. (1987), *Relevance Lost. The Rise and Fall of Management Accounting*. Boston.

Kane, Edward J. (1988), »Interaction of Financial and Regulatory Innovation«, in: *American Economic Review*, Vol. 78, 328–334.

— (2004), »Continuing Dangers of Disinformation in Corporate Accounting Reports«, in: *Review of Financial Economics*, Vol. 13, 149–164.

Kaplan, Robert S./Norton, David P. (1992), »The Balanced Scorecard – Measures that Drive Performances«, in: *Harvard Business Review*, Vol. 70, 71–79.

Knight, Frank H. (1921), *Risk, Uncertainty and Profit.* Boston.

Knorr Cetina, Karin (2003), »From Pipes to Scopes: The Flow Architecture of Financial Markets«, in: *Journal Distinktion*, Vol. 7 (Special Issue on Economic Sociology), 7–23.

Latour, Bruno (1987), *Science in Action.* Cambridge.

Law, John/Akrich, Madelaine (1994), »On Customers and Costs: A Story from Public Sector Science«, in: Michael Power (ed.), *Accounting and Science: Natural Inquiry and Commercial Reason.* Cambridge, 195–218

Lee, Tom A. (1984), *Cash Flow Accounting.* Wokingham.

Levitt, A. (1998), *The numbers game.* Text of remarks delivered at the NYU Center for Law and Business, New York, September 28, 1998.

— (1999) *Remarks to the Panel on Audit Effectiveness of the Public Oversight Board.* Speech by SEC Chairman at the Public Oversight Hearing in New York, October 9, 1999.

Litan, Robert E./Wallison, Peter J. (2000), *The GAAP Gap. Corporate Disclosure in the Internet Age.* Washington D.C.

Luhmann, Niklas (1976), »Generalized Media and the Problem of Contingency«, in: Jan J. Loubser/R.C. Baum/A. Effrat/V. Meyer Lidz (eds), *Explorations in General Theory in Social Sciences Volume Two.* New York, 507–532.

— (1977), »Differentiation of society«, in: *Canadian Journal of Sociology*, Vol. 3, 29–52.

— (1984), *Soziale Systeme.* Frankfurt am Main.

— (2002), *Einführung in die Systemtheorie.* Edited by Dirk Baecker. Heidelberg.

Maghrat, Lorraine/Weld, Leonard G. (2002), »Abusive Management and Early Warning Signs«, in: *The CPA Journal*, Vol. 8, 1–5.

March, James G. (1987), »Ambiguity and Accounting: The Elusive Link between Information and Decision Making«, in: *Accounting, Organizations and Society*, Vol. 12, 153–168.

McGoun (1997), »Hyperreal Finance«, in: *Critical Perspectives on Accounting*, Vol. 8, 97–122.

McSweeny, Brendan (1997), »The Unbearable Ambiguity of Accounting«, in: *Accounting, Organizations and Society*, Vol. 22, 691–712.

Merton, Robert K. (1971), »The precarious foundations of detachment in sociology«, in: Edward A. Tiryakian (ed.), *The Phenomenon of Sociology.* New York, 188–99.

— (1987), »Three Fragments from a Sociologist's Notebook: Establishing the Phenomenon, Specified Ignorance, and Strategic Research Materials«, in: *Annual Review of Sociology*, Vol. 13, 1–28.

Meyer, John (1994), »Social Environments and Organizational Accounting«, in: W. Richard Scott/John Meyer (eds), *Institutional Environments and Organizations. Structural Complexity and Individualism.* Thousand Oaks.

Meyer, John/Rowan, Brian (1977), »Institutionalized Organizations: Formal Structure as Myth and Ceremony«, in: *American Journal of Sociology*, Vol. 83, 340–363.

Meyer, John et al. (1997), »World Society and the Nation State«, in: *American Journal of Sociology*, Vol. 103, 144–181.

Miller, Peter (1990), »On the Interrelations Between Accounting and the State«, in: *Accounting, Organizations and Society*, Vol. 15, 315–338.

— (1994a), »Accounting as social and institutional practice: an introduction«, in: Anthony G. Hopwood and Peter Miller (eds), *Accounting as Social and Institutional Practice*. Cambridge.

Miller, Peter/O'Leary, Ted (1994b), »The factory as a laboratory«, in: Michael Power (ed.), *Accounting and Science: Natural Inquiry and Commercial Reason*. Cambridge.

Miller, Peter (2001), »Governing by Numbers: Why Calculative Practices Matter«, in: *Social Research*, Vol 68I, 379–396.

Mouritsen, Jan/Larsen, H.T/Buk, P. N. D. (2001), »Intellectual capital and the ›capable firm‹: narrating, visualising and numbering for managing knowledge«, in: *Accounting, Organizations and Society*, Vol. 26, 735–762.

Nonaka, Ikujiro/Takeuchi, Hirotaki (1995), *The Knowledge-Creating Company. How Japanese Companies Create the Dynamics of Innovation*. New York.

Piel, Konstanze (2003), *Ökonomie des Nichtwissens. Aktienhype und Vertrauenskrise im Neuen Markt*. Frankfurt a.M.

Polanyi, Michael (1958), *Personal Knowledge*. Chicago.

Power, Michael (2002), »Standardization and the Regulation of Management Control Practices«, in: *Soziale Systeme*, Vol. 8, 191–204.

Rammert, Werner (2002), »The Governance of Knowledge, Limited: The rising relevance of non-explicit knowledge under a new regime of distributed knowledge production«, *TUTS-WP-1–2002*. Technische Universität Berlin, Institut für Soziologie. Technology Studies. Berlin.

Ravetz, Jerry (1987), »Usable Knowledge, Usable Ignorance«, in: W.C. Clarke and R.E. Munn (eds), »Sustainable Development of the Biosphere«, in: *Knowledge*, Vol. 9, 87–116.

Reich, Robert B. (1991*), The Work of Nations: Preparing Ourselves for the 21st Century Capitalism*. New York.

Sassen, Saskia (1999), »Spatialities and Temporalities of the Global: Elements for a Theorization«, in: *Public Culture: Society for Transnational Cultural Studies* 2. Millenial Quartet, 215–232.

Schmidt, Tobias (1998), *Zur Erschließung der Theorie sozialer Systeme für Untersuchungen des Finanziellen Sektors*. Berlin.

Simmel, Georg (1900), *Philosophie des Geldes*. Berlin.

Simon, William H. (2004), »Wrongs of Ignorance and Ambiguity: Lawyer Responsibility for Collective Misconduct«, *Columbia Public Law & Legal Theory Working Papers*, Paper 0480. Columbia Law School, Berkeley.

Strulik, Torsten (2004), *Nichtwissen und Vertrauen in der Wissensökonomie*. Frankfurt a.M.

Suzuki, Tomo (2003), »The accounting figuration of business statistics as a foundation for the spread of economic ideas«, in: *Accounting, Organizations and Society*, Vol. 28, 65–95.

Sveiby, Karl E. (1997), *The New Organizational Wealth: Managing & Measuring Knowledge-Based Assets*. San Francisco.

Teubner, Gunther (1987), »Juridification: Concepts, Aspects, Limits, Solutions«: in Gunther Teubner (ed.), *Juridification of Social Spheres: A Comparative Analysis in the Areas of Labor Corporate, Antitrust and Social Welfare Law*. European University Institute.

Vollmer, Hendrik (2003), »Bookkeeping, Accounting, Calculative Practice: The Sociological Suspense of Calculation«, in: *Critical Perspectives on Accounting*, Vol. 14, 353–381.

Watts, Ross L./Zimmerman, Jerold L. (1986), *Positive Accounting Theory*. Englewood Cliffs/NJ.

Weick, Karl E. (1995), *Sensemaking in Organizations*. Thousand Oaks.

Willke, Helmut (1992), *Ironie des Staates. Grundlinien einer Staatstheorie polyzentrischer Gesellschaft*. Frankfurt a.M.

— (1997a), »Autopoiesis and Organised Complexity«, *Paper prepared for the LSE Complexity Study Group Meeting No.* 3, 18 June 1997.

— (1997b), »Organisierte Wissensarbeit«, in: *Zeitschrift für Soziologie*, Vol. 27, 161–177.

Willke, Helmut/Glagow, Manfred (1987), *Dezentrale Gesellschaftssteuerung. Probleme der Integration polyzentrischer Gesellschaft*. Pfaffenweiler

Zambon, Stefano/Lev, Baruch/Abernethy, Margaret/Wyatt, Ann/Bianchi, Patrizio/Labory, Sandrine (2003), *Study on the Measurement of Intangible Assets and Associated Reporting Practices*. Prepared for the Commission of the European Communities Enterprise Directorate General.

Zorn, Dirk/Dobbin, Frank (2003), »Too Many Chiefs? How Financial Markets Reshaped the American Firm«, *Paper prepared for Constance Conference on Social Studies of Finance: Inside Financial Markets*. University of Constance, May 2003.

Part 3

The Importance of Private Expertise in Financial Governance

The Role of Policy Communities in Global Financial Governance: A Critical Examination of the Group of Thirty

Eleni Tsingou

1. Introduction

The Group of Thirty (G-30) is a non-state organization that, as this chapter argues, has had an important impact on financial regulatory and supervisory practices both at the national and global levels. This chapter provides an overview of the role of the group and its policy-making functions and concludes that the G-30 has played a significant part in altering and harmonising transnational practices of regulation and supervision. The G-30 is, of course, just one player with authority over financial policy-making. However, as part of a developing transnational policy community, it has successfully presented a coherent case in favour of public-private sector interaction and of delegation of authority to private actors and, as subsequent analysis indicates, has been a key factor in the outcome of some important regulatory debates. In doing so, it has contributed to the emergence of a mix of public and private authority in global finance underpinned by expertise and has considerably strengthened the role of private interests in the functions of regulation and supervision.

The G-30 brings together officials from both the public and private sectors and as an organization, can be best characterised as positioned halfway between an interest group and a think tank; it is very much a new form of non-state actor and an example of new patterns of financial governance. The group also represents one instance of public-private sector interchange, and of growing private authority in a vital public policy domain. In particular, the group has been active in the shaping of policy concerning three major financial issues: the efficiency and harmonisation of the clearance and settlement of securities; the regulatory treatment of over-the-counter derivative instruments; and the focus on global institutions in the handling of systemic risk. The analysis explains that the G-30, despite its non-official status, had a key role and considerable influence over the resulting regulatory and supervisory policies for these financial instruments and procedures: the G-30 was purposefully involved in governance processes through explicit delegation of authority or informal assigning of functions; its recommendations were openly adopted by the relevant bodies; and the group was widely and publicly acknowledged for its governance role and its contribution to shaping policy by the wider transnational policy community of public and private practitioners.

The chapter is organised in four parts. The first part draws on theoretical debates in International Political Economy to explain the growing importance of non-state actors in policy processes. Part 2 provides an empirical presentation of the G-30 and Part 3 proceeds to explain how policy communities gain influence and, also, authority functions. Finally, the chapter addresses some normative questions resulting from the changing nature of accountability and legitimacy in global financial governance.

2. Theoretical Debates

The case of the G-30 as an actor with authority in the financial markets is at the center of International Political Economy (IPE) debates on governance and authority. The main conceptual themes raised by the study of the G-30 relate to the nature of financial governance under conditions of financial integration on a global scale; the emergence of private authority in global finance and the new types of actor involved in the process; the position of non-state actors in relation to other actors with functions in the process of governance and their interaction in the making of policy; the principal characteristics of the transnational policy process in terms of preferences and content; the role of knowledge and technical expertise; and the related questions of the legitimacy and accountability of actors with financial governance functions.

Financial markets have changed substantially in recent years, most notably in terms of liberalisation and innovation (Kaufman 2000). Markets are becoming increasingly transnational, and large and key financial institutions favour and promote non-interventionist practices. These developments have taken place against a backdrop of enthusiasm for neoliberal ideas (Helleiner 1994); financial liberalisation followed the economic crises of the 1970s and was backed by the ascendancy of the Chicago school of economic thought and the adoption of the economic principles it advocated by policy-makers. The »ideology of the market« was thus simultaneously being put forward by public officials, international organizations and banks and securities firms (Agnew and Corbridge 1995: 164). The degree of transnationalisation, however, needs further explaining. The transnational restructuring of the financial sector does not only relate to the level at which financial transactions take place but also, the preferred level of policy-making. This analysis, through an examination of the G-30, an organization that operates at that level, sheds light on how and why preferences are determined and formulated on a transnational basis.

With the opening up of markets, business institutions were able to pursue the goal of minimal regulatory interference by exploiting gaps in the system and taking advantage of »convenient jurisdictional locations« (Bratton et al. 1996: 9). In turn, states adapted to these circumstances and acted accordingly, making liberalisation a competitive tool in attracting investment (Cerny 1993; Moran 1991). This trend is only partly mitigated by the existence of multilateral bodies such as the Basel Committee on

Banking Supervision (Basel Committee), which mostly react to financial developments and whose regulatory and supervisory initiatives are lengthy processes. These circumstances have enabled the private sector to take a leading role in shaping of the financial system and policy. The complexity and speed of financial innovation have also put banks and securities firms in a privileged position as knowledge holders. Public authorities lag behind in terms of technical capabilities and expertise. If regulators and supervisors can't keep up with the development of financial products that are complex, often tailor-made and used by a variety of institutions and firms, they cannot regulate effectively (Steinherr 1998). As a result, private initiatives gradually take over important functions and promote standards based on private practice. This transfer of authority is further assisted by the reputation of ›finance‹ as complicated and technical. Financial issues attract limited attention and it appears that there is »low domestic visibility of the issue of financial liberalisation among politicians and the general public« (Helleiner 1994: 19). While several aspects of globalization have caused concern among constituents, finance has to date mostly remained out of the limelight. The topics of derivatives and systemic risk have made it onto the front pages of newspapers, nevertheless, general interest was short-lived and the policy role of the private sector has not been seriously challenged.

What do these developments mean for our understanding of governance and what is the nature of authority in financial markets? The process of the weakening of state authority in financial matters is well documented; »where states were once the masters of markets, now it is the markets which, on many crucial issues, are the masters over the governments of states« (Strange 1996: 4). This »retreat of the state« thesis has been challenged, and it is understood that states often delegate authority and that the latter is made up of a »mix of public and private categories« (Pauly 2002: 77). In order to conceptualise authority we are urged to differentiate between government and governance and incorporate a wider variety of actors, including non-state entities (Rosenau 1992). The concept of »spheres of authority« is also valuable, separating governance from territorial boundaries and associating it with a particular sector (Rosenau 1997). Authority is not exclusively related to the public arena but to legitimacy (Friedman 1990) and »private authority can … evoke a sense of legitimacy and achieve a high degree of acceptance through recognition by others of specific knowledge, expertise, and representational skills« (Cutler et al. 1999a: 18).

This is not a novel trend. Many national economies, predominantly in Western Europe, were organised according to corporatist principles, bringing together the state, business and labour. Delegation of authority to these groups took the form of »private interest government« (Streeck and Schmitter 1985). What we experience today is an altered version of corporatism, with labour out of the equation and increased emphasis on the international/transnational level (Cox 1996). Moreover, there is a tradition of self-regulation in financial industries, especially in the United States and the United Kingdom, and a long history of more or less formal public-private sector interaction (Coleman 1994; Moran 1991). Nevertheless, the crash of 1929 and the subsequent recession brought about strong public agencies and, despite private sector involvement, for most of the twentieth century, there was some clarity with regards to public and private functions, with regulation and supervision firmly in the hands of public authorities. This is now changing.

Non-state actors are independent of state authorities, at least in principle (Josselin and Wallace 2001). In the context of financial market governance, some such actors may be economic agents as such (private institutions) and others aggregate and act for the interests of particular segments of a sector (industry associations). Yet another set of non-state actors has, however, emerged: these often act at the transnational level and provide more informal settings for financial experts with no set representative agenda. These new actors »often convey and/or appear to have been accorded some form of legitimate authority ... They claim to be, perform as, and are recognised as legitimate by some larger public (that often includes states themselves) as authors of policies, of practices, of rules and norms« (Hall and Biersteker 2002: 4). The G-30, a hybrid that is clearly non-state yet both public and private in its membership, having assumed a role in the policy process and benefited from widespread acceptance by the relevant authorities and practitioners, is one such actor. The important role that it played in a series of serious financial policy debates is a clear indication of the significance of looking beyond the state (and the parameters set by state actors) in order to best grasp the nature of global financial governance. Indeed, state-centrism may obscure the phenomena that we are seeking to understand; instead, focusing on the informal aspects of policy-making not only more accurately describes the policy process but also provides analytical explanations of how private and non-state actors assume authority.

One explanation of the growing role of non-state actors is the importance of expertise in the governance of global financial markets. Influence over policy-making is often based on skills and know-how, which can render the regulatory process »captive of knowledge specialists« (Lindblom 1977: 120). The significance of expertise is explored in the concept of »epistemic communities«, which focuses on knowledge in a particular »issue-area« and emphasises that complexity and uncertainty create conditions that are favourable to the prominence of policy communities (Haas 1992). In this configuration, the private sector has an advantage in its capacity as knowledge holder and can thus claim a great degree of authority over technical issues and eventually establish its position of strength on policy decisions of wider scope and implications. A technocratic framework, however, is not interest-free and knowledge and expertise can determine which actors and which ideas are included or excluded in the making of policy (Strange 1994). Nonetheless, the key role of technical knowledge in decision-making has served to ›de-politicise‹ certain financial issues (Radaelli 1995), thus taking some potentially controversial questions outside the public arena. This de-politicisation of global finance has important consequences for the types of priorities advanced by policy makers, including the promotion of efficiency over social equality, justice or democratic accountability. Policy debates are narrowly defined to include economic ideas that favour the prevalence of private sector preferences. Transnational policy processes are captured by private sector interests but this says less about the *imposition* of those interests and more about an evolving and interacting process of their *internalisation* inside the public sector.

The private sector is involved in financial policy processes through the activities of representative pressure groups but also because financial regulation has a long tradition of cooperation between public and private actors (Hancher and Moran 1989). But as this analysis brings to light, we need to think about private sector involvement in policy processes through a different set of conceptual devices that explain its semi-institutionalised position in increasingly transnational policy arenas. Indeed, the analysis shows that the private sector has further enhanced its role through its accepted and dominant presence in a recognised and coherent transnational policy community within which debates and decision-making about the structure, regulation and supervision of financial activities and institutions are taking place. The notion of transnational policy community refers to »experts and professionals that share their expertise and information and form common patterns of understanding regarding policy through regular interaction« (Stone 2001: 6). In the context of global finance, it is argued that such a community has at its core organizations such as the G-30, which bring together relevant public officials and senior industry executives. It provides more or less formal settings for these individuals to reach common ground on the general and the specific of financial architecture. It essentially facilitates the interaction of elites who have strong connections with the main economic players and are often the product of a similar educational, social and ideological upbringing (Gill 1990; van der Pijl 1998). On this basis, and in the context of the practice of ›revolving doors‹ whereby most officials' careers include high-level positions in both the public and the private sector, this public-private distinction becomes blurred.

An additional implication is that the transnational nature of policy communities encourages policy convergence, which in turn offers legitimacy (Dolowitz and Marsh 2000). This is important; the transnational policy community as a whole and the G-30 in particular have in recent years presented neoliberal economic principles as the only path to long-term stability, efficiency, growth and development. Economic ideas are not innocent (Jacobsen 1995). Groups such as the G-30 have not only legitimised private sector involvement in policy-making but have also enabled private interests to be internalised in financial policy decisions.

The legitimacy of non-state actor influence and authority is mostly based on the gaps left by public governance arrangements, especially at the transnational level, which need to be filled, and on the technical expertise of the private sector at a time of rapid financial innovation. It becomes problematic, however, when we examine accountability patterns relating to the activities of these actors. Agnew and Corbridge argue that »the trend from boundaries to flows that is associated with globalization is also bound up with a more general crisis of representation« (Agnew and Corbridge 1995: 216). This is particularly true in finance, where policy making remains »esoteric« and leads to a »limited democracy« (Coleman 1996: 10). Against this background, the »power of the vote in shaping public policy decreases« (Reinicke 1997: 3) while at the same time, the private actors that hold authority are not part of a mechanism that assigns appropriate responsibility. »Market actors are neither elected nor politically accountable« (Cohen 1999: 135). An apparent democratic deficit has emerged, highlighted in the reality of »substantial decisions…frequently [being] taken by unaccountable officials operating in arcane and secretive forums [and exerting] strong pressure on, even if they do not formally bind, national decision-making processes« (Picciotto 1996: 118). Indeed, the democratic deficit in global finance is not only the outcome of non-state actor influence and private authority but results from institutional arrangements as a whole, despite some progress towards the inclusion of a wider range of actors (Porter 2001). There are currently no procedures to guarantee that the policies decided with more or less private sector and non-state actor input are »fair« or »equitable« (Cutler et al. 1999b: 369). Moreover, many financial discussions take place among experts and are isolated from political debates; the views of the public are heard, if at all, following a scandal or a market disruption (Underhill 1995: 273–274). Financial governance patterns have been left outside democratic political debates because of the low visibility of finance; financial matters are of a technical nature and »no specific popular social group [is] directly affected in a negative way« (Helleiner 1994: 203). There are some advantages to the secretive character of financial decision-making. Underhill argues that »the very private and closed nature of the policy communities« in effect facilitates the managing of crises (Underhill 1997: 43) and warns that integrating financial debates in more traditional forums could lead to »the chaos and paralysis« associated with trade negotiations (Underhill 1995: 278).

The role of the G-30 in the policy process is part of a more general trend towards growing private authority in the operation and governance of financial markets. The influence of the G-30 calls attention to developments in the financial markets which have brought about the emergence of new actors and moreover, it highlights the formation and evolution of transnational policy communities and their use of alternative forums for the promotion of ideas and policies. Specifically, the study of the G-30 offers the opportunity to observe certain financial policy debates as they unravel and to identify a less traditional actor, which played a major role in shaping policy agendas and had a significant effect on final outcomes. In building its policy role, the G-30 relied on a transnational coalition of public and private actors and made use of traditional sources of authority: expertise, economic power and the clout of elites. The analysis also shows that the G-30 played a part in keeping policy debates among financial experts and resisting serious public scrutiny.

3. Non-state Actors, Transnational Policy Communities and Changing Patterns of Governance – Understanding the Role of the Group of Thirty

Formally described as a ›Consultative Group on International Economic and Monetary Affairs‹, the G-30 is, in the language of its own official documents, a »private, nonprofit body composed of senior representatives of the private and public sectors and academia«. Founded in 1978 with the support of a grant from the Rockefeller Foundation, its aim has been to »deepen the understanding of international economic and financial issues, to explore the international repercussions of decisions taken in the public and private sectors, and to examine the choices available to market practitioners and policy makers« (G-30 1998). The G-30 is an organization comprised of thirty members at any one time. The individuals involved all have strong credentials in the fields of economics and finance. Appendix 1 provides a list of current members; the list is impressive as the group brings together high profile people from major international institutions, national supervisory agencies, and major banks, along with some prominent academic economists. While some members are reaching the end of their careers, the vast majority remain active participants in financial system activities. Hence, the group is not just a discussion forum for people with vast experience but also a meeting ground for individuals who are currently responsible for the activities within, and the supervision of, financial markets. These people often interact in other forums as well and have the opportunity to exchange opinions in meetings of supervisors or in conferences and symposia of private associations. Furthermore, they are frequently members of other organizations. G-30 members have gone through a particular educational and professional route and their paths often cross, although the G-30 still offers a rather unique environment in the extent of its institutionalisation of the interaction of public and private officials.

The group meets twice a year. Meetings include a general discussion on current issues and also an examination of ongoing work and new proposals. This is where ›study topics‹ are chosen and decisions are taken on future reports. There are three types of publicly available material. First in importance and exposure are the study group reports, which are prepared by special experts and are rigorous research exercises. The group also publishes a series of occasional papers and has established a series of lectures on major financial topics, which are also published. Study group reports covered very ambitious topics in the early days of the group, ranging from exchange rates to the energy situation. In the late 1980s, however, the group's efforts turned to global financial issues, and the published output became more specialised and practical. The G-30 concerned itself with the ›plumbing and wiring‹ of the financial system and found that its ability to provide expert recommendations on technical issues gave it a place in the structure of financial governance and put it at the forefront of (self-)regulatory and supervisory initiatives.

Forging for itself a position at the core of an emerging transnational policy community, the G-30 started its work on the details of the financial system with a comprehensive project on the technical and essentially non-controversial subject of clearance and settlement in the securities markets. The widespread adoption by policy makers of the recommendations put forward by the group established the G-30 in the transnational policy community and provided the opportunity for further work on yet another technical but far more contentious topic: the use of over-the-counter derivatives. This effort proved another successful undertaking for the group, which saw its proposals adopted by all the relevant public and private authorities. In turn, the G-30 acquired the authority and, arguably, legitimacy among the relevant policy community to make a bold policy statement on self-regulation and self-supervision, giving the private sector a clear policy-making role and self-policing functions. In this step, the G-30 report reflected the policy agenda of an emerging transnational policy community. The group's preoccupations and recommendations on global institutions and systemic risk, the third case in this study, have been replicated in the developing framework for regulation and supervision, most notably in the recently revised Capital Accord (Basel II).

The G-30 presents pressure group characteristics in its promotion of views associated with private sector interests; its membership, however, includes personalities from both the public and private sectors and most importantly, it is made up of people and not banks or securities firms. The group also resembles a think tank in its production of high quality and thorough reports, yet it does not have the capabilities and perceived independence of a research institute. Finally, the G-30 shows elements of a private members' club, bringing together people who are part of a policy community and know each other well both on a professional and a personal level. The G-30 defies traditional distinctions of public, private and academic. It is a hybrid organization that has been at the forefront of some of the battles won by the private sector, while retaining a reputation for responsible work among finance practitioners and becoming an arena where both public and private officials feel comfortable.

The G-30 has specifically shown the importance of a transnational policy community governance mode in three major financial policy issues. The first such case deals with clearance and settlement of securities, the topic of the first study on the details of the financial system that was undertaken by the group. In the late 1980s and early 1990s, the G-30 produced a thorough and responsible study on how to improve the efficiency and reduce the risks associated with clearance and settlement and played a leading part in the monitoring of implementation worldwide. The report and subsequent monitoring and implementation work established the group as an actor in the financial transnational policy community. This case suggests that delegation of authority to private groups can be facilitated by the functional, complex and, for most, remote nature of a topic and stresses that a very technical and expert initiative can open the door to groups such as the G-30 to contribute to larger policy issues.

Another major topic to which G-30 contribution has been significant is that of the governance of over-the-counter derivatives instruments. In the 1990s, the group tackled an emerging and contentious topic of interest to practitioners and public authorities. It relied on the expertise of its members and study group participants to produce and promote high quality recommendations on the sound and effective use of these instruments. The project was initiated and conducted by the private sector and endorsed self-regulatory practice; it was also a thinly disguised attempt to pre-empt potentially intrusive official measures. Close examination of the evolution of the policy debate and regulatory and supervisory practices shows that the G-30 effectively defined the issues on the agenda and offered specific solutions (which were adopted) to a controversial policy concern. It did so by claiming to demystify derivatives and by determining policy parameters that met the approval of public bodies prior to the instruments hitting the headlines as the root of major financial losses. The G-30 framed the issues by providing guidance at a time of uncertainty and by limiting wider debate by establishing derivatives as a technical yet regular financial issue, best dealt with within the confines of financial institutions. Through this process, the G-30 advanced its position as an authoritative private body and at the same time, internalised private sector interests in the policy process.

The G-30 was also influential through its project on global institutions and systemic risk. In the late 1990s, the G-30 made a bold statement on self-regulation and self-supervision in the treatment of global financial conglomerates. The group modified its role by moving away from reports that scrutinised specific aspects of the financial markets and produced a study of the system as a whole; this was a significant step that saw the group provide overall policy directions. Self-regulation and self-supervision as advocated by the G-30 are now the policy preference adopted by the transnational policy community, including public authorities, as manifested in the revised Basel Capital Accord (Basel II). In addition, the report, and the widespread acceptance of the principles that it endorses, testify to the central position held by the group in financial policy-making. The role of the group suggests that transnational policy communities can be instrumental in the effort to substantially alter regulatory and supervisory traditions; indeed, in this case the G-30 report worked as a ›tester‹ and prepared the ground for Basel II. It may be concluded that delegation of authority to a non-state actor on matters that appear technical and specialised (e.g. clearance and settlement) can legitimise private sector involvement and lead to influence over issues of wider significance, thus altering the role of the private sector in governance from one of providing expert advice to one of articulating policy preferences.

4. Explaining Influence – A Transnational Policy Community at the Heart of Complex Policy Processes

A close examination of financial market activities and their governance reveals a significant degree of transnationalisation as well a significant place for private sector interests and concerns in the prevailing arrangements. Large global financial institutions have increasingly more in common with each other across borders than with the more domestically oriented entities of their home markets. Similarly, their regulators and supervisors cooperate on an international basis to develop regulatory and monitoring frameworks which, as is the case with the work of the Basel Committee, become predominant; they do not always enjoy the same level of agreement over sets of priorities with other public sector officials in their home jurisdictions. At the same time, a well-established engagement with neoliberal economic practice (which has also become progressively more transnational) has brought private sector concerns to the forefront of policy-making.

The analysis shows that the principal source of influence of the G-30 is its technical expertise and more generally, the power of ideas and that of those who control them. G-30 members are the ›movers and shakers‹ of finance and they hold both useful ideas and an influential position in institutions of great economic and political influence. The growing complexity of financial activities gives the private sector a justified leading position in terms of expertise; additionally, however, it has become important for public officials to maintain good relations with the largest financial players, arguably the most relevant players for the stability of the financial system, and to keep them on board any policy initiatives. The influence of the group is specifically enhanced through its membership pattern, which has important implications for the G-30's intellectual and ideological position. A close look at the individuals involved confirms that both the group and its members are part of the transnational policy community in principle favourable to global financial integration and espouse neoliberal economic thinking. The process is two-fold: members and their institutions follow a particular understanding of regulation and supervision and thus approve of G-30 projects that pursue these objectives. On the other hand, members have the chance to discuss developments in the financial markets with their peers in the context of the G-30 and in turn, this communication shapes their ideas and courses of action. This is reinforced by the situation of ›revolving doors‹ among practitioners, which also blurs the public/private divide. The vast majority of G-30 members have worked in both the public *and* the private sector.

G-30 influence stems from its membership but it is primarily through its study group reports and their publication that the group has become an important actor in financial governance. The prestige, assembled expertise and financial strength are put to good use in the formation of study groups that assemble the most prominent experts in a particular field. The interaction between public and private also leads to documentation that is in the public domain and has been explicitly or implicitly endorsed by both public and private sector officials. This is what differentiates the G-30 from a number of non-state actors and private organizations and gives it authority that is often direct and acknowledged. The perceived quality of G-30 proposals and studies, their portrayal as accurate representations of best practice and responsible standards for widespread adoption, have also been instrumental in the development of the group's role in the policy process.

The G-30 is also an example of how private groups find their niche; by focusing on certain aspects of the operation of financial markets, the G-30 was firstly able to make a meaningful contribution to subjects that were relatively obscure, technical or specialised. Yet the trend towards public-private sector interaction and the adoption of a largely private interest agenda by the nascent transnational policy community on specific technical issues can also have implications for general policy preferences. The work of the G-30 has promoted the adoption of principles and practices which have substantially altered the nature of financial regulation and supervision, resulting in the development of a private regime of self-regulation and self-supervision in the financial markets. One indication of this development is the promotion of flexibility and the endorsement of often-voluntary best practice standards as opposed to rules-based regulation. Further evidence is provided by the widespread reliance on the internal risk assessment models of financial institutions for the purposes of supervision. The empirical study of the G-30 is therefore also significant in linking the category of actor involved in the policy process to the resulting financial practices of regulation and supervision.

The G-30 mostly deals with the specifics of the system, but how do the ›nuts and bolts‹ of financial market governance relate to higher policy issues? Formally including the private sector in policy making and delegating authority on technical and specialised financial subjects can gradually lead to private influence and authority over a wider spectrum of issues, including financial matters that are potentially controversial and touch upon vital public policy areas. It also shows that this trend, along with the developments in liberalisation and innovation that have made financial markets more complex, encourages a bias in favour of treating financial issues in technical terms and minimising scrutiny of activities and policies. This chapter does not argue that this situation is the result of an elaborate private sector strategy; rather, it makes the case that giving a role to the private sector encourages the latter to position itself at the forefront of policy-making and use its advantage of being one step ahead of public authorities on financial market processes, i.e. translate power into governance arrangements. Regular public-private sector interaction leads to issue-specific policy outcomes but also long-term policy directions that may initially be unintended.

The analysis deals with authority, exploring which actors have it and the extent to which private actors have emerged as major players in the formulation of policy. The financial environment in which groups such as the G-30 operate is the product of simultaneous transformations in both states and markets. The findings suggest that public and private actors hold varying degrees of authority and that, even for an industry where, historically, private sector participation has been considerable, the balance has shifted in favour of the private sector. Moreover, debates and decisions about financial policy have moved to the transnational level as can be seen by policy harmonisation across systems. These trends are expressly manifested in the developing role of a transnational policy community, which is essentially actively promoting private sector involvement and, more controversially, interests. Markets are set up by interests to work in particular ways and the public and private sectors are working in tandem to shape market mechanisms. The case of the G-30 indicates that state and market actors are not in a position of conflict with each other but have formed a coherent (at least publicly) transnational policy community to deal with financial issues and to liase and find common ground. Disagreements are ironed out and regulators, supervisors and financial institutions present a united front in their policy directions and priorities. In this context, going beyond sterile distinctions of ›state and market‹ and ›public and private‹ enhances our understanding of financial governance and reveals that public and private are working together to get markets to operate in a certain manner and that their combined decisions have an impact on the relative balance of public and private in the proceedings. In turn, this suggests that those same actors and the transnational policy community could express a preference for alternative market structures and a different degree of private sector influence. Thus, the study confirms the usefulness of the concept of transnational policy community in explanations of financial governance but further, explains the process through which private sector preferences are internalised, prioritised and de-politicised within the community.

5. The Normative Dimension: Accountability and Legitimacy in Global Financial Governance

Examination of the G-30 also raises the issue of the link between financial policy and the provision of wider public goods and questions whether the growing influence of private interests can serve the public good. In the context of global finance, the analysis finds that financial stability and market efficiency are identified as the main goals of regulation and supervision. It enquires whether these should not be supplemented by additional objectives; importantly, however, it queries whether those rather limited goals are themselves best met through the emerging financial governance structures. This is examined through an assessment of self-regulation and self-supervision as the policies of choice advocated by the G-30 and widely accepted by the transnational policy community as a whole.

That the private sector has acquired policy-making functions is explicitly manifested in two sets of developments. The first is an emphasis on standards rather than rules. There is a real incentive for the private sector to play the self-regulation game responsibly and thus prevent heavy-handed intervention. The second development is that the advance of self-regulation leaves public authorities in charge of market-based supervision, relying on transparency and disclosure, as well as the competence of internal models administered by financial institutions. Rating agencies and informal market mechanisms, such as flows of information, gossip and employees are also taken into account by supervisors. Together, these two trends reveal that private sector involvement in policy-making has substantially altered the nature of regulation and supervision by shifting the balance away from the ›public‹ aspect of these very important functions. Nevertheless, the prime incentive behind the industry's drive to regulate and supervise itself is self-interest and the wish to avoid intrusive regulation, which costs money, and an interventionist public sector. In this context, what happens to financial stability and market efficiency? Concerns remain as to how responsibly the private sector takes its role, as well as with regards to the safeguards that are in place should something go wrong. The probability of failure for a financial institution cannot and should not be driven to zero, but in the current financial environment, the private sector enjoys a great degree of autonomy without assuming a corresponding level of responsibility; the public sector is thus left with the task of picking up the pieces when private sector decisions prove detrimental to the stability of the financial system.

It is also important to consider the legitimacy and accountability of the governance structure. In particular, the potential costs of delegation of authority to the private sector need to be examined. This is important as it represents the type of practical concern that worries policy-makers but also because in a wider sense, it goes to the heart of actual political economic debates of governance arrangements and assignment of responsibilities. The failure of a large financial institution can cause widespread panic and trigger extensive systemic consequences of uncertainty, dip in confidence and immediate liquidity problems for other key financial players. Institutions are fully aware of this, especially those considered too-big-to-fail. The lender-of-last-resort responsibilities of most central banks mean that for many institutions, a safety net is in place. It used to be that banks were the sole beneficiaries of this provision. However, the rescue of the hedge fund Long-Term Capital Management (LTCM) in 1998 with private money but US Federal Reserve logistical support and initiative, suggests that there are an increasing number of institutions that *matter*. This could bring a considerable burden to taxpayers. The existence of safety nets and deposit insurance, and the central bank function of lender of last resort, especially for institutions that are too-big-to-fail, are allowing private institutions to self-regulate and self-supervise without an adequate framework of penalties for bad behavior. These are strong political functions and considerations, which provide a great degree of security to the private sector; is this the only aspect of global financial governance that remains ›politicised‹?

A second set of issues concerns questions of responsibility and accountability of non-state actors and increasingly, the whole spectrum of actors in charge of financial governance. Patterns of accountability must be improved and efforts towards transparency and superior disclosure, both quantitative and qualitative, must continue. There is some progress in this direction, most notably in the more inclusive institutional arrangements governing global finance, which emerged in the aftermath of the Asian crisis of 1997 (Germain 2004) and the focus on private sector involvement in financial crisis resolution, but much remains to be done. These considerations are important in analysing a group such as the G-30; the group is not elected or appointed, nor is it ultimately responsible for implementation. Despite considerable influence, the accountability of the group is limited. The G-30 might endure damage to its reputation and private sector influence may be curbed, but little of the blame for any difficulties would lie with the group and only a limited amount of the responsibility of dealing with a significant market failure would fall on private institutions. The G-30 might be a small part of the overall spectrum of policy actors but the type of governance style that it represents is replicated in other aspects of financial and economic governance (Sell 2003; van Apeldoorn 2002). This is not only problematic in the event of crisis and greater awareness of the issue at all times is to be encouraged. The G-30 and the transnational policy community around it are presenting a unified front and whereas some debate may indeed be taking place about the public-private balance within the community, no one is openly questioning the process. As a result, the level of controversy that is often associated with important and potentially explosive financial issues is not fully reflected in the making of policy.

6. Conclusions

The analysis in this chapter highlights a series of issues that are crucial to our understanding of global financial governance. The first is the issue of linkages among members of the transnational financial policy community and the importance of interconnections. The G-30 provides ample evidence of the importance of personal relationships and the extent to which a group of people with similar social, educational and professional backgrounds gets to meet on a regular basis in various settings; cross-membership is prevalent for most members. A further theme is the apparent absence of struggle or political conflict in the promotion of G-30 work, its incorporation in policy-making approaches and implementation: this chapter argues that this is primarily explained by the prevalence of specialised expertise in the shaping of the regulatory and supervisory framework. Regulators and supervisors do not have the resources to lead developments and are often lagging behind in terms of information on techniques and practices.

It remains to enquire as to the ›politics‹ of the resulting patterns of financial regulation and supervision. The private sector has an interest in being regulated, but favours regulation that is market friendly. It appears that this interest coincides with the goals of public authorities; the analysis in this chapter indicates that organizations such as the G-30 are instrumental in bringing about this degree of agreement among public and private participants. Regulation and supervision as advocated by the G-30 and practised by official bodies, especially in the United States, is not about controlling the banking system or constraining activities. Regulators are wary of being an obstacle to the market, imposing procedures that are too bureaucratic and slow. Public functions focus on ensuring that activities are conducted in a safe and sound manner, on preventing failure via quality management and on dealing swiftly with the consequences should a problem occur. At the same time, financial issues, as discussed by the G-30 and the transnational policy community as a whole, are defined mostly in technical and expert terms. Efficiency and stability as policy goals supersede possible alternatives such as social justice. Similarly, some actors in charge of financial policy are remote from the political arena and in the case of the G-30, not accountable or responsible for the implementation of their proposals. Importantly, the public sector members of the policy community appear equally reluctant to delve into a political debate of these issues. This, along with the type of policies advocated, suggests that questions of ›capture‹ of the policy process by the private sector need to be continually examined and reassessed.

References

Agnew, John/Corbridge, Stuart (1995), *Mastering Space: Hegemony, Territory and International Political Economy*. London.

Basel Committee on Banking Supervision (2004), *International Convergence of Capital Measurement and Capital Standards – A Revised Framework*. Basel.

Bratton, William W./McCahery, Joseph/Picciotto, Sol/Scott, Colin (1996) (eds), *International Regulatory Competition and Coordination, Perspectives on Economic Regulation in Europe and the United States*. Oxford.

Cerny, Philip G. (1993) (ed.), *Finance and World Politics*. Aldershot.

Cohen, Benjamin J. (1999), »The new geography of money«, in: Emily Gilbert and Eric Helleiner (eds), *Nation-States and Money. The Past, Present and Future of National Currencies*. London, 121–138.

Coleman, William D. (1994), »Keeping the shotgun behind the door. Governing the securities industry in Canada, the United Kingdom, and the United States«, in: J. Rogers Hollingsworth, Philippe C. Schmitter and Wolfgang Streeck (eds), *Governing Capitalist Economies, Performance and Control of Economic Sectors*. Oxford, 244–269.

— (1996), *Financial Services, Globalization and Domestic Policy Change*. London.

Cox, Robert W./Sinclair, Timothy J. (1996), *Approaches to World Order*. Cambridge.

Cutler, A. Claire/Haufler, Virginia/Porter, Tony (1999) (eds), *Private Authority and International Affairs*. Albany.

Dolowitz, David P./Marsh, David (2000), »Learning from abroad: the role of policy transfer in contemporary policy-making«, in: *Governance*, Vol. 13, 5–24.

Friedman, R.B. (1990), »On the Concept of Authority in Political Philosophy«, in: Joseph Raz (ed.), *Authority*. New York, 56–91.

Germain, Randall (2004), »Globalising Accountability within the International Organization of Credit: Financial Governance and the Public Sphere«, in: *Global Society*, Vol. 18, 217–242.

Gill, Stephen (1990), *American Hegemony and the Trilateral Commission*. Cambridge.

Group of Thirty (1989), *Clearance and Settlement Systems in the World's Securities Markets*. London.

— (1990), *Clearance and Settlement Systems, Status Reports: Spring 1990*. London

— (1992), *Clearance and Settlement Systems, Status Reports: 1992*. Washington, DC.

— (1993), *Derivatives: Practices and Principles*. Washington, DC.

— (1997), *Global Institutions, National Supervision and Systemic Risk*. Washington, DC.

— (1998), *Annual Report*. Washington, DC.

Haas, Peter M. (1992), »Introduction: Epistemic Communities and International Policy Coordination«, in: *International Organization, Special Issue on Knowledge, Power, and International Policy coordination*, Vol. 46, 1–35.

Hall, Rodney Bruce/Biersteker, Thomas J. (2002) (eds/), *The Emergence of Private Authority in Global Governance*. Cambridge.

Helleiner, Eric (1994), *States and the Reemergence of Global Finance – From Bretton Woods to the 1990s*. Ithaca.

Jacobsen, John Kurt (1995), »Much ado about Ideas: The Cognitive Factor in Economic Policy«, in: *World Politics*, Vol. 47, 283–310.

Josselin, Daphné/Wallace, William (2001) (eds), *Non-State Actors in World Politics*. Basingstoke.

Kaufman, Henry (2000), *On Money and Markets*. New York.

Lindblom, Charles E. (1977), *Politics and Markets – The World's Political Economic Systems*. New York.

Moran, Michael (1991), *The Politics of the Financial Revolution: The USA, UK and Japan*. London.

Pauly, Louis W. (2002), »Global finance, political authority, and the problem of legitimation«, in: Rodney Bruce Hall and Thomas J. Biersteker (eds), *The Emergence of Private Authority in Global Governance*. Cambridge, 76–90.

Picciotto, Sol (1996), »The Regulatory Criss-Cross: Interaction between Jurisdictions and the Construction of Global Regulatory Networks«, in: William W. Bratton, Joseph McCahery, Sol Picciotto and Colin Scott (eds), *International Regulatory Competition and Coordination, Perspectives on Economic Regulation in Europe and the United States*. Oxford, 90–123.

Porter, Tony (2001), »The democratic deficit in the institutional arrangements for regulating global finance«, in: *Global Governance*, Vol. 7, 427–439.

Radaelli, Claudio M. (1995), »The Role of Knowledge in the Policy Process«, in: *Journal of European Public Policy*, Vol. 2, 159–183.

Reinicke, Wolfgang H. (1997), »Global Public Policy«, in: *Foreign Affairs*, Vol 76, 127–138.

Rosenau, James N. (1997), *Along the Domestic-Foreign Frontier, Exploring Governance in a Turbulent World*. Cambridge.

Rosenau, James N./Czempiel, Ernst-Otto (1992) (eds), *Governance without Government: Order and Change in World Politics*. Cambridge.

Sell, Susan K. (2003), *Private Power, Public Law*. Cambridge.

Steinherr, Alfred (1998), *Derivatives – The Wild Beast of Finance*. Chichester.

Stone, Diane (2001), »Learning Lessons, Policy Transfer and the International Diffusion of Policy Ideas«, *CSGR Working Paper*, No. 69/01. Warwick.

Strange, Susan ([1988] 1994), *States and Markets*, 2nd edition. London.

— (1996), *The Retreat of the State*. Cambridge.

Streeck, Wolfgang/Schmitter, Philippe (1985) (eds), *Private Interest Government: Beyond Market and State*. London.

Tsingou, Eleni (2003), »Transnational Policy Communities and Financial Governance: The Role of Private Actors in Derivatives Regulation«, *CSGR Working Paper*, No. 111/03. Warwick.

Underhill, Geoffrey R.D. (1995), »Keeping Governments out of Politics: Transnational Securities Markets, Regulatory Cooperation, and Political Legitimacy«, in: *Review of International Studies*, Vol. 21, 251–278.

— (1997) (ed.), *The New World Order in International Finance*. London.

Van Appeldoorn, Bastiaan (2002), *Transnational Capitalism and the Struggle over European Integration*. London.

Van der Pijl, Kees (1998), *Transnational Classes and International Relations*. London.

Appendix I – Group Of Thirty Membership

www.g30.org

Mr. Paul A. Volcker
Chairman of the Board of Trustees
Group of Thirty

Mr. Jacob A. Frenkel
Chairman, Group of Thirty
Vice Chairman, American International Group

Mr. Abdalatif A-Hamad
Chairman, Arab Fund for Economic and Social Development

Mr. Leszek Balcerowicz
President, National Bank of Poland

Mr. Geoffrey L. Bell
Executive Secretary, Group of Thirty
President, Geoffrey Bell & Company, Inc.

Mr. Jaime Caruana
Governor, Banco de España

Dr. Domingo Cavallo
Robert Kennedy Visiting Professor in Latin American Studies
Department of Economics – Harvard University

Mr. E. Gerald Corrigan
Managing Director, Goldman Sachs & Co.

Mr. Andrew D. Crockett
President, JP Morgan Chase International

Sr. Guillermo de la Dehesa Romero
Presidente, AVIVA Groupo Corporativo S.L.

Dr. Martin Feldstein
President, National Bureau of Economic Research

Mr. Roger Ferguson
Vice Chairman, Federal Reserve Board
Chairman, Financial Stability Forum

Mr. Stanley Fischer
Governor, Bank of Israel

Mr. Arminio Fraga Neto
Partner, Gavea Investimentos

Mr. Timothy F. Geithner
President, Federal Reserve Bank of New York

Mr. Toyoo Gyohten
President, Institute for International Monetary Affairs

Mr. Gerd Häusler
Counsellor and Director, International Capital Markets Department
International Monetary Fund

Professor Peter B. Kenen
Senior Fellow in International Economics, Council on Foreign Relations

Mr. Mervyn King
Governor, Bank of England

Professor Paul Krugman
Professor of Economics, Woodrow Wilson School, Princeton University

M. Jacques de Larosière
Conseiller, BNP Paribas

Mr. Guillermo Ortiz Martinez
Governor, Banco de Mexico

Dr. Tommaso Padoa-Schioppa
Professor, Instituto Affari Internazionali

Mr. William R. Rhodes
Senior Vice Chairman, Citigroup
Chairman, Citicorp and Citibank

Mr. Lawrence Summers
President, Harvard University

M. Jean-Claude Trichet
President, European Central Bank

Sir David Walker
Chairman, Morgan Stanley International Inc.

Dr. Marina v N. Whitman
Professor of Business Administration & Public Policy,
Ford School of Public Policy, University of Michigan

Mr. Zhou Xiaochuan
Governor, People's Bank of China

Mr. Yutaka Yamaguchi
Former Deputy Governor, Bank of Japan

Mr. Ernesto Zedillo
Director, Yale Center for the Study of Globalization
Yale University

Emeritus Members

Rt. Hon. Lord Richardson of Duntisbourne, KG
Honorary Chairman, Group of Thirty

Mr. Richard A. Debs
Advisory Director, Morgan Stanley & Co.

Professor Gerhard Fels
Former Director, Institut der deutschen Wirtschaft

Dr. Wilfried Guth
Deutsche Bank AG

Mr. John G. Heimann
Senior Advisor, Financial Stability Institute

Mr. Erik Hoffmeyer
Former Chairman, Danmarks Nationalbank

Mr. Shijuro Ogata
Former Deputy Governor, Bank of Japan

Dr. Sylvia Ostry
Distinguished Research Fellow Munk Center for International Studies, Toronto

Mr. William McDonough
Vice Chairman and Special Advisor to the Chairman, Merrill Lynch
Former Chairman, Public Company Accounting Oversight Board

Mr. Ernest Stern
Partner and Senior Advisor, The Rohatyn Group
Executive Director

Mr. Stuart P.M. Mackintosh
The Group of Thirty

Rating Agencies, Ignorance and the Knowledge-Based Production of System Trust

Torsten Strulik

1. Introduction
2. Rating Agencies as Organizations of the Knowledge Economy
3. The Specification and Exploitation of Ignorance
4. Rating Agencies and the Production of System Trust
5. Conclusions

1. Introduction

Is a shift towards a cognitive mode of global finance taking place? Rating agencies are instructive for finding an answer to this question in two respects. First, ratings have obviously become an integral part of the self-regulation of the global financial system in practice. Most notably, the importance of the »global expertise« (Willke 2003) of the major US-American agencies Standard & Poor's (S&P) and Moody's Investors Service (Moody's) has continually grown since the end of the Bretton Woods era. For example, while Moody's evaluated less than 1,000 issuers in 1970 this number increased to more than 9,000 by 2000, including 100 countries, most of the supranational organizations, banks, insurance companies, industrial companies as well as investment funds (Bank for International Settlements 2000: 21). It is therefore not surprising that the agencies describe themselves as »an essential part of the world's financial infrastructure« (Standard & Poor's 2006). Second, recent studies on rating agencies have adopted the postulate of »opening the black boxes of global finance« (MacKenzie 2003) by analyzing the internal structures and processes that direct the self-regulation of the financial system. The work of Timothy Sinclair (e.g. 1999, 2005; see also chapter 4 in this volume) in particular illuminates this undoubtedly highly technical and intransparent economic field, which at the same time offers instructive insights into our contemporary society's treatment of knowledge and ignorance (in the sense of non-knowledge as a necessary corollary of knowledge).

The present essay follows a ›cognitive turn‹ in theory and practice. First, the specific problems that rating agencies are facing in the context of global finance will be investigated in connection with sociological studies on the knowledge economy (part 2). In the following, two further points will be made. One of these is what the example of rating agencies tells us about the dynamics and consequences of the financial system's knowledge production. While theoretical and empirical studies are already focusing on the risks of knowledge-intensive technologies and the details of environmental problems (e.g. Ravetz 1986; Ladeur 1995), analyses of comparable dynamics within the financial system have yet to be carried out. This contribution therefore pays special attention not only to knowledge but also to ignorance and risk. It is becoming conceivable that, given the rapid advance of globalization and the increasing significance of knowledge, the growing intransparency of finance is being accompanied by an increasing relevance of organizations that are capable of exploiting the ignorance of the development of markets, companies and products. While rating agencies are usually described in economics and political science as enterprises specialized in solving problems of coordination, a thesis of this chapter is that rating agencies are knowledge-based organizations that enable themselves as well as other market actors to utilize the profit-making potential of ignorance. Accordingly, rating agencies can be seen as important driving forces of the risks of global finance (part 3).

The second emphasis of this chapter is the interrelationship between ignorance and trust. Contemporary diagnoses of society indicate that ignorance is progressively growing through the advancement of societal knowledge production (Luhmann 1995). At the same time, the establishment of trust is becoming both more important and more difficult. In light of this, it is to be expected that organizations which are generating trust in intransparent decision-making situations will be of ever increasing importance. Although rating agencies have been described as »guardians of trust« (Shapiro 1987), it is still largely unclear both what the sources and consequences of their trust function are and what type of trust it is that they are building. To answer these questions, rating agencies will be described as organizations which earn acceptance on the basis of their specific expertise and exceptional adaptability to changes in their economic environment. Moreover, attention will be drawn to the obviously growing economic demands on »system trust« (Luhmann 1979) (part 4).

2. Rating Agencies as Organizations of the Knowledge Economy

In terms of the modern sociological systems theory (Luhmann 1995), rating agencies operate as organizations in the internal environment of the economy. Therefore, it is instructive to analyze their functions and consequences in connection with recent changes in the economy. As current studies on the »knowledge society« (e.g. Willke 2002) and the »knowledge economy« (e.g. Strulik 2004) show, one characteristic of our contemporary economy is that the knowledge necessary for their operations is no longer mainly based on experience, but is generated through active learning-processes. The knowledge economy is therefore not to be understood trivially as one in which the nature of products and services is knowledge-intensive. The crucial point is that the knowledge economy's basic problem is to generate, organize and manage useful knowledge. Furthermore, if one considers knowledge as the result of learning, it becomes evident that the operations of the knowledge economy are particularly marked by the »reflexivity of knowledge« (Giddens 1991). This means that the initiation and regulation of knowledge-producing processes is more important than the management of existing knowledge. Thus, it is the creation of *new* knowledge that becomes the central imperative in multi-dimensional social and economic changes where the important factors are new technologies, organization patterns and solutions to problems.

The dynamics of knowledge and innovation are clearly visible in global finance. Since the final collapse of the Bretton Woods system in 1973 a risk management industry of entirely new dimensions has emerged and opened new business opportunities to market players. In light of the importance of rating agencies, two lines of development have been particularly meaningful: securitization and disintermediation. A substantial trigger for the securitization trend was the debt crisis in 1982 (Eichengreen/Lindert 1989). Because the credit standing of numerous third-world debtors had drastically decreased and many credit commitments had become questionable, internationally-operating banks increasingly began to give loans in the form of bonded claims and to accept bonded loans. Where there had been fixed obligations for bank loans, there was now a greater flexibility because of the negotiability of obligations. Loan holders and investors were enabled to adapt transactions to individual circumstances and to liquidate capital more quickly. In this way, risks could be shared, and it became possible to expand access to credit. This structural transformation in the finance sector very clearly reflects the increasing significance of the securities trade, which is the basis for the global transaction of innovative and complex financial products. While the net amount of the securities issued in 1987 was at around 100 billion US dollars, in 1999 it stood at about 1,225 billion US dollars (BIZ 1995, 2000a).

As a consequence of this trend towards innovative and knowledge-intensive products, which was reinforced by the increasing competitive pressure in the area of financial services and the investors' growing expectations of profit, the relationship between investors and debtors is becoming more direct. Indeed, while banks are still participating in the credit business, they have shifted their activity to organizing bonds and distributing securities. This process of disintermediation offers investors opportunities not available to them in their relationship with their house bank. At the same time, there are new opportunities for enterprises that are searching for capital to obtain financing directly through the capital markets, and thus to obtain more favorable conditions than they could get through a conventional loan from a house bank. In traditional credit operations, banks largely carried the risk of debtors defaulting on their payment obligation, while investors could, to a certain extent, rely on their banks to behave correctly in view of the fact that they would be monitored by their supervisory boards. Now, however, investors must make their own judgment on the probability of debtors defaulting on their payments.

This is where rating agencies come in: they meet the demand for assessments of creditworthiness. In his work, Timothy Sinclair (e.g. 1995, 1999, 2000) has impressively portrayed how the agencies perform in the context of »new global finance«. Here it is important to note that rating agencies have emerged as knowledge-based and globally-oriented organizations aimed at interpreting information relevant for determining the creditworthiness of countries, companies and financial products. The agencies' evolutionary advantage is recognizable in light of the interests of investors and borrowers. In providing capital, the latter essentially pursue three goals: (1) securing unlimited access to national and global financial markets; (2) minimizing the costs of capital; and (3) maintaining financial security, judged on the basis of liquidity and the capital structure. Borrowers' ability to realize these goals depends on their solvency or the appraisal of their solvency. Investors' interests are opposed to those of the borrowers: their goal is to attain the highest possible return on the respective risk. Before they decide to invest, investors must therefore decide whether the profits they are aiming for are proportionate to the presumed risk. For this decision they need detailed information about the probability that the respective debtor will be unable to make his payments.

From this perspective, it becomes clear that rating agencies position themselves between these two parties. From an economic point-of-view, the agencies contribute to improving the transparency and the information efficiency of the markets. Their service seems to consist of observing markets on the basis of specialized and largely standardized processes, gathering information and preparing risk assessments for investors. With quantitative and qualitative evaluatory processes and with the use of specific symbols, they offer communicative simplifications which help to make the intransparency of the markets manageable. From a sociological perspective, however, this evaluatory activity does not contribute to ›solving‹ the existing information and knowledge problems as rating agencies are not able to grasp the real complexity of their environment and produce ›certain‹ knowledge. In spite of the agencies' best attempts to gain knowledge, every analysis leaves something unknown, a ›blind spot‹. However, with their assessments, they transform an indeterminate complexity into a determinate ›useful‹ one and enable market actors to make ›rational‹ decisions. In a functionally differentiated society ratings are thus to be understood as effective instruments that react to the increasingly important requirement of a »control of intransparency« (Luhmann 1997). At the same time, with respect to the consequences of ratings, it is important that the agencies contribute, through their highly efficient activity of transformation, to the dynamic interplay of knowledge and ignorance. The future is no longer indeterminable merely because it is dependent upon many unknown as well as known factors, but also because it is circularly connected with the decision-making context and thus dependent upon the assessments arrived at by rating agencies.

3. The Specification and Exploitation of Ignorance

When one looks at the expectation structures which guide the operations of the global financial system, the prominence of cognitive, adaptive and learning-oriented expectations become clearly evident. By the end of the Bretton Woods' system and the transition to flexible exchange rates the financial system had adapted itself to the purely cognitive orientation to market dynamics. External points of reference – whether political or economic – that stabilized the financial system are now increasingly substituted by internal subsystems and structures which coordinate the operations of the system and regulate internal learning processes (see Hanno Pahl in this volume). The emergence of cognitive mechanisms of self-regulation can clearly be seen in the growing importance of organizations that are specialized in providing effective decision-making support in highly intransparent fields of business. Examples are the performance of investment banks, consultants and hedge funds. Rating agencies can also be understood as organizations which make use of elaborate selection heuristics to interpret the indeterminateness or orientation uncertainty of markets and translate them into sustainable expectations. The growing importance of the agencies therefore appears to be not only closely related to a high degree of complexity and intransparency, but also to the increasing pace of financial business. With their ratings, they meet the need of the market actors to handle complex and dynamic situations by means of »fast and frugal heuristics« (Gigerenzer 2001). By consolidating extensive assessments into a manageable format, ratings substantially contribute to situations which are characterized by extreme time constraints and the need to selectively reduce information.

For an adequate understanding of the role of rating agencies within the global financial system, it is necessary to take an intense look at the organizational treatment of ignorance. The social sciences have, however, not sufficiently dealt with either the risks or the productivity of ignorance. Within economics, which has only recently – within the framework of the »New Growth Theory« (e.g. Romer 1986) – found a way to draw on knowledge as an endogenous variable for the explanation of economic growth, ignorance is generally considered nothing more than the disagreeable opposite of knowledge and is to be dealt with by sufficient mechanisms to an economically justifiable degree. From a neoclassical perspective, George J. Stigler (1961) notes:

»Ignorance is like subzero weather: by a sufficient expenditure its effects upon people can be kept within tolerable or even comfortable bounds, but it would be wholly uneconomic entirely to eliminate all its effects. And, just as an analysis of man's shelter and apparel would be somewhat incomplete if cold weather is ignored, so also our understanding of economic life will be incomplete if we do not systematically take account of the cold winds of ignorance« (ibid., 224).

Ignorance is taken into consideration here as a kind of factor which influences economic decisions. Its particular functions and consequences, however, remain hidden.

Niklas Luhmann's thoughts on an »ecology of ignorance« (1998) are much more insightful. Presupposing the existence of basically *unsolvable* ignorance, Luhmann asks how people and organizations cope with the relevant questions of modernity, when it is only possible to speak of the future in terms of a fictionally certain reality. Luhmann does not see ignorance as a dysfunctional condition to be remedied as soon as possible. On the contrary, from his perspective, continuing and newly generated uncertainty is the most important resource for the reproduction of social systems. Referring to organizations, Luhmann points out that without uncertainty there would be nothing left to decide upon, absolute self-determination would be the end of an organization. Accordingly, mechanisms emerge which not only enable society to endure the intransparency of the world but which allow it to be used productively.

It is important to note that economic realms are increasingly defined by an utilitarian treatment of ignorance (see Strulik and Hessling in this volume). The manifest functions of rating agencies can be understood as a form of the operative use of the difference between unspecified and specified ignorance (Merton 1987; Luhmann 1995). While unspecified ignorance appears to be an insolvable information problem (unlimited contingency), specified ignorance on the other hand is a solvable information problem (limited contingency). On the basis of this difference it is clear that ratings serve to transfer indeterminate complexity into structured (manageable) complexity. With their assessments of the probability of payment default, rating agencies qualify the essential indeterminateness of the investment business. Their rating classification translates the result of the rating process into a letter combination (e.g. AAA or BB) (for more detailed information see Standard & Poor's 2006) and makes information available that can be easily understood (and interpreted). In light of the uncertain future, the appeal to ratings makes it possible for financial actors (1) to decide with confidence, (2) to ground their decisions ›rationally‹, and (3) to put themselves in a position to sufficiently deal with their risks in case of negative consequences. It is clear that in specifying factual, social, and temporal expectations, rating agencies contribute to dealing with the contingencies of the financial markets in a structured manner. And while they do not have the ability to tell financial actors their fortune, they have at least developed sophisticated techniques which serve to bridge the gap between present and future. On the basis of quantitative and qualitative analysis, they postulate and anticipate causal and statistical connections between future events in order to incorporate them into the present. From an economic point of view, it is clear that this activity is primarily valued because, given the ever increasing complexity and contingency of the financial markets, it not only makes risks calculable, but also reacts to the possibility that favorable options will be lost if a decision is *not* made.

If the rating agencies' functions are viewed under the aspect of a »colonization of future« (Giddens 1991), the agencies can paradoxically be seen as simultaneously contributing to new ignorance. On the one hand, their assessments and letter symbols serve to stabilize expectations. On the other hand, the interpretations they produce can be compared to other interpretations, thus confronting market actors with problems of choice and consequently with decision risk. This is illustrated by Dirk Baecker (1999: 298) with reference to the price formation on stock exchanges. Here every bit of information not only gives rise to more certainty, but also to more uncertainty – for instance, regarding how the price of stock will develop. In addition to substantiating expectations, every bit of information also supports the possibility of counter developments, and thus creates uncertainty. For rating agencies, changes in the environment are not the only reason why future events are becoming more difficult to predict; in addition, for example, every fine tuning of their analytical techniques also increases the number of debatable assumptions about future developments.

This examination of ignorance and the connection between ignorance and risk is also relevant to the ways in which knowledge-based organizations operate. That an organization is knowledge-based means that the activities of that organization are carried out on the basis of relevant knowledge which (1) is continually revised, (2) is always seen as subject to improvement, (3) is not regarded as an objective truth, but as a context-dependent, productive resource, and (4) is inseparable from ignorance, such that it is connected with specific risks (Willke 2002). If rating agencies are defined as knowledge-based organizations in this sense, it is obvious that they burden themselves and their environment with new and different uncertainties. This view is for example supported by the events which occurred in the wake of the Asian crisis. This case shows clearly that rating agencies never reveal all the facts of a case and that their judgments can lead to substantial problems. Moody's first added Thailand to what is known as the »watch list« in February 1997, long after the exchange rate of the Baht had collapsed. The agencies also considered South Korea's debt to be secure as late as October 1997. The depreciation of creditworthiness that followed the rating re-assessments led to massive strains on the stock exchanges affected and to widespread consequences that had effects far beyond the national economies of the region. At the same time, the rating agencies' reputation was considerably damaged. They were criticized for having »not fully read the speed and depth with which the crisis was spreading« and then, as the crisis became considerably clear, for »muscling into the Asian market and pouring ›oil‹ all over the ›fire‹« (Sakae 1999: 3).

Despite such events, it can hardly be disputed that the leading rating agencies have a great deal of authority. Given the developments in global financial affairs, investors, private customers, and even large institutional investors are finding it more and more impossible to carry out the necessary credit analysis on borrowers by themselves. The emergence of a global financial system is being accompanied by decision-making problems which are due to a lack of information about the local conditions of borrowers (e.g. accounting, the legal system) and which are made more dynamic by the new kinds of securities and financing instruments that are continually being created. In this context, *unspecified ignorance* is increasingly important in many areas: for example, in reference to the intransparency of the markets, to unsolvable information problems, and to the de-limitation of contingencies. However, in order to be able to make acceptable decisions, the actors need reference points which they can use to calculate the consequences of their actions. As already shown with regard to the manifest functions of rating agencies, in specifying ignorance rating agencies react precisely to this demand. In calculating the probability that a debtor will default, the agencies contribute to the governance of global finance by specifying ignorance and opening opportunities for productive risk taking. Therefore, rating agencies can be understood as driving forces of the risk production of the global financial system.

4. Rating Agencies and the Production of System Trust

The cognitive orientation of the global financial system is reflected not only in a growing knowledge intensity but also in an increasingly dynamic production of ignorance and risks. What is important for the following considerations is that the knowledge-driven decision-making problems of the financial system point to the special relevance of trust building mechanisms. Trust is becoming more important because it increases the system's tolerance of uncertainty and serves as an effective »mechanism for reducing complexity« (Luhmann 1979: 15). Luhmann points out from a social theoretical perspective that

> »it is not to be expected that scientific and technological development will bring events under control, substituting mastery over things for trust as a social mechanism and thus making it unnecessary. Instead, one should expect trust to be increasingly in demand as a means of enduring the complexity of the future which technology will generate« (ibid.: 15).

This is certainly true for the global financial system. Developments in the highly knowledge-intensive risk management industry have not only brought about effective instruments for ›rational‹ decision-making but have created complex risks. At the same time, the production of trust, and system trust in particular, has become more important. System trust means that participants in transactions rely »on there being sufficient controls over reliability built into the system, and on the fact that these controls function independently of the structure of motives of any of the participants at any given time, so that one does not need to know personally those who worked out that knowledge« (ibid.: 53). From this theoretical starting point, it will be assumed in the following that rating agencies contribute to the building of system trust by means of their specific expertise. Consequently, trust in the global financial system's mode of operation is supported by cognitive mechanisms for the treatment of ignorance.

The credit and securities business, which rating agencies have traditionally based their assessments on, provide an example of how the increasingly dynamic markets are accompanied not only by higher yields but also by growing individual as well as collective expectations regarding safety. Trust appears to be gaining importance as a mechanism for reducing complexity and supporting the reproduction of the financial system. However, another important development must also be mentioned. In a dynamic, interdependent and globally oriented economy, trust in the continuity of financial transactions can no longer be based on personal acquaintance alone. In particular, constellations that are characterized by high uncertainty require alternative mechanisms for fostering trust in the functional capability of systems. With the primarily technology-driven separation of social relationships from the context of local interactions, social action is losing its connection to the face-to-face context and requires extended connections in order to manage the newly emerging uncertainties. To the extent that trust can no longer be exclusively secured through direct interpersonal relationships (facework commitments), social systems must provide depersonalized support mechanisms (faceless commitments) which promote trust in abstract systems, especially in expert systems (Giddens 1990: 83). When uncertainty between potential business partners grows, as in the expansion of global investment strategies, system trust becomes more necessary in order to bridge knowledge gaps in how business partners of the respective transaction will act. Ratings respond to this problem by compensating for the depersonalization of transactions with an alternative trust-building form of business relationship.

With respect to the growing number of opportunities in the knowledge economy as well as the related increase in the contingency of decisions, ratings are a trust good in two respects. On the one hand the agencies are dependent for their profits on the market actors' trust in their assessments, that is market actors have to give them trust in advance. On the other hand rating agencies operate as »trust intermediaries« (Coleman 1982), and as such make an important contribution to trust building in financial transactions. In both respects trust clearly functions as a complexity-reducing mechanism (Luhmann 1979). On the basis of a rating market actors can exclude certain possibilities of development from consideration. Certain dangers which cannot be removed but which should not disrupt action are neutralized. As for trust in the judgments of rating agencies, it must be noted that there are substantial obstacles to an assessment of the quality of their ratings. Not least because of time pressure and scant alternatives, trust in the formal correctness of the rating process as well as the reliability of assessments are of fundamental importance. A verification of ratings at the moment of publication would entail the very information costs that investors hope to save by making use of the rating. Even at the moment that an assessed commitment is made, it cannot be known for certain whether the contractual obligations of debtors are founded upon sufficient conditions of creditworthiness by the rating agency. This is because the simple ex post observation that the risk of default has or has not been realized does not say anything about whether or not, in a specific case, the expected value was correctly determined ex ante. As such, the use of ratings presupposes a considerable amount of trust in advance from market actors. For rating agencies, this means that they must actively build the necessary trust in their services. This is achieved through reputation.

Reputation can be understood as an orientation tool, which – in light of intransparent conditions – serves to relieve decision-makers (Luhmann 1994: 245). The agencies' reputation effectively functions as a kind of auxiliary code to the medium of money and orchestrates the decisions of market actors. Considering the unknown future, competing interpretations and pressure to make decisions, overtaxed market actors have no other choice but to appeal to reputation as a basis for selections. In this way a self-referential process of attention condensation emerges, which establishes and reinforces itself through proven success. For example, some years ago middle-sized German companies that strove for ratings – not least because of the innovations in banking regulation (Basel II) being discussed at the time – were nevertheless very hesitant to make use of the services of small German rating agencies such as EuroRatings, URA or R@S. As was made clear at a conference in May 2000 organized by the rating agencies operating in Germany for representatives of banks and middle-sized companies, the companies were more interested in the major US-American players Standard & Poor's and Moody's. They were even prepared to pay substantially higher fees for the services of the established agencies. The reason for this was the assumption that a rating made by a reputable market leader is considerably more effective in promoting trust in a business's ability to meet financial obligations, and in doing so, improving the business' refinancing and cooperation opportunities.

Reputation is as costly as it is fragile on the rating market. For the rating agencies it is vital to maintain the appearance of being reliable and impartial financial assessors. In particular, publication of the so called default rates (Standard & Poor's 2001: 3) are used by the agencies as proof of the accuracy of their ratings. Furthermore, it is important that the agencies are reacting to the inevitable differences between the ideal and the real quotas with adjustments to their rating systems. This kind of institutionalized readiness to be reflexive and to learn is clearly honored by the extensive trust provided in advance by market actors. In addition, further factors can be identified that promote the agency's reputation and, most importantly, indicate that they are to large extent independent. First of all, because rating agencies can engage in business relationships with a multitude of issuers, they are relatively little affected by the success or failure of an individual contracting party and therefore only obligated to each of them to a very limited extent. It can be assumed that the increasingly large pool of customers reduces their dependency on individual clients. Secondly, by reducing their business activities to ratings, the reliability of the assessments which they publish can be made the agencies only form of capital. In doing so they avoid any impression of being subject to conflicts of interest as can be the case with other financial intermediaries like banks and issuers which may withhold or manipulate information because of short-term advantages in spite of the risk of causing damage to their reputations. Thirdly, many of the agencies' customers are both issuers and institutional investors and it is because of their duel status that they usually have no interest in the agencies which are demonstrably only either borrower- or investor-friendly.

From an empirical perspective, it is clear that the rating agencies do in fact give the impression of being reliable and impartial assessors. All of the internationally operating credit rating providers have reduced their activities – and in doing so, their potential sales – to issuing evaluations of creditworthiness and have foregone other ways of using their expertise to do business. Their customers can therefore assume that the data provided will not be interpreted and used for business strategic considerations other than those intended by the rating. It is furthermore important that the standardization of the prognoses, that is their positioning in a clearly defined ranking system, ensures that the assessments of the providers are comparable and therefore verifiable. The fact that assessments by rating agencies provide important criteria for financial decisions on the one hand but are also continually under market scrutiny on the other, further illustrates the non-hierarchical observer relationship between the agencies and the markets. Rating agencies are not only observers of the market but are in their turn an object of market observation and have to orient themselves to this. In this way, markets always make the final judgment regarding the ›correctness‹ of ratings. For this reason it is doubtful, as one would intuitively suspect, that rating agencies, which are usually paid by their ›objects‹, are economically dependent on them and that this results in one-sided business oriented assessments which put investors at a disadvantage. What such a perspective overlooks is that issuers' willingness to pay depends on investors' assessment of the reliability of ratings. Although the network of rating agencies, issuers and investors is characterized by asymmetrical observer relationships, it can in no way be considered hierarchically or economically dependent. It is however clear that, as intermediaries of trust, rating agencies are in a position not only to structure market observations but to efficiently relate them economically.

When considering ratings a trust good in these two respects, it must also be recognized that their present reliability for market actors, which has been proven over an extended period of time, has led to trust in the assessments of the agencies and that this is a source of fundamental trust in the financial system. To the extent that one can invest money today in a country that one has never visited and in which loans of companies are being distributed with products that one is not familiar with, the economic demand is growing for complexity reducing mechanisms, which do not depend on personal trust. By making use of the assessments of rating agencies system trust is created which makes it possible for the market actors to engage in financial business that would otherwise not be feasible because of incalculable uncertainties. The establishment of orientation services is successful to the extent that the intermediation of trust is achieved on the basis of *authoritative expertise*, which is recognized as particularly relevant. Nevertheless, the importance of expertise appears to be determined, not only by social authority and objectively based trust in the agencies' ability to construct reality, but also by a reflexive trust in trust that other market actors are similarly orienting themselves on the basis of the assessments of rating agencies. Thus investors not only rely on ratings because they recognize the embedded expertise but also because they expect other investors to have similar trust in the assessments of rating agencies. Last but not least, it is interesting to see that, because of their high economic value, the agencies receive extensive trust in advance even though it is clear to all market actors that no agency can possibly be held responsible for their misjudgements. Although trust and responsibility are normally considered complementary factors, market actors are nevertheless willing to tolerate an asymmetric relationship between the trust that is granted the agencies and their acceptance of responsibility.

5. Conclusions

In the light of the recent sociological discussion on the knowledge society and knowledge economy it is discernable that rating agencies contribute to a strategic management of the dynamics of knowledge and ignorance. The agencies' increasing relevance is a reflection of the fact that global finance requires organizations specialized in a knowledge-based exploitation of ignorance. With their global expertise, rating agencies keep a close watch on the creditworthiness of states, firms and financial instruments. What is of central importance is that rating agencies actively grasp the indeterminateness of the markets, interpret it and translate it into practicable expectations on the basis of which market actors can take risks and make profits accordingly. In addition, rating agencies are important elements of the global financial systems' trust architecture. Their significance as intermediaries of trust shows that the increasing complexity of global finance goes hand in hand with a demand for knowledge-based mechanisms, which strengthen trust in the financial systems' ability to function. From both perspectives – the exploitation of ignorance as well as the production of system trust – it becomes clear that rating agencies are not sufficiently described as financial services firms that solve specific coordination problems. Rather, in a systems-theoretical approach, they can best be understood as knowledge-based organizations which expand the risk-processing capacity of the global financial system and – in doing so – inevitably create new decision-problems and societal risks.

References

Baecker, Dirk (1999), »Die Preisbildung an der Börse«, in: *Soziale Systeme*, Vol. 5, 287–312.

Bank for International Settlements (BIS) (1995), *65. Annual Report.* Basel.

— (2000), *Credit Ratings and Complementary Sources of Credit Quality Information*. Working paper, No. 3, http://www.bis.org/(03/06/02).

— (2000a), *70. Annual Report*. Basel.

Coleman, James S. (1982), »Systems of trust. A rough theoretical framework«, in: *Angewandte Sozialforschung*, Vol. 10, 277–298.

Eichengreen, Barry/Lindert, Peter H. (1989) (eds), *The International Debt Crisis in Historical Perspective*. Cambridge (Mass.).

Giddens, Anthony (1990), *The consequences of modernity*. Oxford.

— (1991), *Modernity and Self-Identity. Self and Society in the late Modern Age*. Stanford.

Gigerenzer, Gerd (2001), *Adaptive thinking. Rationality in the real world*. Oxford.

Ladeur, Karl-Heinz (1995), *Das Umweltrecht der Wissensgesellschaft. Von der Gefahrenabwehr zum Risikomanagement*. Berlin.

Luhmann, Niklas (1979), *Trust and power*. Chichester.

— (1994), *Die Wissenschaft der Gesellschaft*. 2nd edition. Frankfurt a.M.

— (1995), *Gesellschaftsstruktur und Semantik. Studien zur Wissenssoziologie der modernen Gesellschaft*, Vol. 4. Frankfurt a.M.

— (1997), »The control of intransparency«, in: *Systems Research and Behavioral Science*, Vol. 14, 359–371.

— (1998), *Observations of Modernity*. Stanford.

MacKenzie, Donald (2003), *Opening the Black Boxes of Global Finance*. http://www.ed.ac.uk/MacKenzie (05/03/06).

Merton, Robert K. (1987), »Three fragments from a sociologist's notebook: Establishing the phenomenon, specified ignorance, and strategic research materials«, in: *Annual Review of Sociology*, Vol. 13, 1–28.

Power, Michael (1997), *The Audit Society. Rituals of Verification*. Oxford.

Ravetz, Jerome R. (1986), »Usable knowledge, usable ignorance: incomplete science with policy implications«, in: William C. Clark, R.E. Munn (eds), *Sustainable Development of the Biosphere*. Cambridge (UK), 415–432.

Sakae, Sakamoto (1999), *Growing Doubt about Moody's. The JCIF-Report*. http://www.jef.or.jp/en/jti/199905_013.html (12/03/02).

Shapiro, Susan P. (1987), »The social control of impersonal trust«, in: *American Journal of Sociology*, Vol. 93, 623–658.

Sinclair, Timothy J. (1999), »Bond-rating agencies and coordination in the global political economy«, in: Claire A. Cutler, Viginia Haufler and Tony Porter (eds), *Private Authority and International Affairs*. New York, 153–167.

— (2000), »Reinventing authority: Embedded knowledge networks and the new global finance«, in: *Environment and Planning C: Government and Policy*, Vol. 18, 487–502.

— (2005), *The New Masters of Capital. American Bond Rating Agencies and the Politics of Creditworthiness*. Ithaca.

Smithson, Michael (1989), *Ignorance and Uncertainty. Emerging Paradigms*. New York.

Standard & Poor's (2000): *Ratings Definitions*. http://www.standard-poors.com/ResourceCenter/RatingsDefinitions. html> (05/01/00).

— (2001), *Corporate Defaults: Will Things Get Worse Before they Get Better?* http://www. standardandpoors.com (10/30/01).

— (2006), *McGraw-Hill Financial Services.* http://www.mcgraw-hill.com/news/kits_fact.shtml (07/05/06).

Stigler, George J. (1961), »The economics of information«, in: *The Journal of Political Economy*, Vol. LXIX, 213–225.

Strulik, Torsten (2004), *Nichtwissen und Vertrauen in der Wissensökonomie.* Frankfurt a.M.

Willke, Helmut (2002), *Dystopia. Studien zur Krisis des Wissens in der modernen Gesellschaft.* Frankfurt a.M.

— (2003), *Heterotopia. Studien zur Krisis der Ordnungen moderner Gesellschaften.* Frankfurt a.M.

Part 4

Basel II – A Cognitive Turn in Banking Regulation?

Governance without Politics? Administration and Politics in the Basel II Process

Boris Holzer

1. Global Financial Governance and Basel II

The field of banking regulation is an example of the possibilities and problems of global governance. It concerns border-crossing risks that can neither be controlled by individual governments nor by the interstate system as a whole because they require transnational cooperation among regulators and the private sector. Banking crises can wreak havoc on a country's economy. Governments therefore seek to minimize the likelihood of bank failures, for instance by requiring banks to keep a certain percentage of reserve capital for all their loans. The interdependence of the banking system across territorial borders however makes it impossible for any single country to manage systemic risks within its own jurisdiction based on national regulation alone. Consequently, there have been continued efforts to reduce the likelihood of individual bank failures – and thus the risk of systemic repercussions. To this end, the G10 countries established the Basel Committee on Banking Supervision in 1975. It has since issued both supervisory principles (in the Concordat of 1975) and capital adequacy standards (in the Capital Accord of 1988) for transnational financial institutions to ensure accountability and liquidity in case of failures. The work of the Committee adopted the principle of ›international co-operation based on home-country control‹, i.e. the premise that supervision and regulation should be exercised by national governments (Kapstein 1994: 10pp).

The Basel Capital Accord is regarded as an instructive example of successful regime formation.[1] The Accord, which formulated capital adequacy standards for international banks dependent on their credit portfolio, was to some degree a logical extension of previous agreements, but it also pioneered a new degree of the international harmonization of banking standards. Efforts to coordinate banking supervision internationally began when the governments of major industrial countries realized that their economies might be vulnerable to the domino-like structure of international banking failures. Many countries' ability to prevent or at least contain bank failures had been hampered by the internationalization of banking. Lending institutions had long started to engage in ›regulatory arbitrage‹, i.e. they sought to bypass regulations in their home country by establishing affiliates in less strictly regulated environments. The policy of ›international co-operation based on home-country control‹ was designed to close such loopholes and establish an international framework of regulation.[2]

However, there were also some problems with the 1988 Basel Capital Accord. Its implementation was soon beset with undesired side-effects (Swary/Topf 1991: 411pp; Eatwell/Taylor 2000: 198). *First*, the weighting system of the 1988 Accord proved to be a rather crude instrument of regulation. By using four categories of risk, it reduced the complexity of risk assessment to a bare minimum. Possible borrowers were assigned to one of four classes of risk which determined how much capital had to be reserved (varying between 100 percent for the private sector and 0 percent

1 The following brief summary of research on the Basel Capital Accord builds on Kapstein (1989; 1992; 1994: Ch. 5), Porter (1993: Ch. 3), Reinicke (1995: Ch. 8) and Genschel/Plümper (1997).

2 It is appropriate to use the term ›international‹ in this context – in contrast to ›transnational‹ – since the regulatory efforts of 1970s were fundamentally predicated on the co-operation of sovereign nation-states and therefore inter-national in character.

for items not subject to default risk). This resulted in a sometimes unwarranted borrowing to governments at the expense of the private sector. *Second*, the Accord focused on counter-party risk exclusively. The capital requirements were not adjusted for the risk-level of a bank's overall portfolio. Measures of market risk did not enter the picture either. Combined with the fact that counter-party risk was only assessed in terms of the broad categorization into four classes of risk the capital requirements thus created an overly additive and linear image of risk. Possible co-variations within a portfolio, for instance, were not part of the risk assessment. *Third*, the concrete shaping of the risk classes resulted in a bias toward short-term lending. Since short-term lending (especially in government securities) carried a lower risk-weight, the Capital Accord basically established an incentive to refrain from long-term lending in favour of short-term lending. Obviously, that was neither in the interest of governments nor in the interest of the private sector.

Taken together, these shortcomings led banks to focus their lending on those sectors with a low risk weighting regardless of whether that implied a strongly biased credit portfolio. Therefore the objective of the Basel Accord to increase the stability of the banking system was undermined. By leading banks to expand their lending in low-risk categories, the overall distribution of lending was distorted. Not necessarily making the portfolio more risky, that shift nonetheless had an undesirable impact on the overall cost of credit. By making government debt less expensive and therefore more profitable, the Basel Accord had the undesired side-effect of making credit more expensive for the private sector – based on a rather arbitrary bureaucratic categorization rather than on the individual borrower's creditworthiness.

Those problems were soon recognized. The resulting reform of international banking supervision including capital adequacy standards has been a long-running project. A revised version (›Basel II‹) was published in 2004 and will be implemented in the next few years. The agreement was the result of several rounds of negotiations with extensive private sector involvement. Both the formulation and the implementation of the new capital requirements rely heavily on the expertise and resources of the banks themselves. Those international banks with the necessary infrastructure will be allowed and encouraged to use their own risk models (›internal ratings‹) instead of the fixed risk categories and weights prescribed by the regulator. The supervision will therefore depend much more than before on direct interaction between banks and regulators who will have to inspect and evaluate the soundness of complex risk models on site. A continuous ›supervisory review process‹ will assess the coherence and reliability of a bank's risk management systems on site and thus involve an increasingly qualitative instead of quantitative approach to regulation (cf. Strulik/Kussin 2005: 122pp). Basel II thus ›outsources‹ parts of the regulatory process to the banks in order to reduce the information asymmetry between the private and public sectors (Reinicke 1998: 112–113). Regarding this reliance on private expertise the emerging transnational regime has some characteristics of a private or at least a ›mixed‹ regime, i.e. of a ›complex of formal and informal institutions that is a source of governance for an economic issue area as a whole‹ (Cutler et al. 1999b: 13). Many observers however regard the paramount role of private actors in the formulation and implementation of Basel II as problematic (see e.g. King/Sinclair 2003). It appears to replicate the increasing role of ›private authority‹ at the expense of governments in many areas of global governance.[3] Large parts of the negotiations and actual monitoring in financial and other areas of governance are delegated to or at least involve non-elected private organizations. Political or even public debate, in contrast, plays a minor role. The Basel II negotiations are a prime example of such a form of policy-making.

2. Basel II in the Press

We can regard the (non-)presence of Basel II as a topic in public discourse as a rough and incomplete yet still instructive indicator of the amount of public, contentious politics involved in the negotiations. The negotiations were by no means uncontroversial and some of the debated points also figured prominently in the press. For instance, an exemplary analysis of reports in three German newspapers revealed that three topics were particularly prominent (cf. Holzer/Beck 2004): the possible consequences for small and medium enterprises (SMEs), the problem of procyclical effects and diverging opinions among regulators. Overall however the Basel II process attracted only sporadic attention in the German press during the

3 See Germain (2001), Porter (2005) and Sinclair (1994; 2005) for private actors in global finance and for various other fields the contributions in Cutler et al. (1999a), Hewson and Sinclair (1999) and Higgott et al. (2000).

period of investigation (October 2002 to December 2003).[4] Just one newspaper, the *Frankfurter Allgemeine Zeitung* (FAZ), carried reports throughout the progress of the negotiations, while the other two newspapers in our sample – *Süddeutsche Zeistung* (SZ) and *Financial Times Deutschland* (FTD) – did not feature Basel II-related articles for some weeks during the years 2002 and 2003. Measured by the number of articles, there were two peaks of interest: the first in November 2002, the second in September/October 2003 (see Fig. 1). Most obvious is the concentration of reporting activity in autumn 2003: The articles in September and October alone account for 36 percent of total reporting over the year (53:75 articles). In between, reports were scarce and mainly not concerned with the Basel negotiations themselves, but with the possible implications of the new Accord for various fields of finance and the economy.

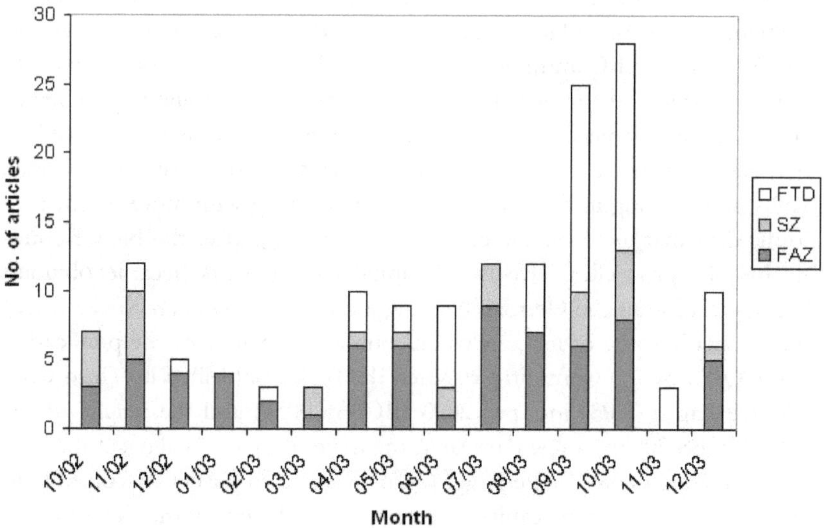

Figure 1: Newspaper Reports in German Print Media 2002/03

The first peak of newspaper coverage in October/November 2002 concerned the possible consequences that Basel II might have for small and medium enterprises (SMEs). While the implications of Basel II for the risk

4 Our sample included newspaper articles from two major German dailies, the *Frankfurter Allgemeine Zeitung* (FAZ) and the *Süddeutsche Zeitung* (SZ), and from the more specialized German affiliate of the Financial Times, the Financial Times Deutschland (FTD).

management of banks or for the economy as a whole are either difficult to pin down or beyond the scope of interest of many people, the possible problems for SMEs are a much more palpable issue. If, put simply, Basel II means that SMEs have to pay higher interest rates for loans because of their traditionally low capital resources or that they may even find it impossible to obtain loans at all, that obviously calls into action many public interest groups. The Süddeutsche Zeitung thus commented near the end of October: ›Basel II … hangs over the German economy like a sword of Damocles‹.[5] Shortly after that statement, the latent threat attracted a host of attention and comments when the European Commission – seemingly under pressure from major European governments including Germany and Italy – publicly announced that it would take all measures to prevent adverse consequences for SMEs.

A second issue that attracted moderate public attention concerned a problem that had surfaced during the third quantitative impact survey (QIS3). The Basel Committee had initiated that survey to assess and calibrate the effects of the new agreement on the banks' capital requirements. In the process, it was discovered that the new risk measures showed an increased sensitivity to macro-economic factors. Because the German banks participating in the survey were now working with more recent economic data that included the economic downswing after the New Economy bubble, procyclical effects on capital requirements became obvious. The association of the German banking industry, the *Zentraler Kreditausschuß* (ZKA), made some of its conclusions public in advance of the publication of the QIS3 by the Committee.[6] When the BCBS published its Third Consultative Paper (CP3) in April 2003 (BCBS 2003a) and the results of the QIS3 (BCBS 2003b) a few days later, the issue of procyclicality set the tone of the ensuing debate.[7] The larger German banks in particular voiced concern that an increase of capital requirements induced by the deteriorating ratings during an economic downswing could exacerbate cyclic fluctuations. If the change of capital requirements were too tightly coupled with the overall probability of default, a rapid increase of capital charges could

5 SZ, 30 October 2002.

6 ›ZKA übt weiter Kritik an »Basel II«‹ (FAZ, 7 April 2003).

7 See »Basel II wirkt prozyklisch« (FAZ, 6 May 2003); ›Testlauf für Basel II mit überraschenden Ergebnissen‹ (SZ, 7 May 2003); this point was later also echoed by Josef Ackermann of Deutsche Bank, Chairman of the IIF (›Banken nehmen Basel II unter Störfeuer‹; FTD, 25 August 2003).

force banks to cut down on their lending – and thereby increase the downswing (ZKA 2003). Data from the QIS3 from four German banks showed that the procyclical effects might negatively affect the banks' ability to lend throughout the economic cycle (BdB 2003). Accordingly, it was suggested that capital requirements should be based on 3–year average ratings of customers and that the risk weight function should be adapted in order to decouple the capital requirements from severe fluctuations (ibid.).

While the debate about procyclicality was a technical rather than a principled one, the debate became more conflictual – and thereby more interesting to the mass media, as indicated by the final peak towards the end of the year – when the Basel II negotiations entered a crucial phase: The comments on the CP3 were designed as the final step in the consultation process; the BCBS planned to finalize the Basel II framework by the end of the year 2003. It is therefore hardly surprising to see the public attention rise towards the end of the year. From the perspective of the media, the efforts of various interest groups and countries to position themselves for the final round of negotiations provided an opportunity to dwell on the resulting conflicts. Comments on the CP3 were due by 31 July 2003, but many groups used the period between that date and the final meeting of the BCBS in October to put their objectives firmly on the political agenda. With the consultation process drawing to a close, members of the EU Parliament in particular realized that changes would be difficult to affect once the deal was done. In the build-up towards the BCBS meeting, it therefore became possible to construe a conflict between two sides – the Americans, who asked for changes, and the Europeans, who preferred quick implementation

The overall rather sporadic presence of the Basel II negotiations in the print media indicates the limited news value of such a transnational policy process. The long duration and technical complexity of the Basel II negotiations made it an unlikely candidate for continuous, extensive reporting. The details of risk weight functions and definitions of regulatory capital are well beyond the scope of interest of a general audience. For a long time, the lines of conflict within the consultation process were also too far removed from the normal requirements of news items. Not persons, but interest groups and business associations were the main actors on the public stage. Therefore it was almost impossible to personalize issues and conflicts. Only the final round of negotiations leading up to the October meeting of the BCBS provided the necessary ingredients. At that point, the clash of interests could be depicted as a transatlantic conflict between European and American positions. Unless such clear lines of conflict could be observed, reporting remained scarce and sporadic.

Generally speaking, transnational policy processes are unlikely to receive much attention in the news media unless they are tied up with domestic interests. Before the ›showdown‹ setting of the October meeting the reports thus concentrated on those issues that seemed particularly relevant for the domestic economy. The majority of the contributions focused on the effects on SMEs, which are a prominent feature of the German economy – and also of its corporatist political system. In comparison, the effects on transnational settings played a marginal role in the debate, despite the fact that the stabilization of the transnational banking system may be regarded as the prime motivation of the old and the new Basel framework. With regard to our initial question about the balance of domestic and transnational interests in the public debate, we can therefore conclude that domestic issues clearly dominated the media discourse in Germany. Although reports repeatedly mentioned that the primary – and welcome – objective of Basel II was to make the banking system ›safer‹, the issue of transnational risk as such never was the motivation for reporting.

It is understandable that members of the European Parliament criticize the lack of participation in transnational negotiations such as Basel II.[8] Yet the sporadic attention paid to the negotiations in the press makes it questionable whether a lot of public or even ›democratic‹ participation in such a matter can be expected even under different circumstances. The call for democratic legitimacy obscures a much more fundamental problem of the regulation of financial risk: legitimacy first and foremost needs to be obtained from those who are the actual subjects of regulation, i.e. the banks themselves. Since transnational regulation cannot take the classical division of labour between politics and administration for granted, it needs to regard the acceptance of decisions by the private sector as more problematical and riskier. In order to understand and interpret the perceived lack of ›democratic‹ policy-making in financial governance, we therefore need to examine the relationship between politics, administration and the public in greater detail.

---

8 In a way, members of parliament thus added the second level to an otherwise incomplete version of a ›two-level game‹, in which international negotiations have to be reconciled with domestic demands (Putnam 1988).

3. Politics, Administration and the Public

The significance of non-elected, non-accountable organizations in global financial governance combined with the relative absence of contentious politics leads to the suspicion that both the Basel II negotiations and the resulting regime suffer from a democratic deficit – just like the institutions of financial governance as a whole (Porter 2001). For some political scientists this raises the question of how legitimate such forms of multi-level governance can be in terms of received principles of democracy. When Pauly (1997) asks: »Who elected the bankers?«, he does not expect any positive answer. Yet ought not the democratic sovereign, i.e. the people, to be the ultimate arbiter – instead of private, profit-seeking enterprises? And should not public authorities, i.e. elected governments, be at the helm of decision-making – instead of regulators and technical experts? To conceive of democratic politics in terms of the literal meaning of ›government by the people‹ can indeed only lead us to the conclusion that transnational politics is inherently undemocratic. Neither is the citizenry much involved in or informed about many transnational negotiations nor is there a lot of public political debate about seemingly arcane topics such as Basel II.

The problem with the democratic deficit argument is that it is based on the classical yet pre-sociological notion of democracy. It presumes that the symbolic notion of ›democracy‹ can be readily translated into a theoretical description. But by taking it for granted that democracy implies a hierarchy of control that puts government and administration at the receiving end of the people's instructions, one is bound to be disappointed. In terms of the actual exercise of power the social reality is complicated by the fact that power in a democratic political system needs to be constantly regenerated. Being instructed by the government, the administration is subject to the sovereign's commands, but so is in turn the sovereign: the public has to comply with administrative decisions that are – at least according to the model – ultimately their own decisions.

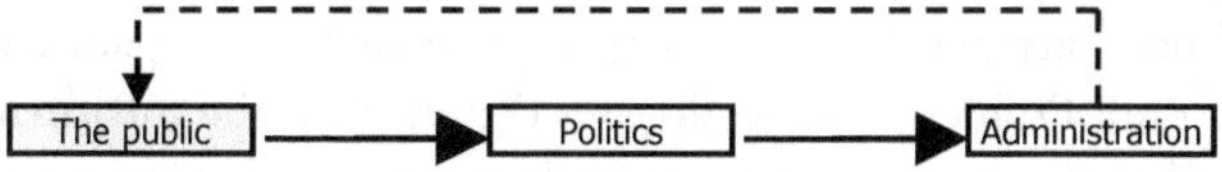

Figure 2: The Hierarchical Model of Democracy

The resulting loop in the exercise of power (indicated by the dotted line in Fig. 2) leads to the model of a *circuit* instead of a *hierarchy* power (Luhmann 1972a: 163pp; 1981; 1987). According to this model of the political system, politics – or rather: *Politics* with a capital P – refers to all those activities that seek to prepare collectively binding decisions by testing und condensing possibilities of consensus, i.e. primarily to ›party politics‹ (Luhmann 2000: 254). The *administration* in contrast is concerned with formulating and implementing decisions based on political premises; it is not confined to merely executing decisions, it also includes the formal stages of parliamentary legislation. The *public* finally consists of the electorate that exercises power by voting while being subject to administrative power itself. However, the flow of power can never be wholly unidirectional. The exercise of power involves cooperation or resistance and thus necessarily opens up possibilities for counter-strategies. Thus, we should expect the ›official‹ circuit of power to be supplemented by another, ›informal‹ one that would flow the other way round.

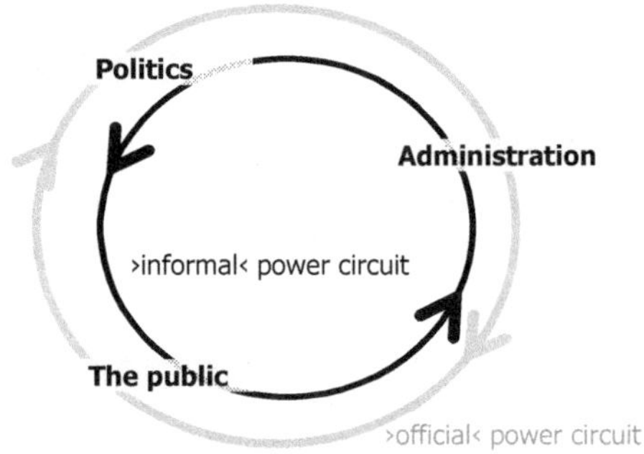

Figure 3: The Power Circuit

An informal power circuit can indeed be observed in modern democracies. In most cases, it concerns the everyday, routine ways of getting things done – that often stand in contrast to the official description. For instance, the administration effectively instructs Politics – rather than the other way round – by formulating possible areas and alternatives for decision-making based on budgetary and legal restrictions. The electorate again has no opportunity to tell Politics what to do, but depends on the information provided by political parties in order to make a choice. But the public is not just a passive recipient of administrative decisions either. It seeks to actively shape them through various interest groups as well as through direct interactions with administrators. Administrative science abounds with examples of ›how great hopes in Washington are dashed in Oakland‹ (Pressman/Wildavsky 1973). In order to actually implement policy decisions, the administration is well advised not to neglect the interests of those affected by them. To the extent that individuals or groups obstruct or facilitate implementation, the public thus wields power over administration. Although there are good reasons to believe that most routine events in the political system are governed by the informal power circuit, the official circuit remains dominant in times of crisis. Political conflicts can be decided in elections, the premises of administration can be changed, and the administration can enforce decisions against resistance. The complexity of everyday decision-making and implementation, however, is more effectively accommodated by the mechanisms of informal power. It thus represents the routine way of coping with political complexity. The exercise of formal power at the interface between administration and the public may be further modulated and circumscribed by another fact: the emergence of informal ›*contact systems*‹ between administrators and their clients (Luhmann 1983: 75pp). The implementation of policies may require or inadvertently lead to regular contacts with particular parts of the public. The social environment of the administration is then increasingly concretized and anticipated based on personal acquaintanceship and past situational experience. That may increase the ability to gauge the acceptance of administrative decisions – but it also gives clients the opportunity to influence the decision-making process.

While the hierarchical model assumes that rule-making is initiated by Politics and then handed down to administration, the power circuit model regards the contacts between administration and its clients as another channel of influence. From an administrative perspective, both Politics and the public are then sources of irritation and change. However, any form of factual dominance of the informal side would be problematic since it tends to reverse the officially anticipated relationship between administration and its public environment. Instead of receiving instructions from Politics and stubbornly executing them, administration would then be open to instruction from the outside. The public would not simply ›learn‹ to accept administrative decisions, but the administration would also learn from its clients. But what would be the consequences for Politics? If we regard contentious Politics as the vehicle for generating *generalized* support for the implementation of collectively binding decisions, it would become dispensable to the extent that administration is capable of securing *specific* support regarding the issue area and clients concerned. It would therefore be hardly surprising that a policy process characterized by such a close cooperation between regulators and the private sector as Basel II should actually involve rather little Politics (with a capital P).

4. The Politics of Capital Standards – Without a Capital P?

The difficulties with turning a policy process such as Basel II into a salient topic of contentious Politics are obvious. Despite its implications for financial stability and economic growth, the regulation of banking does not lend itself to a political debate revolving around traditional distinctions such as left vs. right, progressive vs. conservative or capital vs. labour. Rather, the most salient line of conflict runs between regional banks, small savings banks and small and medium enterprises on the one hand and large global banking houses on the other. Yet the extent to which that fault line can be ›politicized‹, i.e. turned into a salient issue for the political system, appears to be limited to mapping it onto a supposed geopolitical conflict between European and US-American interests. But the problem is not merely that transnational financial governance is too technical, too complex or simply too boring for public debate. It also seems that the role played by contentious Politics within a domestic setting cannot be easily transferred to the transnational level. From a functionalist perspective, the specific role of Politics is to test out and condense chances for consensus so that administrative decisions can count on general acceptance that would isolate any resistance. Yet regarding the problem of acceptance the primary arena of the Basel II negotiations is not the classical political arena. The acceptance by the general public is not that relevant on the one hand – and not enough on the other. Banking regulation does not concern an anonymous population of individual citizens but a more or less defined and known set of organizations. Their cooperation is the main concern, and it is in some ways more difficult to secure. The main risks of transnational financial regulation therefore are the administrative – and not primarily political – risks of decisions, i.e. the risk of regulatory decisions being subverted and rendered ineffective despite generalized acceptance.

It is a general risk of administrative decision-making that rules may have unanticipated side-effects – or no effects at all (Hiller 1994; Vollmer 1997). We noted above that contact systems between the administration and its clients may facilitate the calibration and implementation of decisions. There is, however, no guarantee that anticipated consequences can be realized. Regulation is a form of steering. It thus faces the common problem of policies that aim to achieve some well-defined change in the environment: by reducing one difference, for instance the international variations in supervisory standards, they produce a new difference somewhere else, for instance a new incentive structure for market participants (cf. Luhmann 1997). A regulatory dialectic ensues in which the side-effects undermine the objective of regulation – and thus make new regulation necessary (Strulik 2000: 212). For instance, any kind of regulation based on capital charges represents a cost factor for banks and is thus likely to be circumvented if possible. Banks will have an incentive to engage in ›regulatory arbitrage‹, i.e. to transfer their activities to geographic locations or business areas that are less strictly regulated. Thus both international cooperation (among states) and transnational cooperation (among states and non-state actors) is necessary in order to formulate and implement a system of rule that spans various jurisdictions.

To some extent, increased international cooperation should be able to reduce the arbitrage opportunities for private actors and thus the necessity to bargain directly with them.[9] In practice, however, the international cooperation remains limited both in scope and efficacy. Transnational regime-building therefore regularly is also based on the consensus and the cooperation of non-state actors. Consequently it faces a dilemma: Since transnational regulatory projects such as Basel II have to secure the acceptance of the private sector, Politics appears to be relegated to a minor role. Capital adequacy standards, for instance, are not formulated by political parties but by public administration in cooperation with private sector expertise. The effort to broaden the basis of regulation by actually including those most directly *affected* by it simultaneously fosters the impression of a democratic deficit of transnational negotiations. On the other hand, however, there is no lack of participation by regulators and other administrative staff from countries which by all standards are regarded as democratic ones in the Basel II

9 Many observers of global politics therefore recommend international cooperation including the transfer of national sovereignty as a solution to the new problems of private vs. state power (cf. Beck 2002).

process. Therefore it does not actually seem that there is a lack of *democracy* as such, but rather one of *Politics*. Echoing well-known criticisms of technocracy, the anxiety about democratic deficits therefore primarily concerns the relegation of policy-making to a matter of administration instead of contentious party politics.

Rather than merely to deplore this fact it is important to understand the reasons behind it. In the first instance, the administrative bias of financial governance is due to the fact that it is almost entirely concerned with organizations instead of individuals. In contrast to collectively binding decisions that need to be generally legitimated vis-à-vis an anonymous public, the regulatory decisions have a very specific audience: the relatively mobile, resourceful and knowledgeable organizations affected by them. Individuals usually only have sporadic contacts to administration. Therefore they can wield only situational influence. Organizations however necessarily have more constant relationships with the specialized regulatory agencies or even staff responsible for them. Contact systems between administration and organizations emerge almost inevitably (Grunow 1994: 218). And they are of far greater significance for organizations than for individuals – since organizations have no ›formal‹ power over either Politics or administration, they must rely on the informal channels in order to influence decision-making at all. From the perspective of organizations without access to formal electoral roles, informal contact systems appear as a logical vehicle to prepare, supplement or prevent legal actions. From the perspective of administration, in turn, the knowledge gathered via those channels is vital in order to minimize the risk of (non-)acceptance and obstruction of administrative decisions.

While the hierarchical model only recognizes the official instruction of administration by Politics, we must therefore regard contact systems as another mechanism of adaptation: To the extent that the implementation of administrative decisions depends on and contributes to specific contacts to the affected organizations, a cognitive element is introduced into administrative behavior. The main focus of administrative work is and remains normative: It is primarily based on expectations that are upheld even in the case of disappointment.[10] If some regulatory norm such as the adequate level of capital is violated by a particular bank, that norm is not changed. A normative orientation therefore implies the unwillingness to

10 For the distinction between cognitive and normative styles of expectation see Luhmann (1972b: 40pp).

learn. Backed by legitimate state power, administration regularly refuses to learn. Direct contacts with clients however can only be maintained if the information thus gathered makes a difference within the administration itself. That is only possible if the actual interaction between administration and its clients offers enough flexibility for adaptation. While the traditional model of regulation based on fixed thresholds must regard such flexibility as a potentially corrupt anomaly, new forms of regulation regularly include ›procedural‹ elements that provide more room for negotiation and change and thus combine cognitive and normative orientations.

5. Basel II: From Threshold to Procedural Regulation

It is certainly possible to explain this form of negotiation and bargaining between the private sector and administration – which except for the absence of labour organizations reminds one of traditional forms of corporatism – with reference to the interests of profit-seeking enterprises. On the part of business it is of course a plausible motive to keep regulation at a minimal level. However, it is more difficult to explain why regulators should be willing to play along. The new modes of regulation might not only be due to the economic interests involved (which could probably be served even better in other ways) but also due to the demands of regulation itself. In other words, we should not only look for the constraints but also for the possibilities associated with new forms of financial governance.

For instance, a prime motive behind the Basel II reform on the part of regulators was to remedy the side-effects of the old Accord. But the underlying regulatory dialectic is intrinsic to any form of steering. The problem of perverse effects in banking regulation shows that second-order observation cannot be avoided: Any decision in the political-administrative system is observed in the economic-financial subsystem – and vice versa (Schmidt 1998: 317). Regulation just appears as one among many constraints that have to be taken into account – and not necessarily in a form that the regulators would have anticipated. This kind of problem is common to many fields of regulation in which *thresholds* are used to manage risk. A threshold regime such as the Basel Accord always runs the danger of degenerating into some piece of information that merely stimulates the search for action repertoires whose only motivation is to avoid certain limits and not, for instance, to *minimize* the amount of damage done. In environmental regulation, the limits of the threshold model have long been recognized. As an alternative to fixed rules and limits forms of contextual and procedural regulation have emerged (Willke 1992; 1998; Ladeur 1999). The main point of those models is to concentrate regulation on the formulation of rules of a due process in which the concrete terms of thresholds, standards and so on can be negotiated. It seems that Basel II follows a similar model with regard to financial governance.

Elements of a procedural regulation are discernible in the ways in which Basel II handled both the negotiations and the actual supervision process itself. First, the participation of the private sector in the negotiations made the acceptance of the final result more likely. By giving various organizations and associations the opportunity to present their suggestions and criticisms, the long consultation process made it increasingly difficult for individual participants to dismiss the process as such. The final decision was thus transformed into a series of smaller steps that served to bind the participants into the process. Although it is probably impossible to prevent side-effects completely, the entanglement of the parties concerned can at least help to minimize the problem of a regulatory dialectic in the implementation of Basel II. Second, the supervision process introduces distinctive cognitive elements that stand in contrast to the strictly normative approach of the former threshold model. On the technical side, internal ratings can replace fixed risk categories and thus shift part of the burden of regulation back onto the soundness of the banks' risk management systems themselves. On the side of actual supervision the procedural model involves a kind of ›interactive governance‹: On-site inspections become more and more important as regulatory compliance does not depend on rule-following alone but on the evaluation and testing of risk models. This new kind of interaction between the regulators and the banks means that part of the regulatory work will actually be done on site. Thus, opportunities for informal contact systems will proliferate and potentially become the main vehicles of irritation. That means that regulation itself becomes more cognitive, i.e. it cannot avoid learning from the direct interaction with its clients. However, such a close relationship also bears the danger of a ›de-differentiation‹ of the administrative and the business logic (Hiller 1994: 111). After all, administration can and must be cognitively open to irritating facts and events but it needs to maintain its normative closure regarding the coherence of its own rules. Not the lack of debate or participation of the public, but the potential adaptation of the administrative logic to the one of its organizational environment appears to be the most likely deficit of the new financial governance.

6. Conclusion

The analysis of the relationship between politics and administration shows that the low salience of contentious *Politics* in financial governance cannot be adequately interpreted merely from the perspective of a ›democratic deficit‹ extrapolated from domestic models. It is important to acknowledge that the imbalance between public debate and private authority in the first place reflects the exigencies of transnational policy-making that Basel II and similar policy areas face. In contrast to a domestic policy process, those problems do not primarily lie in securing the generalized support of the public for collectively binding decisions of the political system. The task of transnational financial governance is on the one hand more general: The question of support is not limited to a clearly defined population within territorial boundaries but concerns the capacity for collective action and decision-making among a whole range of states and non-state actors. On the other hand, however, the task is also more specific: Not the support of whole electorates but the cooperation of specific, directly affected organizations in concrete policy areas is at stake.

That means that generic political distinctions such as left vs. right or progressive vs. conservative are not very useful for anticipating alliances and estimating chances for consensus (cf. Luhmann 1998). Instead, transnational governance provokes new lines of conflict such as those between regional and multinational banks and thus has to deal with them primarily. The attending political conflicts and administrative risks lie largely beyond the traditional points of reference of domestic political systems. The emergence of ›governance without politics‹ indicates that administrative responses to this situation may be easier to find than political ones.

References

BCBS (2003a), *Basel Committee on Banking Supervision: The New Basel Accord (Consultative Paper 3).* Basel

— (2003b), *Quantitative Impact Study 3 – Overview of Global Results.* Basel http://www.bis.org/qis3.htm.

BdB (2003), *Potential Pro-Cyclicality of the Basel-2 Framework. Analysis and Possible Solutions*, Working Paper, 30 May 2003, Berlin. http://www.bis.org.

Beck, Ulrich (2002), *Macht und Gegenmacht im globalen Zeitalter. Neue weltpolitische Ökonomie.* Frankfurt a.M.

Cutler, A. Claire/Haufler, Virginia/Porter, Tony (1999a) (eds), *Private Authority and International Affairs.* Albany.

Cutler, A. Claire/Haufler, Virginia/Porter, Tony (1999b), »Private authority and international affairs«, in: A. Claire Cutler, Virginia Haufler, Tony Porter (eds), *Private Authority and International Affairs.* Albany, 3–28.

Eatwell, John/Taylor, Lance (2000), *Global Finance at Risk: The Case for International Regulation.* New York.

Genschel, Philipp/Plümper, Thomas (1997), »Regulatory competition and international cooperation«, in: *Journal of European Public Policy*, Vol. 4, 626–642.

Germain, Randall D. (2001), »Global financial governance and the problem of inclusion«, in: *Global Governance,* Vol. 7, 411–426.

Grunow, Dieter (1994), »Politik und Verwaltung«, in: Klaus Dammann, Dieter Grunow, Klaus Japp (eds), *Die Verwaltung des politischen Systems.* Opladen, 27–39.

Hewson, Martin/Sinclair, Timothy J. (1999) (eds), *Approaches to Global Governance Theory.* Albany.

Higgott, Richard A./Underhill, Geoffrey R. D./Bieler, Andreas (2000) (eds), *Non-State Actors and Authority in the Global System.* London.

Hiller, Petra (1994), »Risiko und Verwaltung«, in: Klaus Dammann, Dieter Grunow, Klaus Japp (eds), *Die Verwaltung des politischen Systems*, Opladen, 108–125.

Holzer, Boris/Beck, Ulrich (2004), *Global Financial Risks and Transnational Regime-Building: Basel II and the German Domestic Policy Discourse* (Research Report to the World Society Foundation, Zurich), Institut für Soziologie der LMU München. München.

Kapstein, Ethan B. (1989), »Resolving the regulator's dilemma: international coordination of banking regulations«, in: *International Organization*, Vol. 43, 323–347.

— (1992), »Between power and purpose: central bankers and the politics of regulatory convergence«, in: *International Organization,* Vol. 46, 265–287.

— (1994), *Governing the Global Economy: International Finance and the State.* Cambridge.

King, Michael R./Sinclair, Timothy J. (2003), »Private actors and public policy: a requiem for the New Basel Capital Accord«, in: *International Political Science Review*, Vol. 24, 345–362.

Ladeur, Karl-Heinz (1999), »Risikobewältigung durch Flexibilisierung und Prozeduralisierung des Rechts – Rechtliche Bindung von Ungewissheit oder Selbstverunsicherung des Rechts?«, in: Alfons Bora (ed.), *Rechtliches Risikomanagment. Form, Funktion und Leistungsfähigkeit des Rechts in der Risikogesellschaft*, Berlin, 41–64.

Luhmann, Niklas (1972a), »Soziologie des politischen Systems«. in: *Soziologische Aufklärung 1*. Opladen, 154–177.

— (1972b), *Rechtssoziologie* (2 Bde.). Reinbek b. Hamburg.

— (1981), *Politische Theorie im Wohlfahrtsstaat*. München.

— (1983), *Legitimation durch Verfahren*. Frankfurt a.M.

— (1987), »Machtkreislauf und Recht in Demokratien«, in: *Soziologische Aufklärung 4*, 142–151.

— (1997), »Limits of steering«, in: *Theory, Culture & Society*, Vol. 14, 41–57.

— (1998), »Politics and economy«, in: *Thesis Eleven*, Vol. 53, 1–9.

— (2000), *Die Politik der Gesellschaft*. Frankfurt a.M.

Pauly, Louis W. (1997), *Who Elected the Bankers? Surveillance and Control in the World Economy*. Ithaca, NY.

Porter, Tony (1993), *States, Markets and Regimes in Global Finance*. New York.

— (2001), »The democratic deficit in the institutional arrangements for regulating global finance«, in: *Global Governance*, Vol. 7, 427–440.

— (2005), »The private production of public goods: private and public norms in global governance«, in: Edgar Grande, Louis W. Pauly (eds), *Complex Sovereignty: Reconstituting Political Authority in the Twenty-first Century*. Toronto, 217–237.

Pressman, J./Wildavsky, Aaron B. (1973), *Implementation: How Great Hopes in Washington Are Dashed in Oakland*. Berkeley.

Putnam, Robert D. (1988), »Diplomacy and domestic politics: the logic of two-level games«, in: *International Organization*, Vol. 42, 427–460.

Reinicke, Wolfgang H. (1995), *Banking, Politics and Global Finance. American Commercial Banks and Regulatory Change, 1980–1990*. Aldershot.

— (1998), *Global Public Policy. Governing without Government?* Washington DC.

Schmidt, Tobias (1998), *Grundlagen einer Systemtheorie des Finanzsektors*. Berlin.

Sinclair, Timothy J. (1994), »Passing judgement: credit rating processes as regulatory mechanisms of governance in the emerging world order«, in: *Review of International Political Economy*, Vol. 1, 133–159.

— (2005), *The New Masters of Capital: American Bond Rating Agencies and the Politics of Creditworthiness*. Ithaca.

Strulik, Torsten (2000), *Risikomanagement globaler Finanzmärkte*. Frankfurt a.M.

Strulik, Torsten/Kussin, Matthias (2005), »Finanzmarktregulierung und Wissenspolitik. Basel II – Die aufsichtsrechtliche Konstitution kollektiver Intelligenz?«, in: *Zeitschrift für Rechtssoziologie*, Vol. 26, 101–129.

Swary, Itzhak/Topf, Barry (1991), *Global Financial Deregulation: Commercial Banking at the Crossroads*, Cambridge.

Vollmer, Hendrik (1997), »Zur Akzeptanzorientierung des Verwaltungshandelns in Risikokonflikten«, in: Petra Hiller/Georg Krücken (eds), *Risiko und Regulierung*. Frankfurt a.M., 11–38.

Willke, Helmut (1992), *Ironie des Staates. Grundlinien einer Staatstheorie polyzentrischer Gesellschaft.* Frankfurt a.M.

— (1998), *Systemtheorie III: Steuerungstheorie,* 2nd edition. Stuttgart.

ZKA (2003), *Comments of the Zentraler Kreditausschuss on the Basel Committee's Consultative Document of 29 April 2003 on a New Capital Adequacy Framework for Banks (›Basel II‹),* Berlin: http://www.bis.org.

Making Use of Cognitive Standards: On the Logic of a New Mode of Governance in Global Finance

Matthias Kussin and Sven Kette

1. Introduction

Our contribution aims to shed light on the operational logic of global standards as elements of soft law.[1] We intend to focus particularly on the cognitive quality of such standards and the implications for the governance of the global financial system.[2] Furthermore, questions concerning global legal coordination are also taken into account.

A great number of the regulations that currently determine the framework for transactions on the global market are produced by so-called standard setting organizations (Brunsson/Jakobsson 2002: 1). On the capital

---

1 For a discussion about soft law and ›non-binding international legal agreements‹ see the contributions in Shelton 2000.

2 We think of the financial system as a social system. For further analyses see the contribution of Helmut Willke in this volume.

market, the banking or insurance industry multi-national committees are implementing standards to establish premises for the stability and efficiency of the financial system.[3] This applies not only to public legitimized regimes but also to private authorities (Cutler/Haufler/Porter 2004).[4] The diversity of regulations on a supra-national level can also be considered as an answer to the challenges of the knowledge society that has left its traces particularly on the financial system in recent years. Together with the accompanying deterritorialization in some areas of the finance industry, the exigence of coordination requires a new regulatory framework on a supra-national level. Standards will play an important role in this context.

The common function of standards is to provide a form of social coordination – for economical, technical as well as scientific questions. So far – at first sight – standards do not seem to differ from norms. Thus it is hardly surprising that the terms »standard« and »norm« are often used synonymously. However, one thing becomes clear when we focus on the application method of standards in different contexts: We are dealing with a type of social coordination that goes beyond the effects of norms on specific constellations. Standards undoubtedly comply with similar tasks in many social situations that can also be considered for norms. They have a homogenizing and regularizing effect regardless of the real context. At the same time, however, some other empirical examples indicate a different but extended mechanism of standards. Standards – apart from their stabilizing and homogenizing effects – also entail potential for change in the sense that they render (self-)changes possible and do not reject but productively embrace heterogeneity.

Thus, standards provide both a normative and a cognitive coordination potential. The combination of both forms – as described in this paper – gains particular importance in complex and heterogeneous constellations. The reform of the framework for the governance of globally active banks serves as an example for this. It explains how the cognitive side of standards deals with the problem of a lack of (classical) legitimacy and allows handling organizational heterogeneity. So the questions at hand are: Why

3 An example of Capital Market regulation is the Financial Action Task Force on Money Laundering (FATF). With regard to the banking sector – which we refer to in the following – it is the Bank of International Settlement (BIS), while in the case of the insurance industry among others the International Association of Insurance Supervisors (IAIS) can be quoted.

4 Examples of this are the Accounting Standards. See also the contribution of Alexandra Hessling in this volume.

do (non-binding) standards become an important mechanism for legal coordination? How do they work? And which capabilities do they provide compared to (classical) legal norms?

In order to explore these issues, the following chapter looks at the societal developments of globalization and knowledge society and describes the resulting problems for social coordination of the financial system. The third chapter contains a theoretical demonstration of how political and legal mechanisms for coordination are encountering limiting factors in view of these developments. In the fourth chapter an alternative (cognitive orientated) mechanism of coordination is defined by the term »standard«. Here, we intend using different theories concerning standards to show that on the one hand standards are similar to norms in the way they operate, while on the other hand legitimating principles and acquiring potentials constitute an apparently different mode of coordination. Chapter five contains examples of cognitive standards and their differentiating performances for adequately dealing with challenges of the knowledge society and globalization in new forms of banking regulation (Basel II).

2. Challenges for the Governance of the Global Financial System

The complexity of the financial system and new forms of risk have made other, more adequate forms of risk regulation not only necessary but also conditional. Above all, the exigence of regulation is a result of the systemic character of these risks. On the one hand, liberalization of global financial flows and the available digital data processing and transfer have led to a deterritorialization of the financial system during the final third of the last century, while on the other, the complex knowledge-based information processing and the highly innovative orientation of the financial system expand normal risks to so-called systemic risks.[5] In line with the increasing

5 Those systemic risks are characterized by no longer referring to single elements of labour division or mechanistic contexts but having consequences for the kind of systemic operations, as certain individual risks are bumping due to the integration of elements and lead to a systemic destabilization (Willke 2002: 30). Both the emergence and development of such risks are hard to redict and neither prevention nor an appropriate reaction in any crisis

distribution of knowledge-based financial instruments[6] risks are broken down, resold and multiplicated. This leads to an evolution and accumulation of single risks. The governance of the financial system is thus confronted with special challenges in factual as well as temporal and social terms. With regard to the fact dimension, coping with ignorance becomes a core problem – a problem that originates from the particular characteristics of knowledge society.

The debate on knowledge society started earlier than scientific theories about the societal importance of knowledge, which date back to the early 1970s.[7] However, in our context two aspects of the latest scientific discourse on knowledge society are particularly effective in solving problems: *heterogeneity of knowledge* (Rammert 2002a; Willke 2003: 258–309) and the *relevance of ignorance* (Willke 2002). Because of growing knowledge-based communication of all societal functional systems, knowledge is no longer just truth but rather a resource. Science also loses its exclusive position as the place of knowledge production (Willke 2002: 66–67). As a consequence of this differentiation of societal knowledge, a heterogenization of the societal knowledge stock follows. Growing knowledge production and increasing complexity lead to the problem of how to cope with ignorance. Ignorance – be it specific or unspecific[8] – comes up as a correlate of knowledge production, as the corollary of knowledge.[9] This problem will have consequences in the context of the financial system in particular (Strulik 2004).

---

can be achieved. For details and analyses of the definition of systemic risks in the financial system see Alexander/Dhumale/Eatwell 2006. See also Eatwell 2004.

6 Here insurance derived of credits, loans and other activa, which are dealt with globally, do not have balancing effect in the long term (see Bernauer 2000: 165). Since the early 90s financial instruments like swaps, futures and options, etc. have functioned like bets and distinguishing in so far that their market value and other basic values (shares, loans, gold or recently even the weather conditions) have become important and that conclusions and performances of contracts fall apart. For a detailed overview see Hull 2006.

7 See above all Bell 1973 but also Stehr 1994.

8 For this differentiation see Merton 1987. Specific non-knowledge defines knowledge over lacking knowledge, while unspecific non-knowledge refers to an area including non-knowledge about lacking knowledge, which is principally unreachable so far. Also instructive: Japp 2000.

9 The kind of knowledge within the knowledge society particularly distinguishes that non-knowledge becomes the counter-definition of knowledge and former kinds of knowledge (knowledge/belief; knowledge/power) are put aside. See Willke 2002: 27pp.

Thus, as far as the governance of the financial system is concerned, a primary problem arises from the need to deal with regulatory ignorance. Under these circumstances classical forms of political-legal risk regulation encounter limiting factors. The legal system does not have the necessary expertise to efficiently regulate the financial system. Likewise, politics can no longer decide authoritatively and without considering the distributed information, expertise and opportunities for implementation. For this it simply does not have the formal competence to decide (Willke 2006: 106). When we also consider the temporal dimension, the (conditional) program structure[10] of the legal system turns out to be past-oriented (Luhmann 2004: 196pp); and adaptation through legislation is very time-consuming. This relates to the difficulties experienced by legal systems in keeping pace with the highly innovative and forward-looking financial system.

The differentiation of diverse knowledge orders and the process of coping with regulatory ignorance merely point to the problems in financial system governance. A second complex of problems relate to the global operation of the financial system, which has almost entirely lost its territorial aspect (O'Brien 1992). This relates to issues of legitimacy and acceptance, which are rooted in the social dimension. In this case, neither the legal nor the political system can keep up with the extended globalization of the financial system. This is because both systems are linked to nation-states (Willke 2001a). The legal system, however, follows a global logic as the principal difference legal/illegal and the function of counterfactual stabilization of expectations (Luhmann 2004: 199) is almost unlimited. However, as far as programs are concerned, the legal system is particularly characterized by segmentary internal differentiation into nation-states. When it comes to the function of providing capacities for collectively binding decisions and resulting legitimated jurisdiction the same is true for the political system (King/Thornhill 2003: 70pp). A globally imposed law would need a global state, which – as reference level of a legitimate jurisdiction – obviously does not exist. However, in order to stabilize expectation on a global level, politics and law need to use mechanisms of preventive acceptance that can exist without any direct link to a democracy-legitimated imposed law. The same is true for sanctions: Laws, jurisdiction and sanctions are linked with the legislation of a state and thus with nation-

10 In the sense of legal sentences like laws, orders, administrative regulations etc.

states. Without national legislation, law cannot be implemented legitimately, nor can a mandatory jurisdiction be realized.

In all, four aspects can be seen as the main reasons for the complexity of the financial system: The knowledge base of the financial system, the dynamic character of innovation, the ongoing production of knowledge and ignorance as well as the globalization facilitated by digitalization and deregulation. As mentioned above, classical political-legal regulation is not suited to provide problem-oriented governance. Firstly these difficulties are based on the legal reconnection to nation states (social dimension). Secondly they are based on the lack of expertise/regulatory ignorance (factual dimension) and thirdly, they depend on the past-oriented logic of legal norms (temporal dimension). Thus, an adequate mode of governance would need to comply with at least two premises in order to adapt to these conditions: First, because there is no democratic legitimacy on the global level, this must be based on a derived form of legitimacy for securing acceptance. Furthermore, it has to be grounded on an alternative for securing expectations, which is more oriented towards variability than towards stability, in order to increase its own ability to acquire and reduce length of time required to respond to environmental changes. Consequently, it may be possible to deal more adequately with a future-oriented dynamic and innovative financial system.

3. The Classical Logic of Governance Within the Nation State

Alternative forms of political and legal regulation in response to the challenges of knowledge society and globalization cannot be achieved by reforms of content alone. Instead structural changes of political and legal processes are required. Until now, both social systems concentrate on producing and stabilizing normative expectations and therefore, both are hedged by norms. The reference to norms is an elementary part of the (classical) operational mode of legislation and policy, as it offers specific construction forms of social structures as coordination mechanisms. Thus, norms implement social consensus[11] in relation to the definition of acceptable/unacceptable, right/wrong or good/bad (Luhmann 2004: 145). This

11 Consensus in this context does not comply with Habermas' »intersubjective communication« but is rather seen as form of actual social coordination.

is how norms comply with important requirements for social coordination. If, for example. repayment of debts is refused or cannot be realized by a debtor, the generally accepted norm will remain in force. This is precisely where norms apply. If they are not fulfilled, they do not change, but rather insist on the expectation. Of course, this fact does not guarantee that norms will not be infringed. However, a general certainty of expectation about the meaning and lack of meaning of norms is outlined in a social context (Luhmann 1995: 326). This particular form of social coordination makes anything possible. This is because norms do not merely allow infringements. Instead their basic operational mode does not allow any alterations and therefore implies there is no readiness to learn. It is, however, beyond doubt that norms can be changed and these changes can be observed empirically. But the norm itself does not adapt to the empirical situation. This is the only mechanism that allows a limited certainty of expectation with regard to an uncertain future. It may be expected – to refer to our example again – that debts will be repaid after all.

The political and legal systems in modern society are established as privileged components participating in the production and stabilization of social norms. Laws and their interpretation secure this type of norms. They are *legal* norms. Thus, a degree of certainty of expectation may become true as it allows the realization of risky operations that otherwise would be impossible. As in complex societies, a certainty of expectation can no longer be secured by personal or interactive mechanisms, the recourse on such legal norms is essential for producing a certainty of expectation (Luhmann 1988). Banks often lend credits not only for personal reasons but also for contractual reasons by trusting in compliance. This confidence may be disappointed, because a functioning legal system does not always protect against infringements of norms. However, particularly legal consequences in the case of disappointment are imaginable: The norm will either be met on the basis of jurisdiction (additional as legally supporting measure) or legal sanctions will be exerted on the legal system by taking recourse to the power potential of the political system. This interrelation between the political and the legal systems and the resulting stability of norms represent a basis of complex forms of social coordination (Luhmann 2004: 162). This stability does not only have a factual but also a spatial dimension. Again, within territories, political and legal systems determine *who* may expect the influence of *what* codified norms and *where*. Even if norms apply to several addresses e.g. natural persons, legal persons, courts or authorities, the target group and territorial domain are clearly defined and does not usually reach beyond national borders. The result is a juxtaposition of various political and legal regulations on a global level.[12]

On the one hand both social systems (political and legal system) render important services for the financial system. They produce normative structures of expectation through policymaking and stabilize them by instruments of legal regulation. This normative structure makes it possible to establish certainties of expectation even under conditions of complex risks. On the other hand – as we outlined above – this normative orientation triggers financial market regulation problems. The fact is that forms of regulation based on norms are hardly prepared to comply with the described dynamics of the financial system that are coming into effect in knowledge society. The legal regulation is permanently confronted with innovations where not only no consequences have been established but even are not yet understood as facts to be dealt with at all. This is how mechanisms of social coordination, such as risk regulation in the financial system, are losing their effectiveness.

Thus, a solution of this problem cannot – as we explain in this paragraph – simply be attained by »more« regulation through reforms of the content. On the contrary, the political and the legal systems are faced with a challenge because the financial system permanently withdraws from the regulation of risks by constructing new financial instruments. The consequences are new impulses to regulation.[13] In this way, the here outlined operational mode of legal norms collides with the specific innovation dynamic of the financial system. By imposing a defined norm, extra problems are arising and negating the assumed productive intentions of the legislator.

Looking at the dynamic financial system, not only the particular ways of operation are coming up against limiting factors but also the related requirements of politics and law. In connection with a globally interconnected financial system, it becomes less possible for a territorially limited genesis and stabilization of expectation for extra-determined persons to be maintained. This problem cannot just be reduced to the fact that capital flows or banks can withdraw from the regulatory authorities of the nation

12 Phenomena like the international warrant for arrest, applications for extradiction or even mutual appreciation are proving that laws need specific instruments to attain inter- and transnational value.

13 Edward Kane calls this phenomenon »regulatory dialectic« (Kane 1981).

states by transferring investments or subsidiaries to other countries (Cerny 1994: 328).[14] Furthermore, its forms of expectation regarding stability and change principally neglect the logic of territorial boundaries as can be observed on the financial markets.[15]

4. Standards as Cognitive Mechanisms of Legal Coordination

In order to avoid systemic dangers, modern society relies on forms of social coordination that go beyond the norm. An alternative style of social coordination seems to be necessary that can comply with both the readiness to learn and the segmentary internal differentiation of the political and legal systems. This seems to be the only way to avoid the potential dangers described. Instead, confidence in the (inevitably risky) continuation of financial market operations can be built up. According to Johann Galtung, one theoretical characteristic of such a mode is called a cognitive style of expectation (Galtung 1959: 228). If disappointed, cognitive expectations will no longer be maintained. On the contrary, the expectation will be usefully adapted to the factual situation. If, for example, it is expected that debts will be repaid on due date, this expectation will either be adapted in case of disappointment, or, it will be rearranged to e.g. installments or an alternative form of compensation. At first, Niklas Luhmann used this diversification exclusively to distinguish social processes within his theory of society and for the description of primary operational logics of functional systems: While law and the political system are primarily operating on the mode of producing normative expectations by means of the function of stabilizing expectations, other social systems operate rather on the basis of cognitive styles of expectation.[16] The science system, for example, is primarily cognitively oriented. Expectations within the context of scientific

14 Helmut Willke points out that the problems of nation-state legislation result from the fact that this has been prepared above all to control natural persons, but in a society dominated by organizations does it loose its efficiency – especially because organizations cannot be »impressed« by the thread of physical violation (Willke 2003: 82).

15 Here the global definition of the often Salomonic expressions of Alan Greenspan should be thought of, which have been considered as central for the construction of expectation on the financial markets (Frankfurter Allgemeine Zeitung 2006).

16 With this decision for a theory the system theory clearly differs from classical sociologies, where norms represent the base of social acting. See also Niklas Luhmann 1995: 325.

research are that a convincing falsification of theories leads to abolition or relativization but never to insistence despite the facts. The production of cognitive expectations also appears to be prevailing in the economic sphere. The marketing of goods presupposes a permanent observation of markets and an application of adequate strategies.[17] However, normative expectations also play a role in these functional contexts. In science quality criteria do exist that have to satisfy research results (Luhmann 1992: 143). And in the economy, for example, product norms control the patterns of expectation in business communication. This ratio of normative and cognitive styles to expectations can also be shown in the political as well as in the legal system. Certainly, legal norms persist to be normatively orientated. But instead, with the use of standards, a different form of social coordination comes into play that allows for a combination of normative and cognitive styles of expectations.

The distinction of norms and standards as different types of social coordination is not apparent at first sight. After all, standards often operate in a similar way as norms – especially in technical processes, where their efficiency is proven (Blankart/Knieps 1993). With regard to studies from the field of law, political science but also sociological theory, it becomes clear that standards also possess »cognitive qualities«. Particularly in legal contexts, this cognitive potential seems to permit a more adequate form of social coordination. Karl-Heinz Ladeur e.g. differentiates standards from nation-state legislation norms but grants them legal qualities when developing in very specific contexts (Ladeur 1999: 34). »These standards try to formulate expectations and rules of appropriateness for behavior under conditions of risk and for quality requirements, long term contracts on corporation, etc« (ibid.).

From a political scientists' point of view, Khalid Nadvi and Frank Wältring mention the developments of standards – from basic generic, through sectoral, to enterprise-specific standards – which number is constantly increasing (Nadvi/Wältring 2002: 12). Here, the definition of standards for processes of political deregulation and liberalization seems to become important (Mattli 2001: 239). Arguments for the increased importance of standards can also be observed in sociological, (neo-)institutionalist analyses. Nils Brunsson argues that standards serve as forms of social coordination that, above all, gain relevance within the context of globalization

17 The definition of markets and prices for information acquaintance in economic processes see Friedrich A. von Hayek 1945: 525.

(Brunsson 2002: 36). Following Brunsson's analysis, further characteristics of standards can be seen, pointing to enlarged, cognitively oriented coordination potentials as compared to (legal) norms. Standards are formally distinguished by their voluntary nature. They only acquire legitimacy through this mode of voluntariness (Brunsson 2002: 23). While the real coordination potential of legal norms develops through the mode of sanctioning, standards have to convince by practical application. Brunsson talks about best practice solutions in this context (Brunsson 2002: 24). The permanent performance of standards can only be produced if developers can prove the performance of standards or the users accept them. These characteristics again indicate that standards must be seen as different modes of social coordination that differ from the norms of the nation-state. This becomes clear in the social-, factual, as well as temporal dimension.

In the social dimension the aspect of legitimacy becomes important. While legal norms are based on formal political legitimacy, standards are based on (Best-Practice) knowledge (Brunsson 2002: 24). Standard-setters cannot – like political authorities – refer to the possibility of sanctions. On the contrary, they can only emphasize the »benefit« of the standard in question. Consequently, standards can merely ceaselessly rely upon scanning their own relevant societal processes and – if necessary – learn in view of their own logic.[18]

This modified setting in the social dimension corresponds to changed conditions in the factual dimension. Standard-setters are forced to observe relevant social processes, continually and to make adaptations, if necessary. Thus, the reflexivity of standards reacts to the reflexivity of its users. Hence, a potential of cognitive expectations must be accepted by side of the standard-setters as well as by standard-users – a fact that must not necessarily apply to legal norms. Instead of a counterfactual stabilization, standards prefer to operate in a more evolutionary mode by connecting aspects of stabilization with those of change and re-stabilization. Finally, this new mode also becomes obvious in the temporal dimension. Standards seem to make it possible to cope with uncertain futures in a different way. One main reason can be seen in its potential for coping with heterogeneity. While norms bind the future and consequently limit options, stan-

18 This does not mean that this cannot be observed in every situation. In fact there exist or have existed many standards which have not been adequately modified – consequence of which was that others replaced them.

dards enable forms of self-modification as results of learning-processes.[19] This does not mean that this cognitive potential is always exploited in the context of any standard setting. Standards operate in a similar way to norms, especially in technical processes, but they also have an homogenizing effect on the construction and reproduction of normative expectations with regard to the consequences of legal norms. However, with regard to the significance of standards in the context of governance, the following aspects are of primary importance: Firstly, standards gain their legitimacy from a mode of operation, that entirely differs from the political norm setting and legal stabilization. Secondly, standards may and must contain the potential to adapt to particular constellations but also to experience general modifications in response to changed social conditions. Comparing norms and standards, one can see that both forms of social coordination cope differently with the personalized problems in the three dimensions of meaning (see figure 1). This is especially grounded in the varying mixed ratios of normative and cognitive styles of expectation.

Dimensions of meaning	*Focal problem*	*Norms*	*Standards*
Factual dimension	Coping with ignorance	Fade out of ignorance	Processing of ignorance
Temporal dimension	Coping with an (uncertain) future	Counterfactual stabilization of expectations	Capabilities of procedural adaptations
Social dimension	Coping with questions of legitimacy	Legitimacy based on the authority of the nation state (Power)	Legitimacy based on (Best Practice-) Knowledge and the voluntariness of its applicator

Table 1: Comparing Norms and Standards

19 Under these circumstances the question concerning alternatives for securing expectations has to be posed. Trust may appear as a functional equivalent to norms. While trust does not play an essential role in the context of normative expectations, it gains importance with regard to cognitive expectations. For the role of trust in the knowledge based economy see the contribution of Torsten Strulik in this volume.

Taking these characteristics into account, there are indications that standards proceed with the challenges of globalization and knowledge society in a different way compared to norms. The conditions for possible real effects of coordination do not merely depend on supra-national political and legal authorities, but also on the practicability for the user. In fact, the problem of reconnection with nation-state territories, which has been a decisive criterion for classical forms of operation of the political and legal system, does not arise. On the other hand, standards – due to the demand for »best practice« – deal with the dynamic of innovation of the knowledge society in a different way from norms. There follows an explanatory example of how the political system and law exploit the different coordination potentials for financial market regulation. Such forms of social coordination may be expected in the field of the financial market regulation above all, and here particularly with the dynamics of globalization and innovation.

5. Basel II: A Cognitive Standard in Global Banking

Up until the 1970s banking was regulated on the basis of national legal norms. This mechanism of social coordination was obviously congruent with the dynamic of innovation as well as with the expansion of capital flows of the financial system up to that time. Triggered by the breakdown of the Bretton-Woods-System (1971) and the associated abolition of the stable exchange rate, a liberalization of the financial flow began that formed the basis for the globalization of the financial system (Strulik 2000; Wood 2005). This globalization of the financial system mainly concerns the intensified activities of banking organizations in the international banking business.[20] Becoming aware of the first destabilizing consequences[21] of such a deregulated financial system in 1974, the Basel Committee on Banking Supervision (BCBS)[22] constituted itself as a supra-national stan-

20 To this aspect see Kapstein 1989.

21 The currency turmoil of 1974 and the bankruptcy of the German Herstatt-Bank as well as the US-American Franklin National Bank should be considered in this context. For details see Dale 1984: 156–161.

22 The BCBS is hosted at the Bank for International Settlements. Initiated in 1974 by representatives of the Central Bank of the G 10–States and without the authorization to set legal norms, the Basel Committee develops minimum standards of the banking supervision, aiming at international convergence for the standards of banking regulation for the guarantee

dards organization for the global banking system. In order to meet with the main objectives of the Basel Committee – the implementation of comprehensive and adequate banking supervision – the committee published a series of recommendations for the banking practice since 1975. Not later than the Basel Accord of 1988 (Basel I) was published supra-nationally imposed standards became the most important basis of coordination for the global banking system.[23] Against the background of the Latin-American debt crisis in the early 1980s the member states agreed to implement a consistent minimum standard for the coverage of equities. This minimum standard obliged banks to cover their credits with eight percent of the equity from then on. This homogenizing minimum definition of the capital ratio was intended to increase the capacity of the global financial system.[24] This intention, however, could not be realized due to drastic changes in the financial system. Especially the growing importance of the knowledge-intensive derivatives business[25] and the advanced internationalization of banking business exerted a regulatory force to action. Both developments endangered the efficacy of Basel I (Strulik 2000: 212–220). In addition, the banking industry developed efficient instruments for risk evaluation that measured the existing risks more exactly. As a result it became possible to picture a bank's risk structure in a more differentiated and adequate way.[26] Furthermore, the financial crises of the 1990s and their outcome made the banking system sensitive to the previously inadequate rules.[27] Soon after Basel I had been introduced it became obvious that the rigid and less market sensitive regulations would never meet the (regulatory) requirements of an international networking and dynamic financial system. Also several

---

of a greatest stability of the financial system. See also the self-description of the Basel Committee: BCBS 2004a.

23 BCBS 1988.

24 Regarding formation and details of the Basel Accord see Kapstein 1996 as well as Genschel/Plümper 1996.

25 The growing importance of derivative business (transactions) has been pushed (indirectly) by the implementation of Basel I, as in the following period these banks were trying to reduce their equity commitments by exploring balance-ineffective business sectors. For this problem see Strulik 2000: 176–177.

26 The consequence of this was among others, that two risk-evaluation procedures of were run in parallel: One for business management and the other for supervisory matters.

27 The »Asian-Crisis« (1997/98) and the »Russian-Crisis« (1998/99) has to be considered in this connection.

corrections and revisions, amendments and supplements[28] did not meet with any expectations. Against this pressure was exerted on the Basel Committee from different sides, i.e. not only from the credit institutes' side but also from the supra-national representatives of interests[29], while there was also increased criticism from nation state supervisory authorities as standard users. Following on from this, the Basel Committee announced in September 1998 a revision of the Basel Accord of 1988.

In June 1999, the Basel Committee initiated a (multi-level) process of consultation by publishing the first proposals for Basel II. For several months, the interested public[30] had the opportunity to comment on each paper. On the basis of the more than 200 comments received in response to the first consultation paper, the Basel Committee published a second consultation paper in January 2001. Finally, a third phase followed in April – July 2003. Taking the responses and comments in relation to this paper into account, the final version of the Basel II framework entitled »International Convergence of Capital Measurement and Capital Standards – A Revised Framework« (BCBS 2004b) was released. During the course of this consultation process on global as well as national level, there was a permanent dialogue between the banking industry and bank watchdog organizations.[31] On the one hand this permanent analysis by financial and scientific experts increased the chances that Basel II would be accepted by the banking industry. On the other hand this procedure facilitated mutual learning processes among regulators and regulated institutions and thus opened up the chance of finding adequate regulations adapted to risk models.

Basel I and Basel II must be understood as voluntary agreements on a supra-national level, only becoming binding through the imposition of national laws. However, insofar as Basel I is exclusively based on sanctions, it can be understood as a more normative standard. The (self-related) potential to amendments was restricted to later »Amendments« (see above)

28 Apart from smaller amendments (BCBS 1991; BCBS 1994a; BCBS 1994b) the inclusion of market risks represented – above all – the development of the Basel Accord of 1988 (BCBS 1996).

29 For example Institute of International Finance, Group of Thirty.

30 Above all, credit institutes, banks (and banking associations), insurances, finance services and rating agencies, but also consultancies, auditors and banking supervisory authorities. Furthermore, statements from the science' side were received by the Basel Committee.

31 Since 2003 in Germany this dialogue was taking place in the study group »Umsetzung Basel II« as well as in sub-teams of experts, which were established by banking supervision.

and has not been flexible enough to respond adequately to the dynamic innovation oriented financial system and its knowledge intensity.

On the contrary, Basel II can be seen as primarily a cognitively oriented standard. To this extent it corresponds with the knowledge intensity of the financial system for these regulations and emergence meant as trials of reciprocal exploitation of learning potentials could be realized. On the one hand, with Basel II, cognitive adaptations contribute to sanctions as forms of coping with derivations. On the other hand Basel II does allow diversity instead of transferring it into homogeneity. Consequently, the differences between the regulations of Basel II and Basel I can be characterized by two principles: heterogeneity and the ability to learn.

Thus, the Basel-II-framework contains a series of rules, that are already developed for detailed adaptation to national (market) conditions within the framework of national implementation processes. Moreover, the regulations concerning capital ratio (Pillar I)[32] guarantee that more sorts of risks are embedded in the evaluation process.[33] And the (rigid) capital ratio of eight percent is replaced by flexible capital ratios, based on the relevant credit risk – meaning the individual creditworthiness of any borrower. Three different complex models are provided for the calculation of solvency. These models reach from a rough classification of the borrower by external rating-agencies up to a model allowing banks to install their own rating processes for the purpose of solvency. In addition, the Supervisory Review Process of Pillar 2, leads to the opinion that Basel II entails a paradigm shift (e.g. Deutsche Bundesbank 2001; FED Bulletin 2003) within the banking supervision. In this context, the essential novelty lay in the move from quantitative, financial ratio-oriented banking supervision, to a qualitative mode. Core instruments for the revision of risk management systems for banking institutes are regular on-site-inspections and meetings with bank managers and staff. In this way the focus of bank supervisory inspections shifts from results of a risk management to the appropriateness of

---

32 Comment: The details of Basel II are organized as 3–pillar-architecture. The first pillar aims at the requirements for equities in view of credit risks and operational risks. The second pillar refers to the supervisory process – the so called –Supervisory Review Process (SPR). Additionally, there is a third pillar containing regulations for transparency and disclosure to »the market«. Basel II is a framework that is not only takes account of the regulation of equity coverage by banks but also describes the banking supervisory process and thus refers to both banks and banking supervision.

33 Compared to Basel I, which was related to the credit risks, focuses Basel II additionally on Operational Risks as well as further risks (e.g. Market risks) directly by means of the SRP.

procedures and processes of the risk management of banks. This mode of banking supervision allows (bank-)organization-specific conditions to be included so that heterogeneity can be noticed for revision as well. With these organizational contexts in mind, a further clear difference from the non-differentiated rules of Basel I can be seen. Basel II differentiates the capital requirements depending on the borrowers' solvency. Furthermore the framework allows calculating the creditworthiness by internal risk models converging with supervisory legal requirements. Thus, Basel II rules provide a framework complying with an organization-specific supervision and therefore – beyond all nation state divergence – allow organizational heterogeneity.

On the one hand, this form of supervision allows potential bank internal risks to be handled appropriately – because it focuses on the individual bank organization. In doing so, it allows potential bank internal risk to be handled adequately. But on the other hand this mode provides new challenges in view of aspects of compatibility. This is particularly true for the fact that globally acting banks often maintain various subsidiaries in several countries. In this context, the question arises as to which national supervision is responsible for which sectors and how a coordinated regulation can be realized.[34] While the »eight-percent-regulation« of Basel I – in spite of the numerous deficits – could provide at least convergence between national forms of supervision a regulation based on heterogeneity produces compatibility problems. In the context of Basel II these aspects have become difficult to resolve by home/host solutions or cross-border implementation. Actually, the trend towards the resolution of these problems lies in reciprocal learning of the supervisors and inter-national processes of consensus. An US-American banking supervisor puts it as follows:

»So we do anticipate having Basel experts – more Basel experts and also enhance coordination and communication with our foreign supervisors. Now that's Basel going to be implemented cross-boarder we expect our relationships become much

34 The Executive Director of an US-banking association points out, that this problem already arises when choosing the date of implementation: »The big issue now we are worrying about is the different implementation date. It's regrettably … the US got into a situation where they lost their consensus and that gonna delay it – a year or to. So you're going to get different implementation dates and it's obvious that an American bank that has a big European subsidiary – European subsidiaries that gonna have to comply with Basel II under the European implementation date. […] And we're worried about what will it to in between.« (Interview 091105)

stronger. Some, obviously – as you can see more enhancements to our already existing process.« (Interview 051110)

This mode of supervisory dialogue not only considers the challenges of globalization but also aspects of the knowledge society. Basel II particularly differentiates using the chances for reciprocal learning processes through an increased rate of interaction resp. density between banks and supervisors and thus comes to terms with an innovation-oriented mode of banking supervision. This means that bank organizations can profit from bank supervisors' scope of estimation and their experiences. A US-American agency consultant with long lasting experience as banking supervisor explains his role as follows:

»The regulators in the US [...] do share what they consider to be best practice, that they see in other institutions. In other words: I mean they wake you up in terms of saying what they think that you may do that – this is one way to solve it. And so we advice [...] our clients that you should – particular if you're new to the industry – you should view the regulator as a source of information for you. [...] Because of the ›examine approach‹ thy do see a lot of things. And they see if something seems to be working particular well in one institution. And if another institution has a similar issue or problem they can say well this is one way you may want to look at it or you want to deal with it. You know, they not gonna give up confidential, proprietary information but just in terms of processes – suggestions.« (Interview 051115a)

Moreover regulators can learn by this procedure and are able to adapt their supervision procedures. The opportunity to learn from each other through high quality discourses between supervisory authorities is explained by an US-American supervisor as follows:

»Now we have a resident person there [in the bank]. That person gets significant reports about the banks' activities. They also attend meetings at certain points in the year to understand what the bank is doing and changes in their objectives and strategies of course ... and just general information. We feel that by being on-site an speaking with people just in the normal course of business you have a better insight to what's going on with the institution. And therefore we are able to better identify concerns as they come up or things that we think might be concerns.« (Interview 051110b)

Thus, Basel II helps allay the antagonism of banking organizations and supervisory authorities through a reflexive, learning-oriented form of coordination, promising any support to the heterogeneous knowledge-backgrounds of banking industry and banking supervision and in this way providing a way to resolve the problems of regulatory ignorance (paragraph 2).

6. Conclusions

This article aimed to demonstrate the extent to which a standards-based form of regulation can cope with the globalized and knowledge intense financial system. Furthermore, it was intended to explore the special capacity of non-binding standards as elements of soft law (in comparison with norms). The observation that norms as classical instruments of political and legal regulation cannot keep up with the global and future oriented logic of the financial system provided our point of departure. This insufficiency – the argument goes – is grounded on the inner logic of (legal) norms: the normative mode of expectation.

In contrast to this, Basel II can be seen as a standards-based framework, which enables social coordination through the complementary usage of normative expectations with elements of a cognitive mode of expectation. Thus, the new framework does not make use of total homogenization and generalization of expectations but focuses on heterogeneity and the adaption of expectations through learning processes. This does not imply that the normative mode of expectation will become completely irrelevant. Far from it! Stabilizing expectations – even when disappointed – rests necessary to avoid chaos, at least on an abstract level. It serves as Archimedes' *fixed point* needed to make use of the flexibility potentials inherent to cognitive expectations.[35] It is more about a new ratio between cognitive and normative expectation modes with a movement towards the exploitation of the implications of cognitive expectations. The capacity of such a mode of governance is based on the internal logic of cognitive expectation, which can be shown in the factual as well as in the temporal and social dimensions.

With regard to the *factual dimension,* a cognitive oriented mode of governance prevails over norms because of its specific capability to cope with ignorance. While norms hide ignorance and avoid the communication about ignorance, standards hold ignorance present as in the occasion of disappointment learning process are evoked and lead to an adaption of expectations. In the context of Basel II, this can be observed particularly with the constitution of the Supervisory Review Process. It institutionalizes the expectation to discover unknown risks: and to process them. To put it

35 So at least the (second order) expectation that the occasion of disappointment leads to modifications of the expectation in question, has to be stabilized normative. In this sense Helmut Willke talks about »possible disorder« in contrast to »impossible order« (cf. Willke 2003).

another way: The SRP includes dealing with (regulatory) ignorance. And that means its existence is foreseen. Instead of examining management or financial ratios that hide ignorance,[36] qualitative dialogic forms of supervision allow — an exploratory approach to ignorance because they are detached from the observation schema ›limit‹. In this sense, with regard to the factual dimension a cognitive opening means an unlimiting of ignorance. This mode of coping with ignorance is closely linked to special conditions in the temporal and social dimension.

Comparing standards and norms with regard on the *temporal dimension* it is clear that standards operate flexibly and consequently enhance variability, so that learning results can take operational effect. This means a shift from persistence to change, which is functional to the same extent as the counterfactual stabilization of expectations becomes dysfunctional in dynamic fields of regulation and (the ability to) change the basic requirement for stability at all. In the case of standards, a strict if/then-logic, on which norms are based, is added to the idea of an uncertain future. This makes it possible to include learnt knowledge continuously in supervisory decisions. This implies a reduction of (regulatory) response times. While norms operate on the basis of past knowledge due to their conditional if/then-logic, cognitive oriented standards are ›up to date‹ by virtue of their goal-orientation. For instance the Supervisory Review Process allows to *continuously* exploiting ignorance.

With respect to the *social dimension,* the cognitive expectation stylization refers mainly to questions of legitimacy and acceptance. Unlike norms grounded on democratically-legitimated power in the case of standards (best-practice) knowledge serves as source of legitimacy and acceptance. With regard to Basel II, the increased relevance of knowledge leads to consequences in two aspects. First, the (inter-)relationship between national supervisory agencies has to be focused. As the relevance of multinational banking grows, the transnational cooperation of supervisory agencies gains in importance. In the context of Basel II this problem is met by the home/host-regulations discussed above in which complementarity rather than convergence is the characteristic guiding principle behind cooperation. It is about modulating through reciprocal learning – with all empirical observable difficulties.[37] Even if a central coordinated world order of fi-

---

36 For the relation of numbers and ignorance see also the contribution of Alexandra Hessling in this volume.

37 See our explanations above.

nancial regulation has not yet been achieved, these efforts can be understood to constitute a policy-network that fulfills these tasks in a complementary way.[38] Secondly, the relationship between banking organizations and supervisory agencies is subject to change. It is obvious that directive and power based forms of communication are not compatible with a cognitive oriented mode of governance. On this note the Supervisory Review Process intends to base its regulatory decisions on dialogical talks. This inclusion of the perspective of the regulated also improves the chances of acceptance.

These aspects of the cognitive orientation in the factual, temporal and social dimension mark the productivity of standards. Taken together it becomes clear that, finally, the central problem is how to cope with complexity in a controlled way. This is the main service standards perform with regard to governance matters. By enriching normative expectations with elements of cognitive uncertainty, standards gain processing capacities for heterogeneous and knowledge based circumstances that enable a form of social coordination that does not negate contingency but rather foresees it. Besides a (classical) form of governance by reduction of complexity governance by increasing complexity emerges as an alternative form that provides special capabilities to keep up with the global, knowledge-based and innovation-oriented financial system. That is not to say that every standard entirely exhausts its cognitive potential.

By contrasting norms with standards, we tried to show in how far standards are more likely to be able to deal with the challenges of globalized and knowledge based fields of regulation than norms are. Taking Basel II as example, we have shown this for the financial system. The empirical observation that the marked nature of the cognitive elements varies from standard to standard remains unquestioned. In this sense Basel I for instance is largely extent based on normative expectations. However, it is important to see that standards have a particular impact on governance that must be differentiated from norms and grounds in their specific capability to integrate cognitive expectations.

---

38 See Torsten Strulik 2000. A justifiable objection might be that Basel II only has been concluded by 13 nation-states and thus does not have the acceptance of all nation-states. But on the other hand it can be expected that many nation-states outside the G-13 will adopt Basel II. This is what has happened with former guidelines from the Basel committee and is also foreseen in the framework itself (BCBS 2004b: 2).

References

Alexander, S. Kern/Dhumale, Rahul/Eatwell, John (2006), *Global Governance of Financial Systems. The International Regulation of Systemic Risk.* Oxford.

BCBS (1988), *Internationale Konvergenz der Eigenkapitalmessung.* http://www.bis.org/publ/bcbs04ade.pdf (03.02.06).

— (1991), *Amendment of the Basel Capital Accord in respect of the inclusion of general provisions/general loan-loss reserves in capital.* http://www.bis.org/publ/bcbs09.pdf (12.01.06).

— (1994a), *Amendment to the capital accord of July 1988.* http://www.bis.org/publ/bcbs12b.pdf (12.01.06).

— (1994b), *Basel Committee: Amendment to the 1988 capital accord recognition of collateral.* http://www.bis.org/publ/bcbs14a.pdf (12.01.06).

— (1996), *Amendment to the capital accord to incorporate market risks.* http://www.bis.org/publ/bcbs24a.htm (12.01.06).

— (2004a), *History of the Basel Committee and its membership.* http://www.bis.org/bcbs/history.pdf (19.05.05).

— (2004b), *International convergence of capital measurement and capital standards: A revised framework.* http://www.bis.org/publ/bcbs107.pdf (31.05.05).

Bell, Daniel (1973), *The coming of post-industrial society, a venture in social forecasting.* New York.

Bernauer, Thomas (2000), *Staaten im Weltmarkt. Zur Handlungsfähigkeit von Staaten trotz wirtschaftlicher Globalisierung.* Opladen.

Blankart/Knieps (1993), »State and standards«, in: *Public Choice*, Vol. 77, 39–52.

Borowicz, Frank (2001), *Strategien im Wettbewerb um Kompatibilitätsstandards.* Frankfurt a.M.

Brunsson, Nils (2002), »Organization, markets and standardization«, in: Nils Brunsson, Bengt Jacobsson (eds), *A World of Standards.* Oxford, 21–39.

Brunsson, Nils/Jacobsson, Bengt (2002), »The Contemporary Expansion of Standardization«, in: Nils Brunsson, Bengt Jacobsson (eds), *A World of Standards.* Oxford, 1–20.

Cerny, Philip G. (1994), »The dynamics of financial globalization: Technology, market structure and policy response«, in: *Policy Sciences*, Vol. 27, 319–342.

Cutler, Claire A./Haufler, Virginia/Porter, Tony (2004), »Private authority and international affairs«, in: Timothy J. Sinclair (ed.), *Global Governance. Critical Concepts in Political Science*, Vol.3. London, 319–342.

Dale, Richard (1984), *The Regulation of International Banking.* Cambridge.

Deutsche Bundesbank (2001), *Basel II – Die neue Baseler Eigenkapitalvereinbarung.* http://www.deutschebundesbank.de/bankenaufsicht/bankenaufsicht_basel.php (01.08.05).

Eatwell, John (2004), *International Regulation, Risk Management and the Creation of Instability.* Speech at the IMF, 10/01/04. http://www.cerf.cam.ac.uk/publications/files/IMF%201.10.04.pdf (08.02.06).

Frankfurter Allgemeine Zeitung (2006), »Die Greenspan-Jahre. Viel gelobt und auch gescholten«, January 31, 2006, 12.

Galtung, Johan (1959), »Expectations and interaction processes«, in: *Inquiry*, Vol. 2, 213–234.

Genschel, Philipp/Plümper, Thomas (1996), »Wenn Reden Silber und Handeln Gold ist: Kommunikation und Kooperation in der internationalen Bankenregulierung«, *Discussion Paper, MPI für Gesellschaftsforschung*. Köln.

Hayek, Friedrich A. von (1945), »The use of knowledge in society«, in: *The American Economic Review*, Vol. 35, 519–530.

Hull, John C. (2006), *Options, Futures and other Derivatives*. Upper Saddle River.

Japp, Klaus Peter (2000), »Distinguishing Non-Knowledge«, in: *Canadian Journal of Sociology*, Vol. 25, 225–238.

Kane, Edward J. (1981), »Impact of regulation on economic behavior. Accelerating inflation, technological innovation, and the decreasing effectiveness of banking regulation«, in: *The Journal of Finance*, Vol. 36, 355–367.

Kapstein, Ethan Barnaby (1989), »Resolving the regulator's dilemma: International coordination of banking regulations«, in: *International Organization*, Vol. 43, 323–347.

— (1996), *Governing the Global Economy. International Finance and the State*. Cambridge.

King, Michael/Thornhill, Chris (2003), *Niklas Luhmann's Theory of Politics and Law*. New York.

Ladeur, Karl-Heinz (1999), »The theory of autopoiesis as an approach to a better understanding of postmodern law«, *EUI Working Paper Law*, 1–45. http://www.jura.uni-frankfurt.de/ifoer1/vesting/Dokumente/Rechtsphilosophie /law99_3–Ladeur.pdf (06.03.06).

Luhmann, Niklas (1969), »Normen in soziologischer Perspektive«, in: *Soziale Welt*, Vol. 20, 28–48.

— (1988), »Familiarity, confidence, trust: Problems and alternatives«, in: Gambetta, Diego (ed.), *Trust, Making and Breaking Kooperative Relations*. New York.

— (1992), *Die Wissenschaft der Gesellschaft*. Frankfurt a.M.

— (1995), *Social systems*. Stanford.

— (2000), *Die Politik der Gesellschaft*. Frankfurt a.M.

— (2004), *Law as a Social System*. Oxford.

— (2005), »Die Weltgesellschaft«, in: *Soziologische Aufklärung 2. Aufsätze zur Theorie der Gesellschaft*. Wiesbaden, 63–88.

Lütz, Susanne (2002), *Der Staat und die Globalisierung von Finanzmärkten. Regulative Politik in Deutschland, Großbritannien und den USA*. Frankfurt a.M.

Mattli, Walter (2001), »The politics and economics of international institutional standard setting: An introduction«, in: *Journal for European Public Policy*, 328–344.

Merton, Robert K. (1987), »Three fragments from a sociologist's notebook: Establishing the phenomenon, specified ignorance, and strategic research materials«, in: *Annual Review of Sociology*, Vol. 13, 1–28.

Nadvi, Khalid/Wältring, Frank (2002), *Making Sense of Global Standards*. Institut für Entwicklung und Frieden der Gerhard-Mercator-Universität Duisburg. Duisburg, 1–46.

O'Brien, Richard (1992), *Global Financial Integration: The End of Geography*. London.

Rammert, Werner (1999), »Produktion von und mit Wissensmaschinen. Situationen sozialen Wandels hin zur »Wissensgesellschaft«, in: W. Konrad, W. Schumm (eds): ›*Wissen und Arbeit. Neue Konturen von Wissensarbeit.*‹« Münster, 40–57.

— (2002a), »Zwei Paradoxien einer Wissenspolitik. Die Verknüpfung heterogenen und die Verwertung impliziten Wissens«; *TUTS Working Paper 08/2002*. http://www.tu-berlin.de/fb7/ifs/soziologie/Tuts/Wp/TUTS_WP_8_2002.pdf (10/01/05).

Rüthers, Bernd (2005), *Rechtstheorie. Begriff, Geltung und Anwendung des Rechts.* München.

Shelton, Dinah (ed.) (2000), *Commitment and Compliance. The Role of Non-Binding Norms in the International Legal System*. Oxford.

Stehr, Nico (1994), *Knowledge Societies*. London.

Strulik, Torsten (2000), *Risikomanagement globaler Finanzmärkte*. Frankfurt a.M.

— (2004), *Nichtwissen und Vertrauen in der Wissensökonomie*. Frankfurt a.M.

Strulik, Torsten/Kussin, Matthias (2005), »Finanzmarktregulierung und Wissenspolitik. Basel II – Die aufsichtsrechtliche Konstitution kollektiver Intelligenz?«, in: *Zeitschrift für Rechtssoziologie*, Vol. 26, 101–129.

Willke, Helmut (1983), *Entzauberung des Staates. Überlegungen zu einer gesellschaftlichen Steuerungstheorie*. Königstein.

— (2001a), *Atopia. Studien zur atopischen Gesellschaft*. Frankfurt a.M.

— (2001b), *Systemtheorie III. Steuerungstheorie*. Stuttgart.

— (2002), *Dystopia. Studien zur Krisis des Wissens in der modernen Gesellschaft*. Frankfurt a.M.

— (2003), *Heterotopia. Studien zur Krisis der Ordnung moderner Gesellschaften*. Frankfurt a.M.

— (2005), *Symbolische Systeme. Grundriss einer soziologischen Theorie*. Weilerswist.

— (2006), *Global Governance*. Bielefeld.

Wood, Duncan (2005), *Governing Global Banking. The Basel Committee and the Politics of Financial Globalization*. Aldershot.

Authors

Alexandra Hessling is graduate student in the DFG-post graduate programme »World Concepts and Global Structural Patterns« at the University of Bielefeld. Her Ph.D. thesis is concerned with »Accounting Standards in the Financial and Knowledge Economy«. Her research interests include: sociology of organizations; economic sociology; sociology of accounting; and studies on knowledge economy.

Boris Holzer, Ph.D., is lecturer in the Department of Sociology, Ludwig-Maximilians-University Munich, and associated with the Research Center »Reflexive Modernization«. His current research focuses on economic and political sociology; globalization; and social networks.

Herbert Kalthoff is Assistant Professor for Sociology at University of Konstanz, Department of History and Sociology. His research focus is on economic sociology; sociology of education; and qualitative research methods.

Sven Kette is research fellow at the University of Bielefeld. His Ph.D. thesis is concerned with the societal and organizational effects of a cognitive mode of governing global banking. His research interests are: sociological theory; sociology of organizations; and sociology of risk and regulation.

Matthias Kussin is research fellow at the University of Bielefeld. His Ph.D. thesis is concerned with the consequences of the new qualitative approach in banking supervision. His research interests are: sociological theory; sociology of organizations; political sociology; and media sociology.

Hanno Pahl is graduate student in the DFG-post graduate programme »World Concepts and Global Structural Patterns« at the Universtity of Bielefeld. His Ph.D. thesis is concerned with the emerge of world economy and world finance as subject to societal theoretical reflections in the theories of Karl Marx and Niklas Luhmann.

Timothy J. Sinclair is Associate Professor in the Department of Politics and International Studies at the University of Warwick. His research interests include theories of global governance; the politics of international finance; and institutional change in market societies.

Torsten Strulik is Assistant Professor at the Faculty of Sociology at the University of Bielefeld and Heisenberg-Fellow of the German Research Foundation (DFG). His main areas of research and practice are: economic sociology; sociology of finance; political sociology; social theory.

Eleni Tsingou is research fellow at the Center for the Study of Gobalisation and Regionalisation (CSGR) at the University of Warwick (UK) and Project Coordinator of an EU-funded Network of Excellence on ›Global Governance, Regionalisation and Regulation: The Role of the EU‹.

Hendrik Vollmer is Assistant Professor at the University of Bielefeld. In his post-doctorial thesis he is working on »Social order through its state of exception«. His research interests are: sociology of organizations; sociological theory; historical sociology; political sociology; sociology of knowledge; and sociology of calculation.

Helmut Willke is Professor of State Theory and Global Governance at the department of sociology of the University of Bielefeld. He was visiting professor at Washington D.C., Geneva and Vienna. His main areas of research and practice are systems theory; state theory; global governance and global regime building as well as organizational development; systems dynamics and systems guidance; and knowledge management.